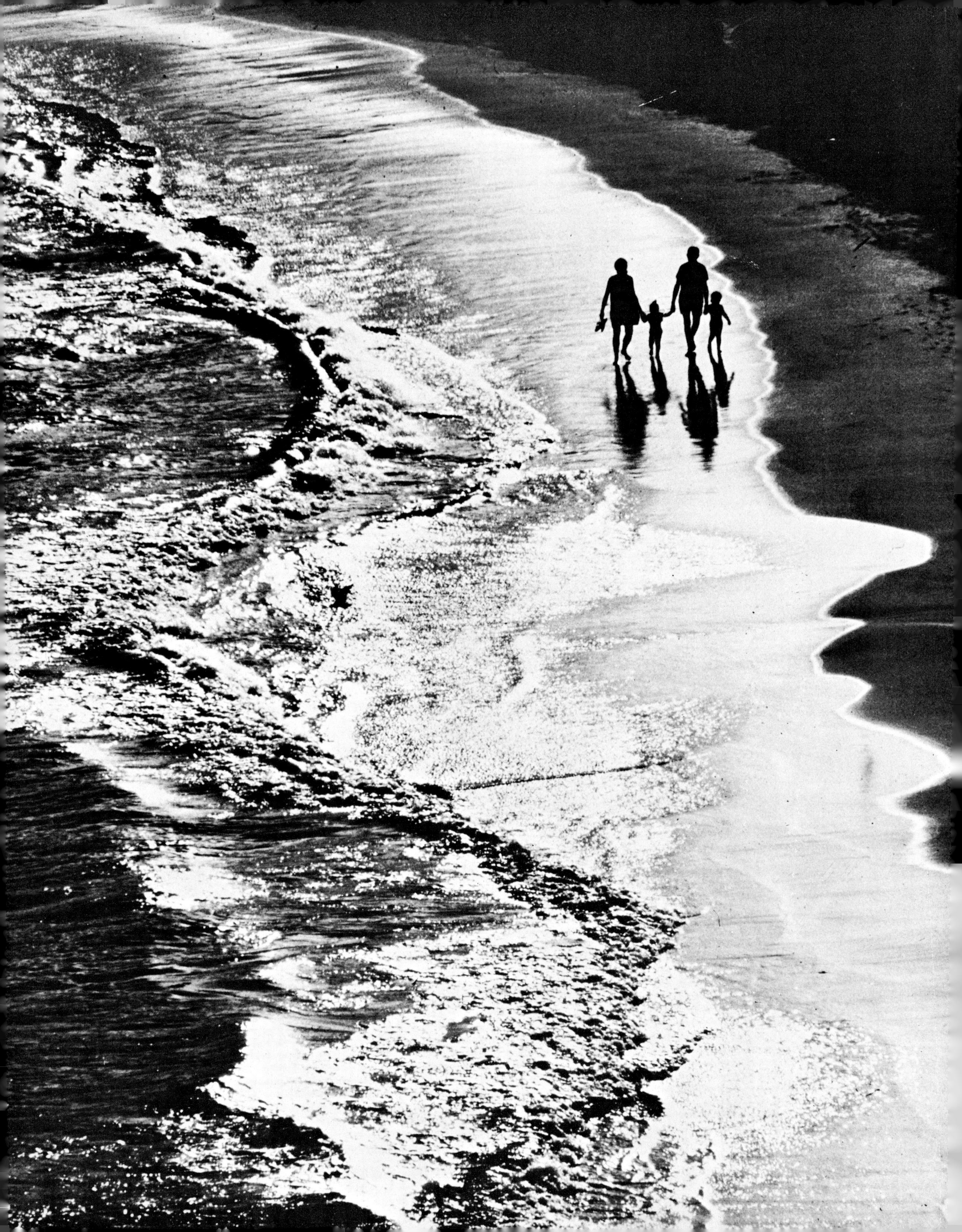

LIFE IN AUSTRALIA

Text edited by **Craig McGregor**

Photographs edited by **David Beal**

Golden Press

Published 1971 by
Golden Press Pty Ltd
10–16 Dowling Street
Potts Point N.S.W. Australia
©Lloyd O'Neil Pty Ltd

An earlier edition
was published in 1968 by
Southern Cross International Pty Ltd
Printed in Hong Kong

DU
105
M24
1971

Contributors

Geoffrey Dutton
Harry Gordon
Douglas Lockwood
Craig McGregor
Ian Moffitt
John Douglas Pringle
Gavin Souter
Patrick Tennison
Richard Walsh

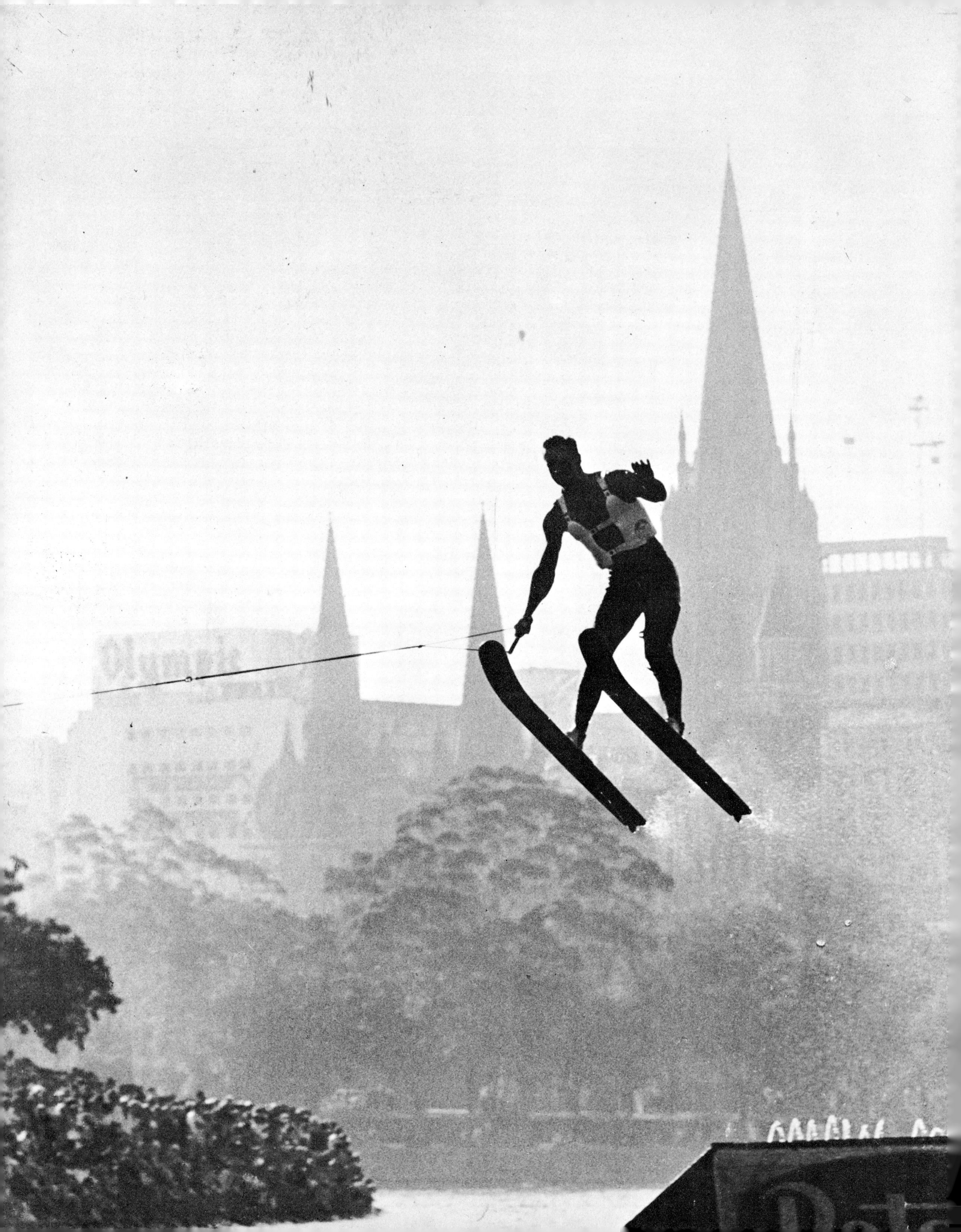

Contents

1. Introduction—
   What does it mean to be an Australian?
   Craig McGregor

2. The Bush—
   Change and Challenge
   Douglas Lockwood

3. The Cities—
   Ten Shades of Difference
   Gavin Souter

4. The People—
   In Search of a Dream
   Ian Moffitt

5. Pleasure—
   Happiness without Guilt
   Craig McGregor

6. Sport—
   The Great Australian Talent
   Harry Gordon

7. Culture—
   Artists and Flatlanders
   Geoffrey Dutton

8. Progress—
   Chipping Away at a Continent
   Patrick Tennison

9. Young Australia—
   Pacemakers from the Cults
   Richard Walsh

10. The Future
    John Douglas Pringle

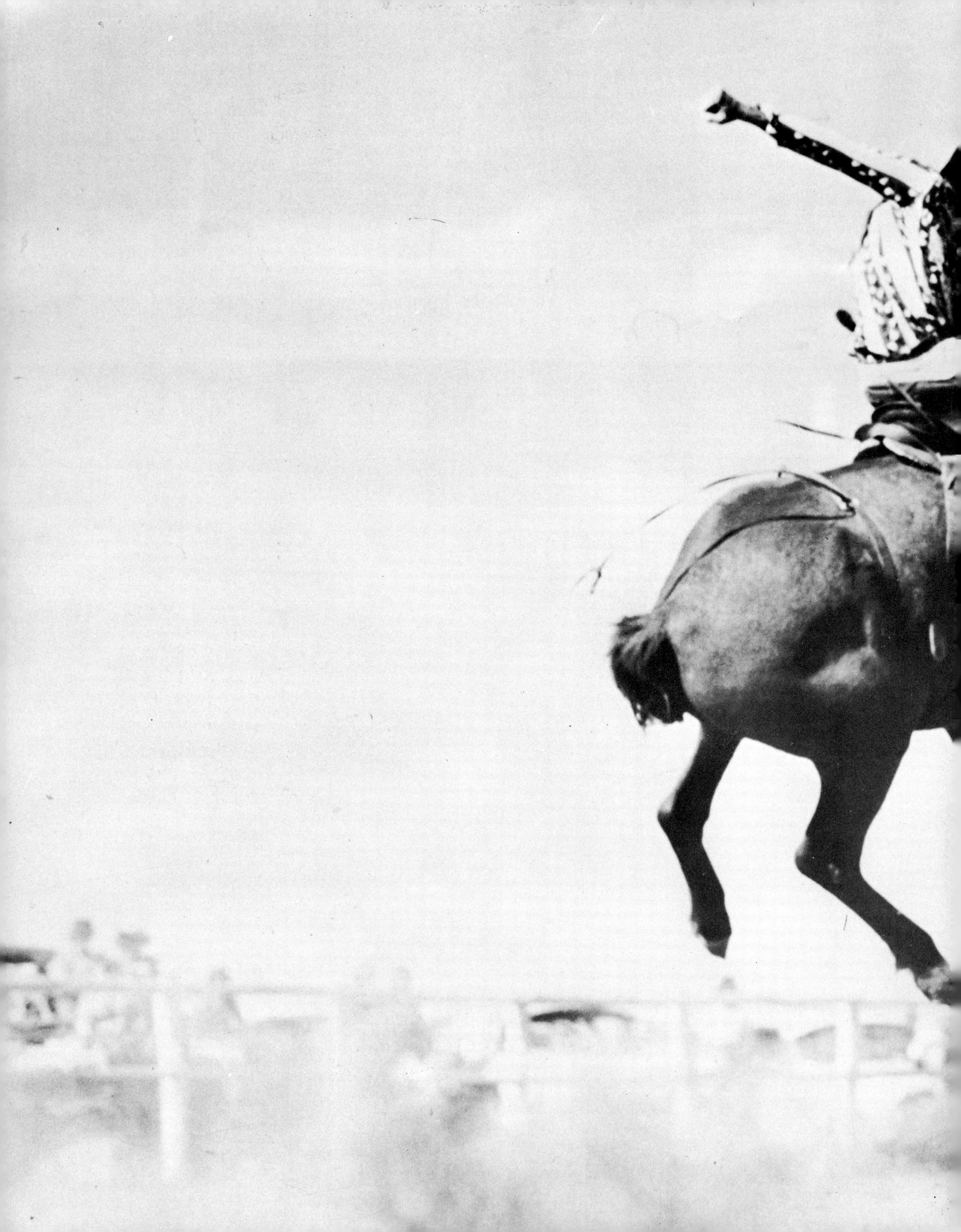

Photographers

ANDERSON James
BEAL David
BEAUMAN Nick
CARNEMOLLA John
CLIFFORD Beverly
CROWE Pat
DUNDAS Kerry
DUYCKERS Leo
GRITSCHER Helmut
LIPMAN George
MARSTON Jane
MOORE David
MURRAY Neil
McARDLE Brian
McFARLANE Robert
McQUILLAN Ern
NELSON Lance
O'GRADY John
POTTS David
RAE Peter
SIEVERS Wolfgang
SMITH Robin
STANYER Ray
STRIZIC Mark
VISSEL Jozel
WEIGHT Gregory
WITZIG John
WOLDENDORP Richard
WONG John

INTRODUCTION

WHAT DOES IT MEAN TO BE AN AUSTRALIAN?

Craig McGregor

The faces drift by in the street, young faces, old faces, faces lined with the sorrow of years, faces still eager for experience, Depression faces with the mark of the battler upon them, faces of worried businessmen in hornrims, button-down shirts and outsize necks, hippies in military coats and long hair, teenagers in high leather boots, mini-skirts and ironingboard hair, fat pudgy Mums with moustaches and shopping bags, dainty models with rigid sacroiliacs clip-clipping aristocratically over the cigarette-strewn pavement like Japanese geishas with tied ankles, tiny Spaniards with false teeth and frightened eyes, Italian grandmas in Catholic mass black for husbands who died 20 years before at Rimini, homosexuals holding white poodles with fastidious fingernails, lesbians in drag, Fascists disguised as industrialists, art students disguised as Bob Dylan, plainclothes men disguised as plainclothes men, a motley mass of sharpies, trendies, oldies, teenies, rockers, surfies, mods, bikies, junkies, camps, queers, poofters, hamboners, ravers, nymphos, femlins, gremlins, Alfs and Ednas, Berts and Francescas, Nolas and Nancys, packers and drapers, wharfies and waiters, handsome garbo men, not-so-handsome stockbrokers, plus a fair sprinkling of aborigines, Chinese, Italians, Greeks, Balts, Malts, bananalanders, apple-eaters, rock choppers, god botherers, jesuschristers, popsters, kicksters, dragsters, and all that mob from Fitzroy, Collingwood, Highgate, Malvern, Moonee Ponds, Warrawee, Warringah, Wahroonga, Woollahra, Surry Hills, Sarsaparilla, Moorabbin and Pleasantville, to say nothing of those timepayment crucifix martyrs who live in bungalows called Kia Ora, Emoh Ruo, Wyework and Bella Vista and catch the 8.5, 8.8, 8.14, 8.20, 8.30, 8.32, 8.45 and 8.50 commuter special to work each day . . . they are all of them, every one, Australians.

What do they have in common? Very little. Once everyone was sure what it meant to be an Australian. It meant being Alf, Mate, Digger, a Good Bloke, with a fag in your mouth, an R.S.L. badge in your lapel, a chip on your shoulder and a Jack's-as-good-as-the-next-man attitude to the whole bloody world. The Typical Aussie was a rather heroic figure, extravagantly admired overseas, the inheritor of the cornstalk-Anzac legend, the bushie in a battered worker's hat, one of The Weird Mob, Horne's icecream-licking lucky bastard, Albert Tucker's Antipodean Man, a beaut mate, a hard case, the Common Man in all his glory. But the mirror-image shatters, time cracks the face smiling beneath the slouch hat, fragments splinter against a new reality. Mass migration, the fat years of the 'fifties' and 'sixties' and the emergence of a new postwar generation have destroyed the old social matrix which stamped Australians as clearly as die-cast Button Day medallions, the Queen on one side and Digger on the other. For better or worse Australia has been flung into an era of change, subjected to new and crucial pressures, forced to make decisions about everything from Vietnam to town planning to aboriginal rights which once would have drifted slowly past the closed eyes of the sunbathers. The white collar revolution has come, the White Australia policy has gone (almost). The sheep's back has sprouted burrs, four million cars ride the motor industry boom. Americans build the computers which tell Australians what to do,

Japanese own the minerals which tell Australians what they can import. As the flood of British migrants recedes the flood of Europeans increases. It is absurd to force a spurious unity upon a nation of 13 million people in which two million were born overseas, three million are of immediate foreign descent, four million are still children. The splits have occurred, the matrix broken open; what characterises Australia today is diversity and contradiction, and the difference between the thousand and one minorities (aborigines, New Australians, students, mods, financiers) which make up the majority has never been greater. It isn't any use searching for the Typical Australian any longer: there ain't no such animal.

And yet Australians have some bonds to yoke them together. One is the land itself, the huge, sprawling three million square miles of dry and ancient continent which gives all Australians a common frontier and a common subsoil for their imagination. The bush looms large in their minds and memories, even those for whom it is little more than a composite of Hans Heysen gumtrees, Brownie Downing aborigines and a drive through the market gardens on a Sunday arvo. There has always been a close link between the city and the bush, which is rather surprising in the most highly urbanised nation in the world. The "drift to the cities" which the politicians bemoan underlines the fact that many city Australians originally came from the country; the Depression put many city workers on the track and heightened an easy fluidity between country and city labour which was evident, earlier, in Henry Lawson's short stories; and the nation's pioneering past is so recent that time has not yet eroded the link between it and Dad and Dave's cityfied descendants. Many urban Australians still have relatives in the country, visit them on holidays, send postcards home from Mt Lofty and Toowoomba and Bourke; some of the nation's most exclusive boarding schools, such as Frensham and Geelong Grammar, are located miles from the capital cities. The bush is ubiquitously present in contemporary Australian life: Timbertop, Namatjira prints on suburban walls, aboriginal art in Myers, bushwalking clubs, Scouts, Outward Bound, bush barbecues, outback tours, posters at Kings Cross advertising a grizzled stockman smoking a flip-top King Size. It's as though Australians were determined to hold on to their bush tradition while it still exists, much as Sidney Nolan has tried to pin down myth-figures like Ned Kelly before they vanish. The bush mystique still colours the imaginations of Australians who have long since deserted waterbags, drip-safes and saltbush for the workbench, the telly, and an Esky in the boot.

As well as the bush Australians have in common their history, the concrete record of a dream which failed. The dream had its beginnings in the convict days when red-coated troopers and shackled criminals struggled together to wrench a living from the sand and stunted scrub of Botany Bay. You can hear its harsh birth in the tales of the convicts who rebelled against the social system which had transported them halfway across the world, took to the bush and gave Australia the first of its national heroes: the bushranger. You can hear it in the half-forgotten memories, passed down from genera-

Saturday crowd

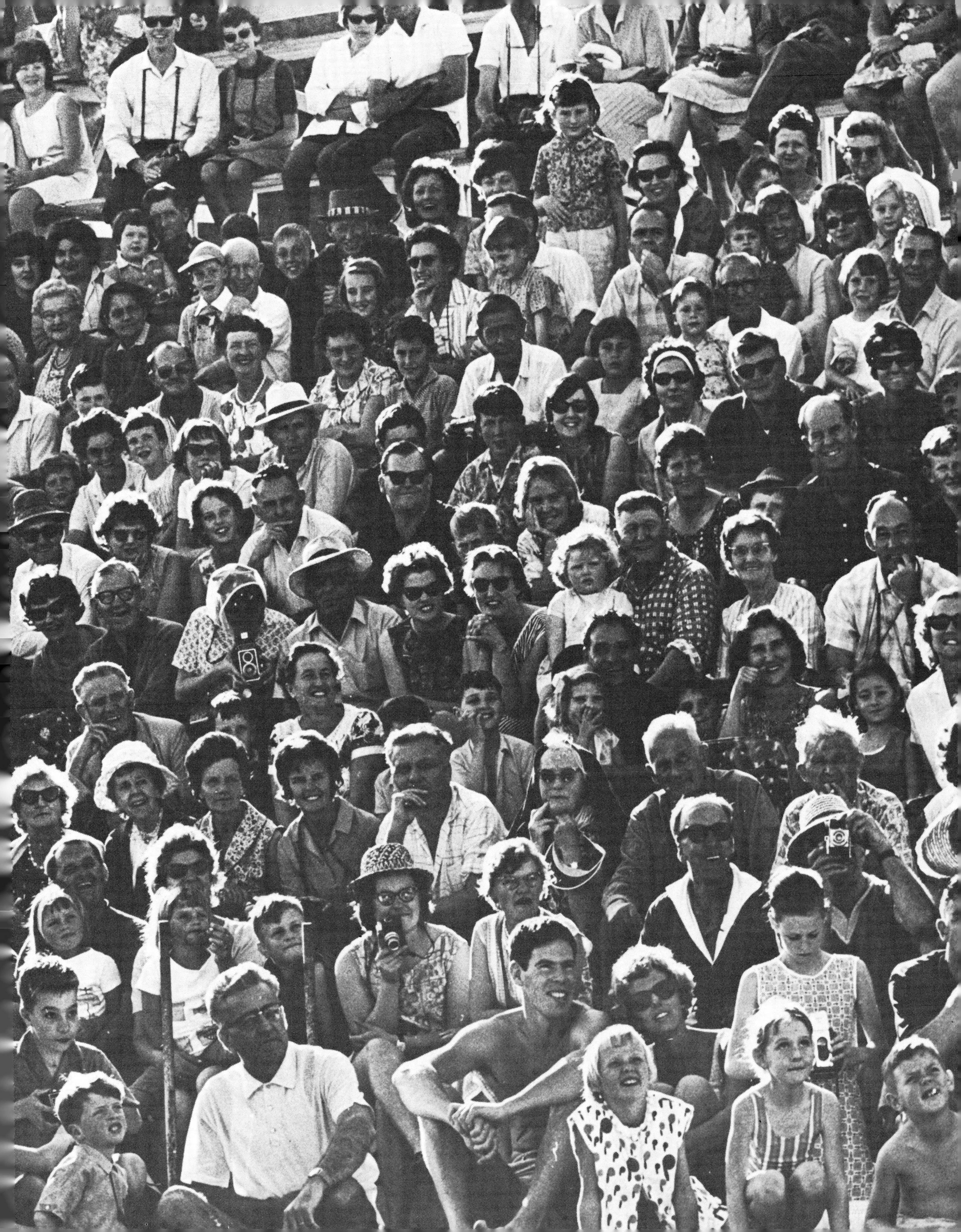

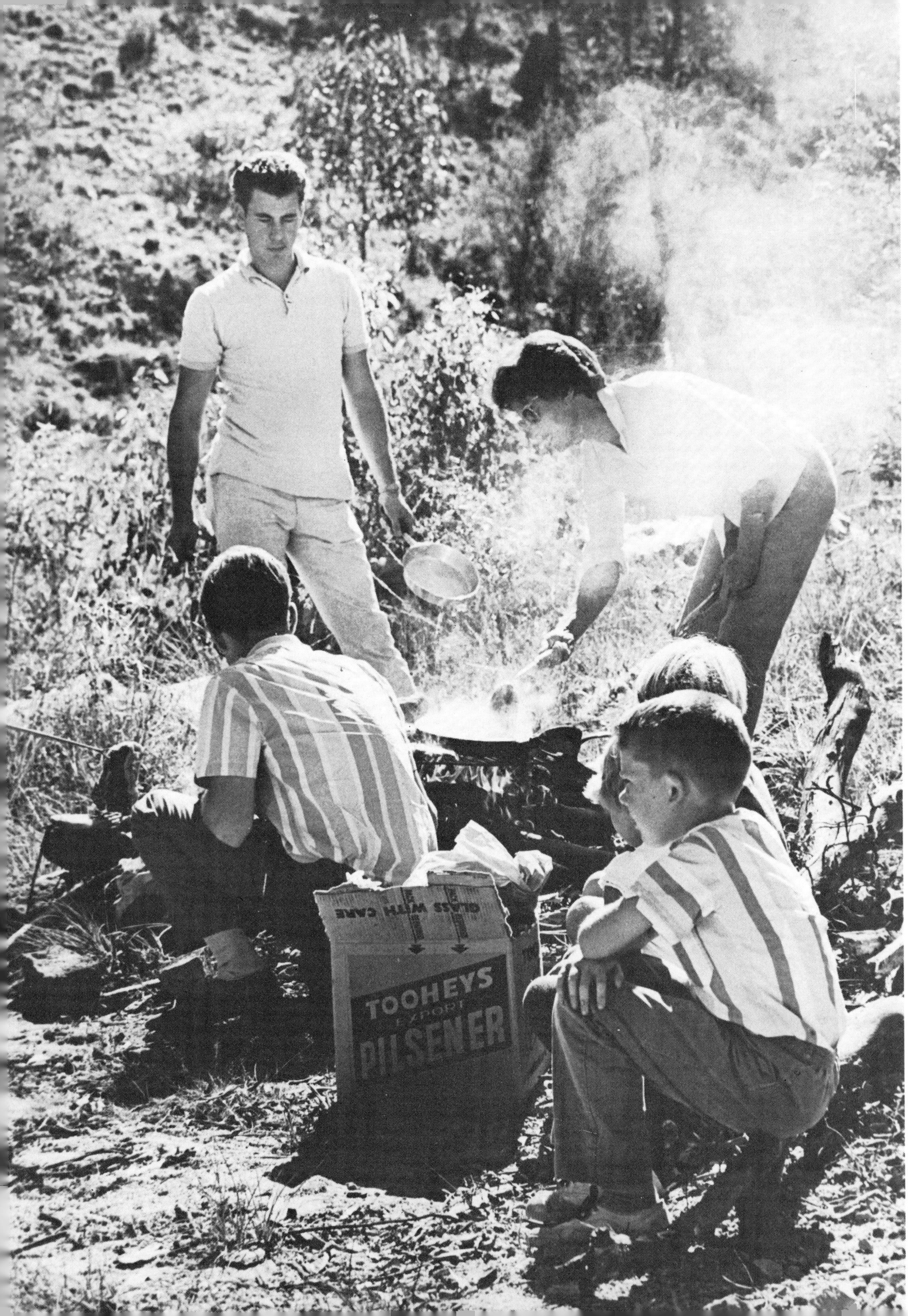
GLASS WITH CARE
TOOHEYS
EXPORT
PILSENER

tion to generation, of bloody insubordinations and futile rebellions, of the uncomprehending thick-wristed Irish who were lashed to death in the barrack-square, of the Scots and English who were banished to the prison island of Van Diemen's Land. And you can hear it again in the songs which sprang up around the men who were lucky enough to escape from the penal system and began a life for themselves as ticket-of-leave men, farmers, seamen, brothel-keepers, carpenters—and outlaws:

> 'It shall never be said of me that Donahue the brave
> Surrendered to the peelers or became an English slave,
> I'd rather roam the bush so wild like a dingo or kangaroo,
> Than work one day for the Government,' says bold Jack Donahue.

It was a dream of freedom which, as the century wore on, also became a dream of equality. A flood of the world's rebels and dispossessed and footloose surged into Australia. They were an extraordinary amalgam: hardy Scots and English farming families, forced from their land by poverty and the chaos of the industrial revolution; Chartists who had turned their back on the old country and hoped to build a better society in the antipodes; wandering adventurers, drawn by the chance of easy money and a good life; goldseekers who swarmed into the country after the news of the big strikes flashed around the world; Irish rebels and Liberty men who were shipped to Australia chained to their dead companions; free settlers thirsty for land and room to grow in; deserting seamen, remittance men, traders and tarts, professional soldiers and professional criminals, businessmen, blacksmiths, tradesmen, harlots and whores and pimps and scoundrels, speculators and investors, manual labourers and murderers. From this unlikely material Australia had to fashion a nation and, incredibly, the amalgam began to jell. For whatever else soured and divided them, whatever else flared up into the race riots at Lambing Flat and the clash between troopers and bushrangers at Collector, they at least had their dream in common. Colonial society, of course, was never unified behind it. The Eureka Stockade rebellion was brutally crushed. Squatters took over the rich inland pastures, so that half a century later the cry of "unlock the land!" went up all over the nation. Wentworth proposed a 'bunyip' aristocracy. The new colonies soon bred their own discontents and tensions and power struggles. But by the 1890s the Australian Legend was a reality, and the nation experienced the onrush of national consciousness and pride which made mateship and equality the ethics of the new society and forged the colonies into a single Commonwealth.

The dream failed. Today Australia is a conservative, affluent, predominantly white collar and middle class society which has incorporated many of the class distinctions, privileges and social injustices of the Old World. The wilder frontiers of the world are littered with dead utopias, and the visionary new society dreamt of by Lawson, O'Dowd, William Lane and the Chartists never arrived. But the very importance of utopias is not that they succeed (by their very nature success is impossible) but the way in which they fail, which ideals are sacrificed and which aren't, what the nation still

Sunday lunch

clings to. Australians today are marked by their history as strongly as the convicts were marked by the arrow. The characteristic flavour of Australian society is still egalitarian, though each day brings fresh evidence of inequality; and the belief in mateship is still strong, reaffirmed in every strike and over the bar of every pub. In State and Federal parliaments the politicians boast about progress, no party dares call itself conservative, the taxi-driver and the bus conductor and the plumber still proclaim Jack's bloody well better than youse. Nations live by the myths they believe in, and it is the myth of equality which still orders and explains much of life in Australia.

But for how long?

As well as their land and their history, Australians have the present in common. They have a common accent, and some would say a common face as well ("you can always pick an Australian by his ears: they stick out!" someone told me once). They share common attitudes, such as disliking class snobbery and admiring manliness above all else. Much of present time revolves around images of unity: Anzac Day, the Melbourne Cup, Christmas, the beach. People still talk about "Australians" as though they were a unique, definable and indivisible race of people who can be summed up in a few bold strokes of black and white, a few provocative generalisations. But the harder you look at these sacred vessels which are supposed to contain a nation's identity, some precious essence of Australianness, the less valid they become. A common accent? It has already split up on class lines; the phoneticians discern three major kinds of accent, innumerable minor ones. Anzac Day has become The One Day Of The Year, a playwright's symbol of the clash between the generations in Australia, the clash between old patriotism and new rebellion. Trams still stop for the Melbourne Cup, but in the nation's technocratic capital, Canberra, the buses grind remorselessly on and the Cup matters less than whether young Richard has made the Sub-Atoms team on Saturday. To many Australians the New Year, Easter, May Day, Holiday and Pay Day are more important than Christmas. Conflict has even reached the beach: surfies v. rockers, boardriders v. lifesavers, transistor bugs v. the rest! Things shatter at the centre, the extremes draw further apart. These days the characteristic tone of Australian life is one of disunity (over Vietnam, conscription, university students, the Bomb) and conflict (between one generation and another, New Australian and Old Aussie, pre-war and post-war life styles). Protest marches, demonstrations and melees in the street are signs of a more general disturbance which has been felt throughout Australian society. In seeking to describe life in Australia the writers of this book have come back again and again to senses of difference, change, conflict. Gavin Souter has polarised the nation's cities into two distinct blood groups. Richard Walsh has delineated the gulf between the generations, the impossibility of communication. Geoffrey Dutton has charted the rapids which divide artists from their audience, the astronomers from the flat-earthers. John Pringle has refracted the uncertainty which so many Australians feel about the future of their country. Ian

Brisbane city, from Kangaroo Point, Queensland
18, 19) Country races, Betoota, Queensland
20, 21) Sydney Harbour at dusk
22, 23) Lady bowlers, Sydney

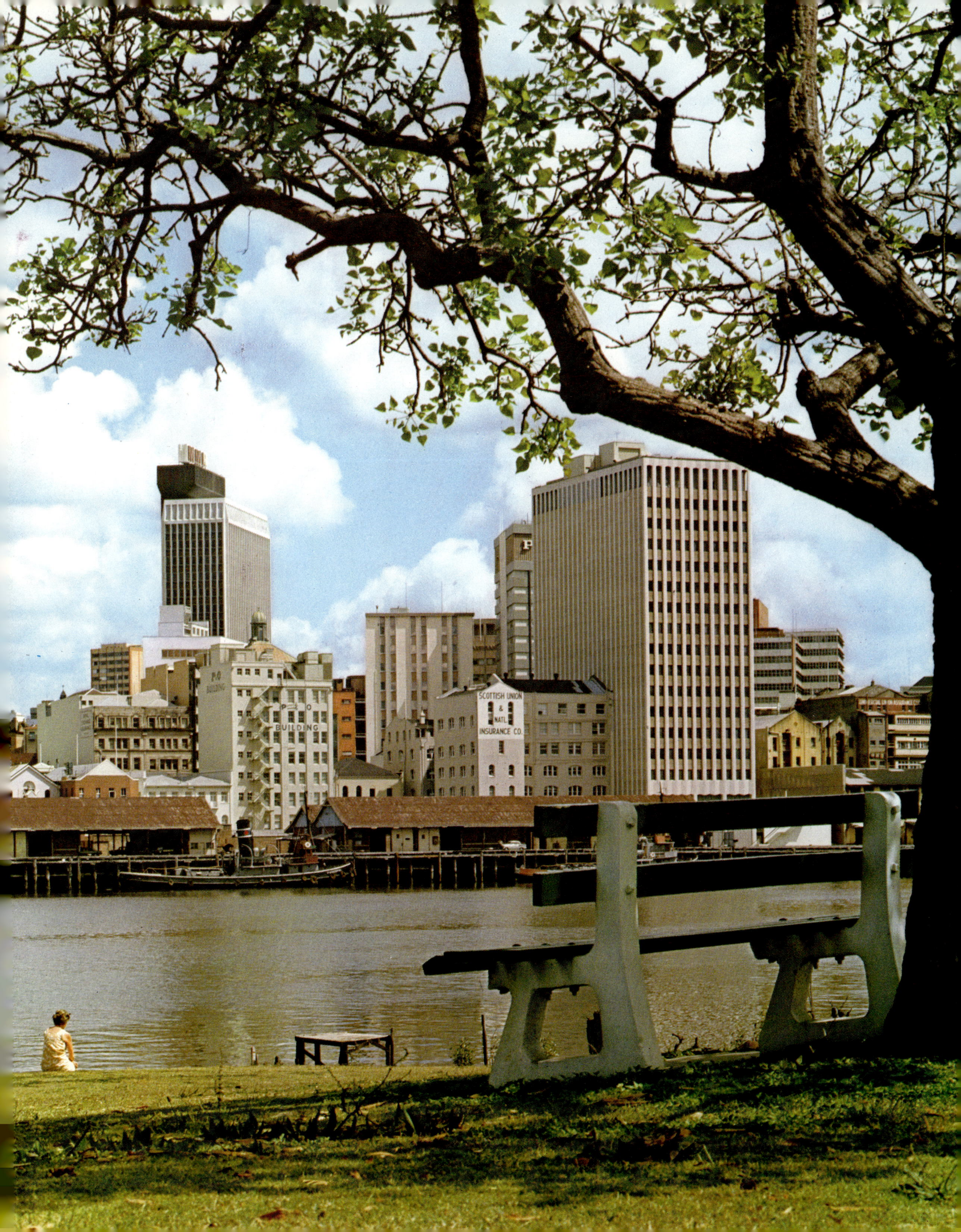
P&O BUILDING
SCOTTISH UNION & NATL. INSURANCE CO.

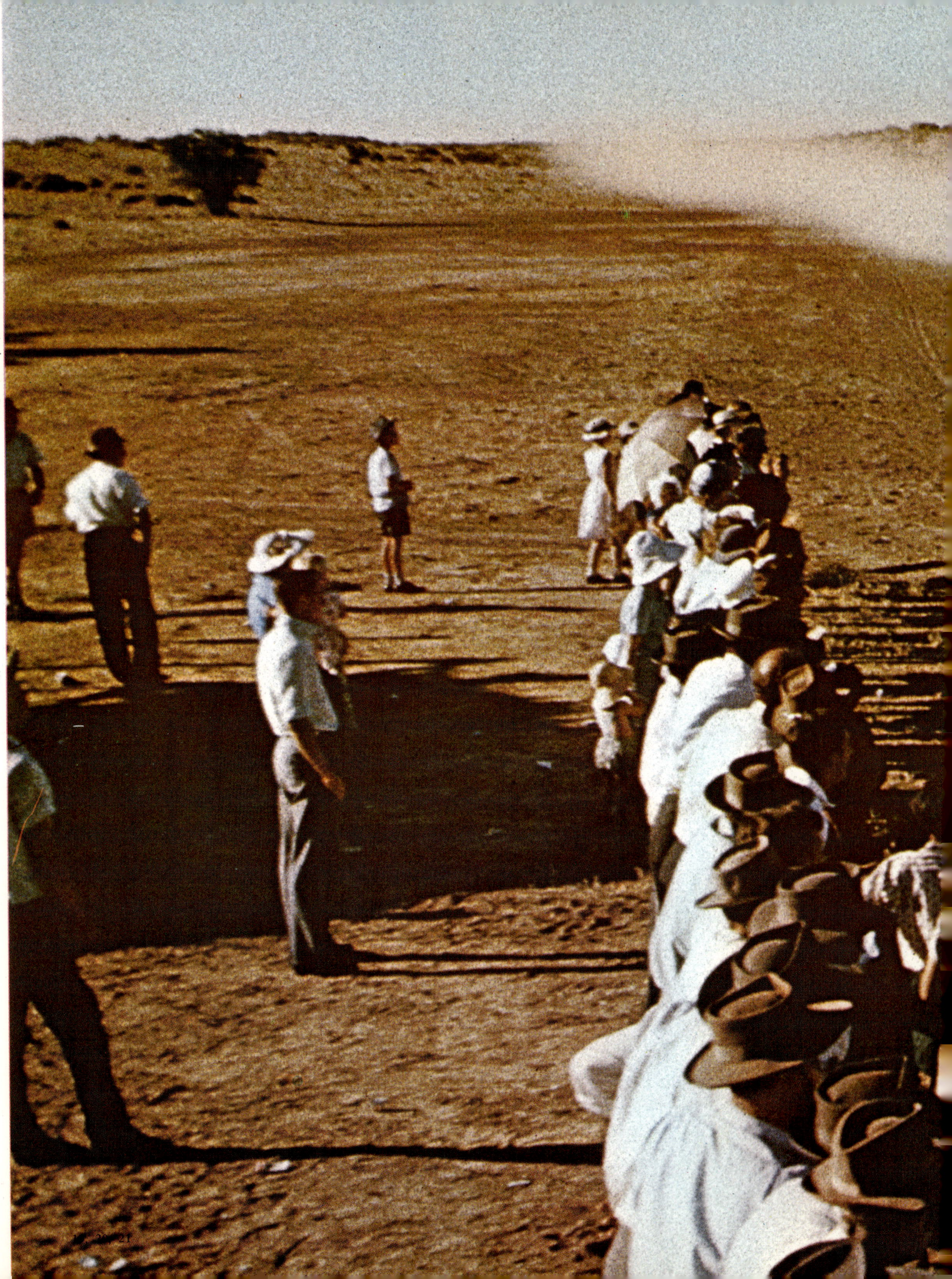

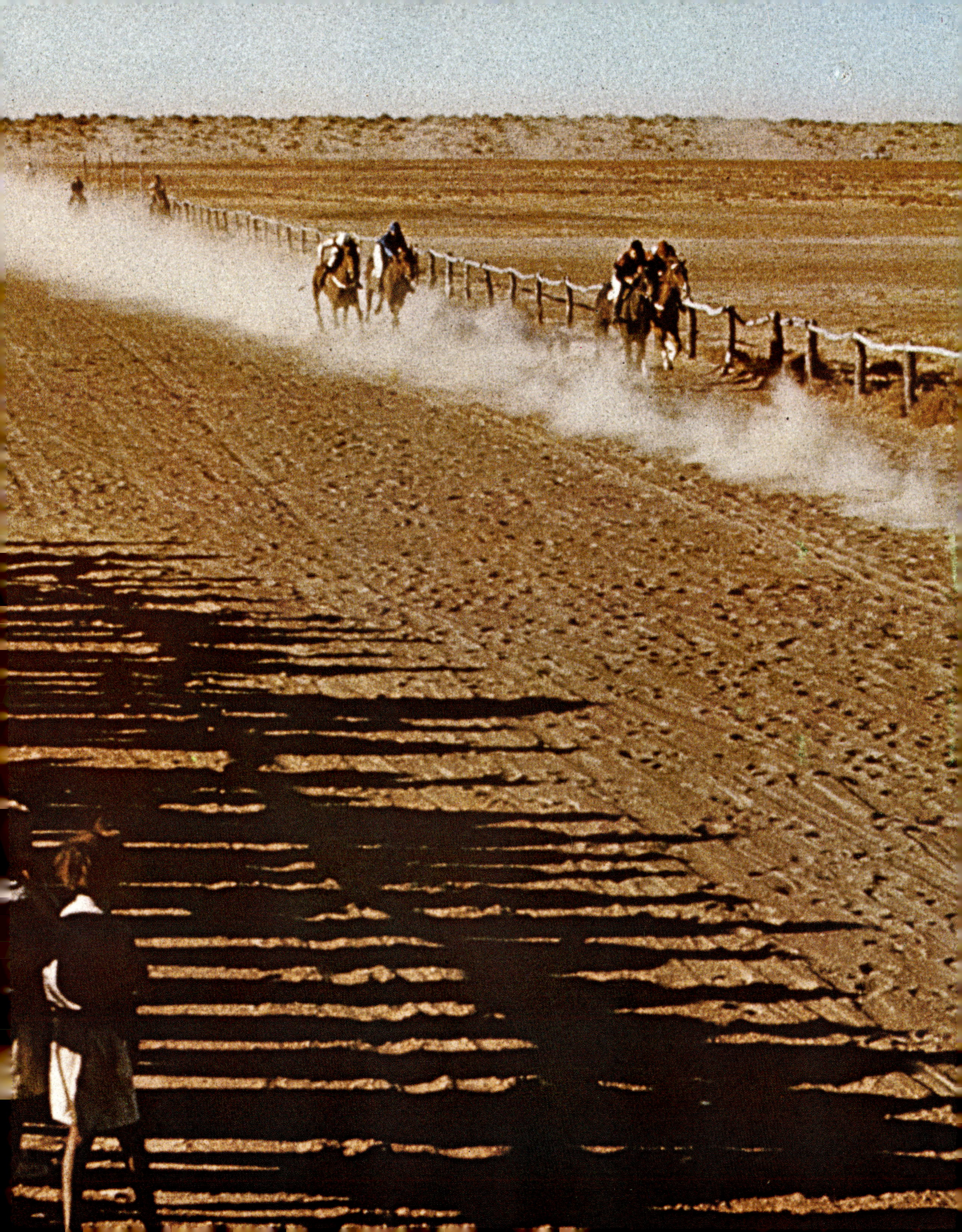

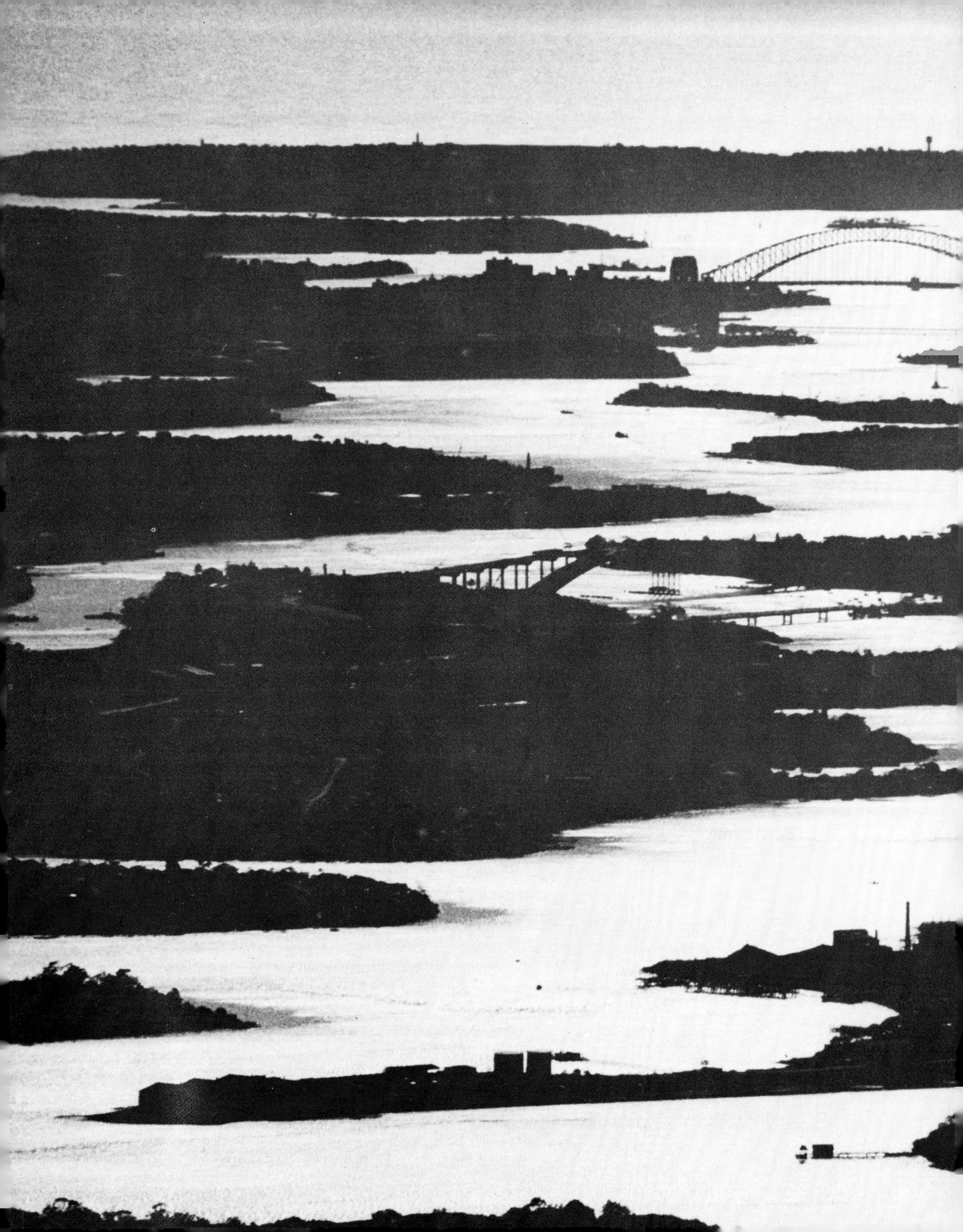

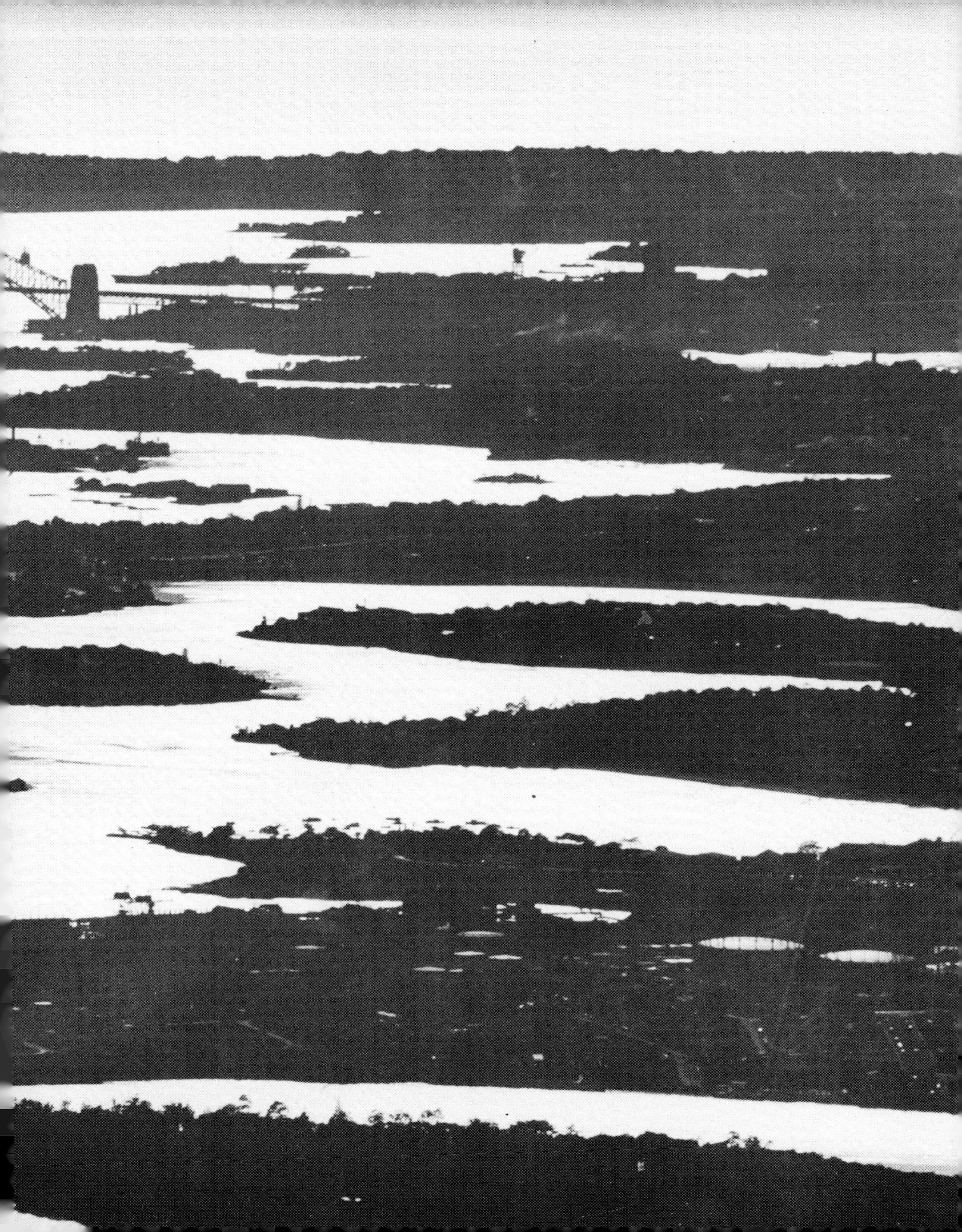

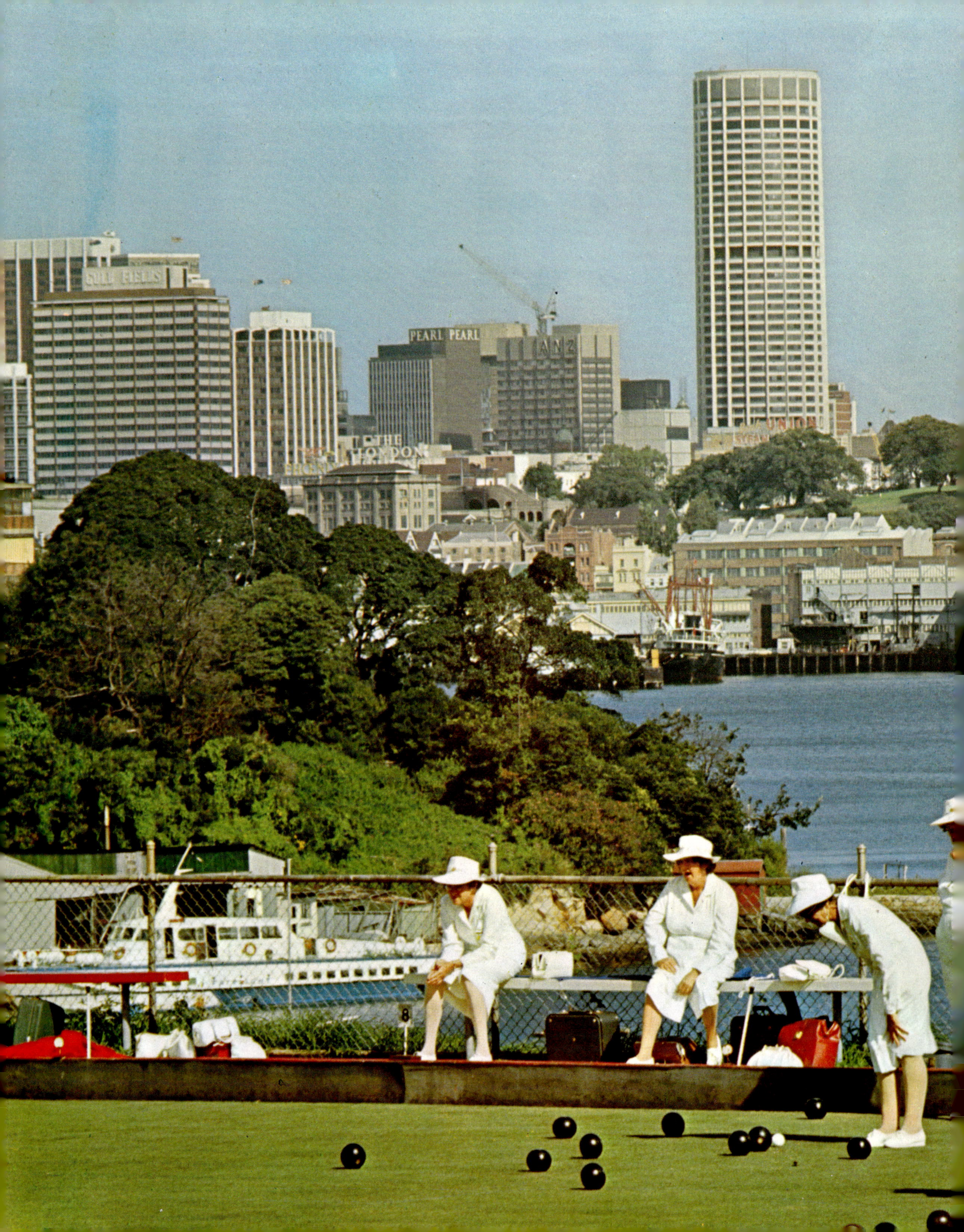
PEARL PEARL
THE LONDON

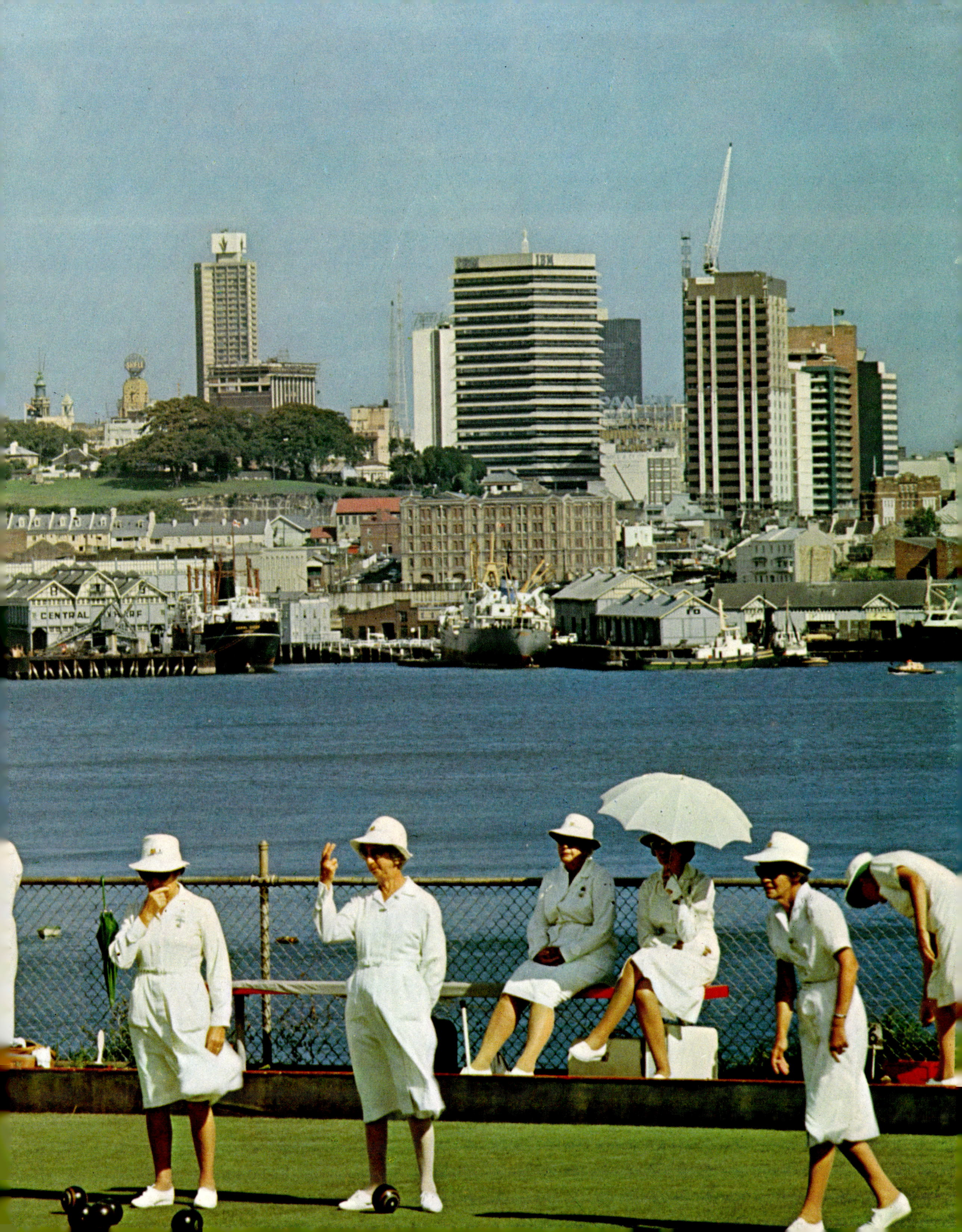
CENTRAL

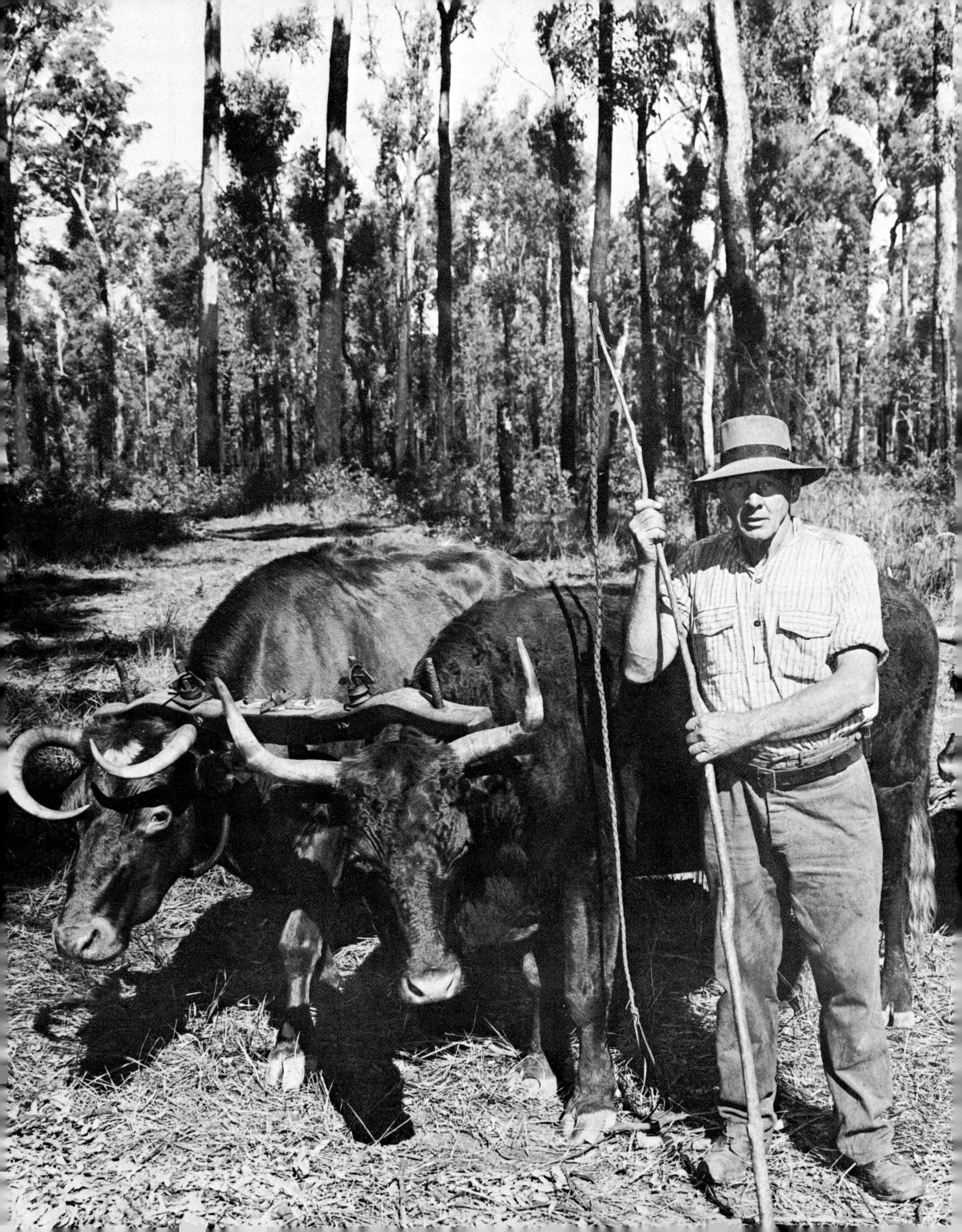

Moffitt has described the search for a new dream to replace the old, broken one. Douglas Lockwood, Harry Gordon and Patrick Tennison have all focussed upon the dynamic of change.

These days the molecular groups which make up Australian society are so disparate, so heterogeneous, so extreme that they have more in common with similar groups overseas than with each other. The fact that one is an Australian no longer defines one's being; the fact that one is an artist, or a white-collar worker, or a Greek migrant, or a surfie, does so far more satisfactorily. The search for a national identity is, in many ways, an absurdly old-fashioned one, a parochial preoccupation which an international age is making irrelevant. People just *are,* in all their multiform complexity; they cannot be simplified or defined away in terms of flags, prime ministers and national anthems. The Australian today is a prism, a kaleidoscope, a diamond with 13 million faces, and the life he leads is a microcosm of life the world over. The Family of Man lives next door.

Ancient ... and modern

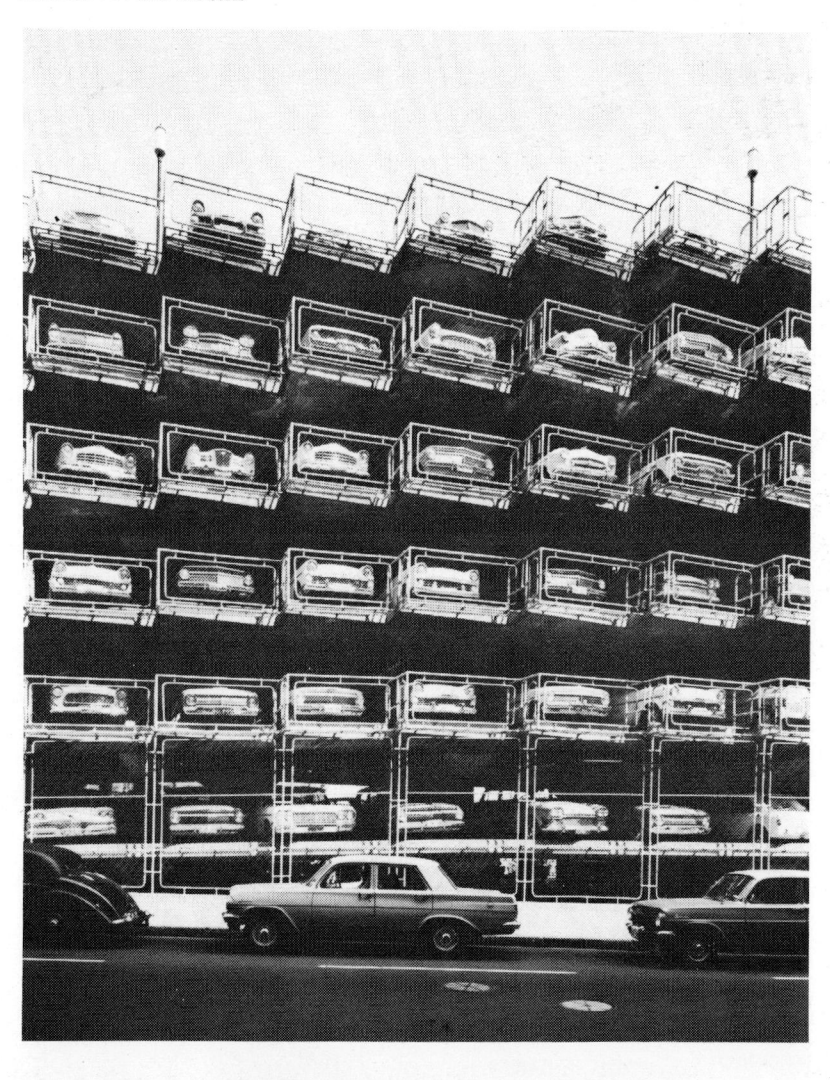

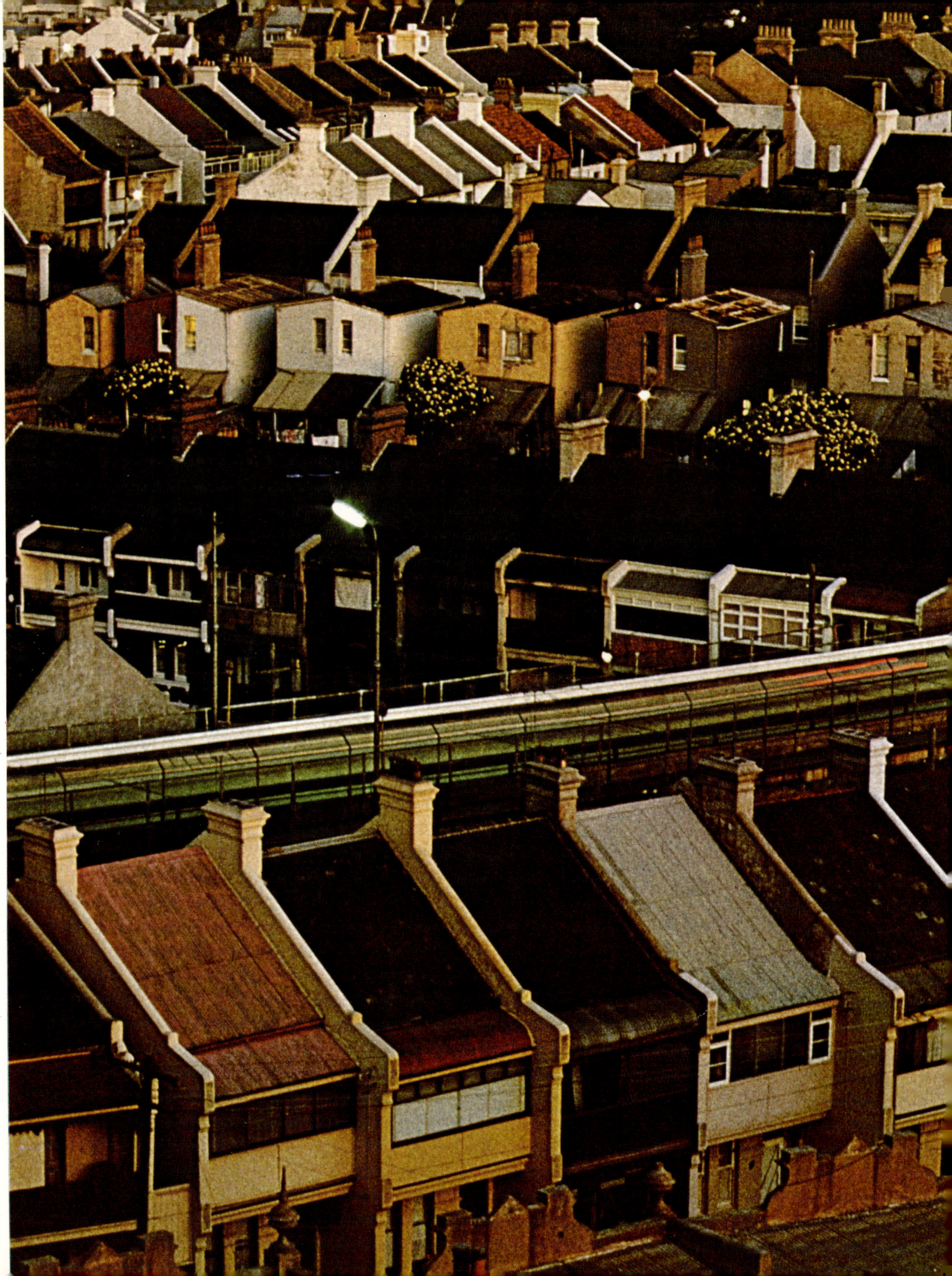

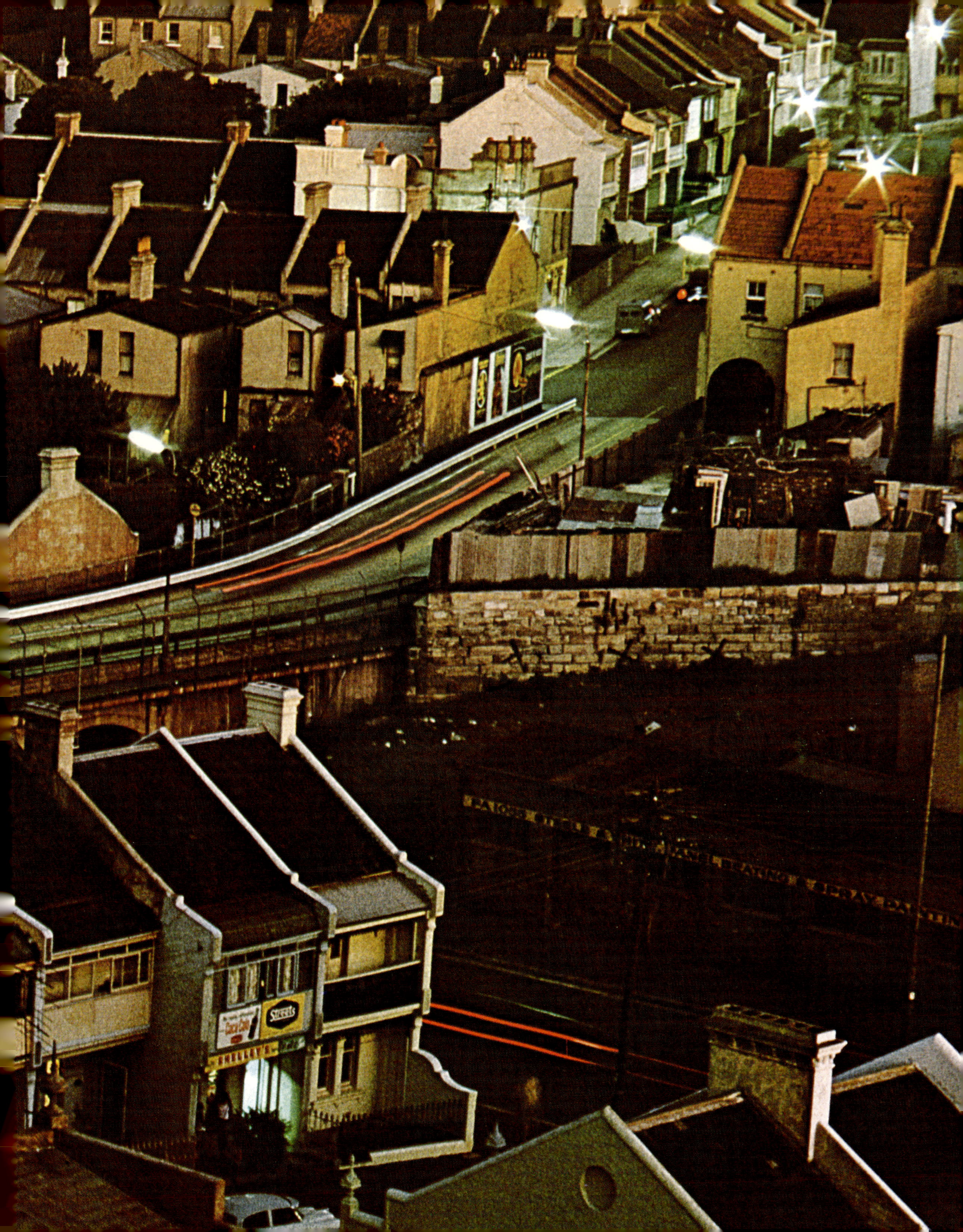
Streets

Kapunda, South Australia

26, 27) Terraces at night, Sydney

THE BUSH

CHANGE AND CHALLENGE

Douglas Lockwood

30, 31) Main street, Tibooburra, N.S.W.

God sits on a mountain crest in the Australian bush. He sits somewhere out there, I believe, because he regards it as his supreme accomplishment, as his own particular bit of terrestrial heaven.

Of course, I agree with God's judgment. I think I have proved that by giving more than quarter of a century to foretasting the Might-Be of man's future. In any case, I dislike everything urban. Cities are anathema to me. They restrict my breathing. I can't walk carelessly. I am made giddy by movement and insensible by sound. All I ever need to convince me of the wisdom of remaining in The Bush is an occasional visit to the big cities and their proliferating suburbia. Within a week I am thinking of The Quiet Places and The Wide Spaces, scheming for means to cancel appointments that prevent me getting back . . . to Borroloola and Beyond. I become annoyed at having allowed myself to compete in the Rodent Stakes, a lemming led by two million others in the daily quest for necessities, for a share of the roadway and the pavement and a patch of pansies. God has many protagonists in these uncomfortable places, and his biggest houses are there, yet I am convinced he must look upon cities as the work of the devil. He is against war, and life in the cities is war, equally distressing, almost as lethal.

Nevertheless, if this is to be an honest account of The Bush today it must begin by stating that it isn't what it used to be. Wheels and engines have seen to that. Now the hermits complain and beachcombers on the Gulf of Carpentaria lament the invasion of mining men, and their white women, and the hot and cold sliding doors.

Take Harry Blumantels for instance. He is a Baltic migrant who came to Australia at the end of the war with a torn body and memories he wanted to forget. When I first met him twenty years ago he was living on the fringes of the Gulf, lying around Limmen Bight in sand that was disturbed only by the tracks of turtles and crocodiles. They laid eggs conveniently close at hand. There were fish in the river. The bush and its wallabies were behind. But then the Limmen was taken up as a cattle station. Ringers moved in, and Blumantels moved out. He tried the lonely places between Burketown and Borroloola. Invariably, he was found; finally, disgusted, he accepted the inevitability of urban existence.

He chose Borroloola, with its population of about a dozen Europeans and a hundred or so Garawa and Anula aborigines. For the first time in his life he owned a house—a splendid 5000-gallon water tank turned upside down so that its iron bottom gave him a roof. The door was a hole cut in the tank's side. He bought it from an aboriginal woman for £26/11/1½, a rather odd sum but presumably all he had. The tank's previous owner had been Roger Jose, a man of astonishing wit who gave the world away when he went to Borroloola with a packhorse mail fifty years earlier. The aboriginal woman was his widow. Blumantels has since added a second storey—another tank. And there he sits, the base from which he wanders barefoot, complaining about the helicopters and aeroplanes and heavy machinery

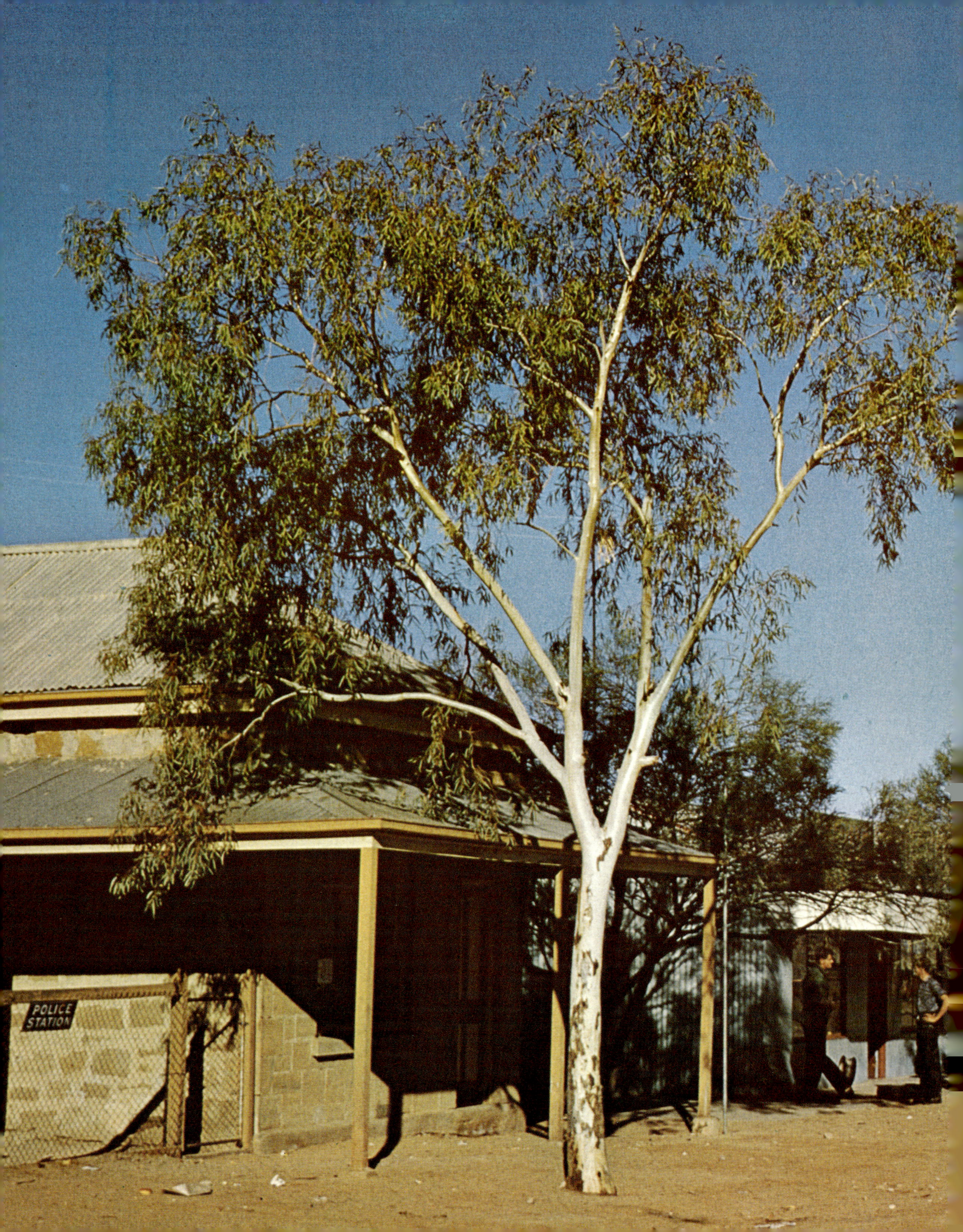
POLICE
STATION

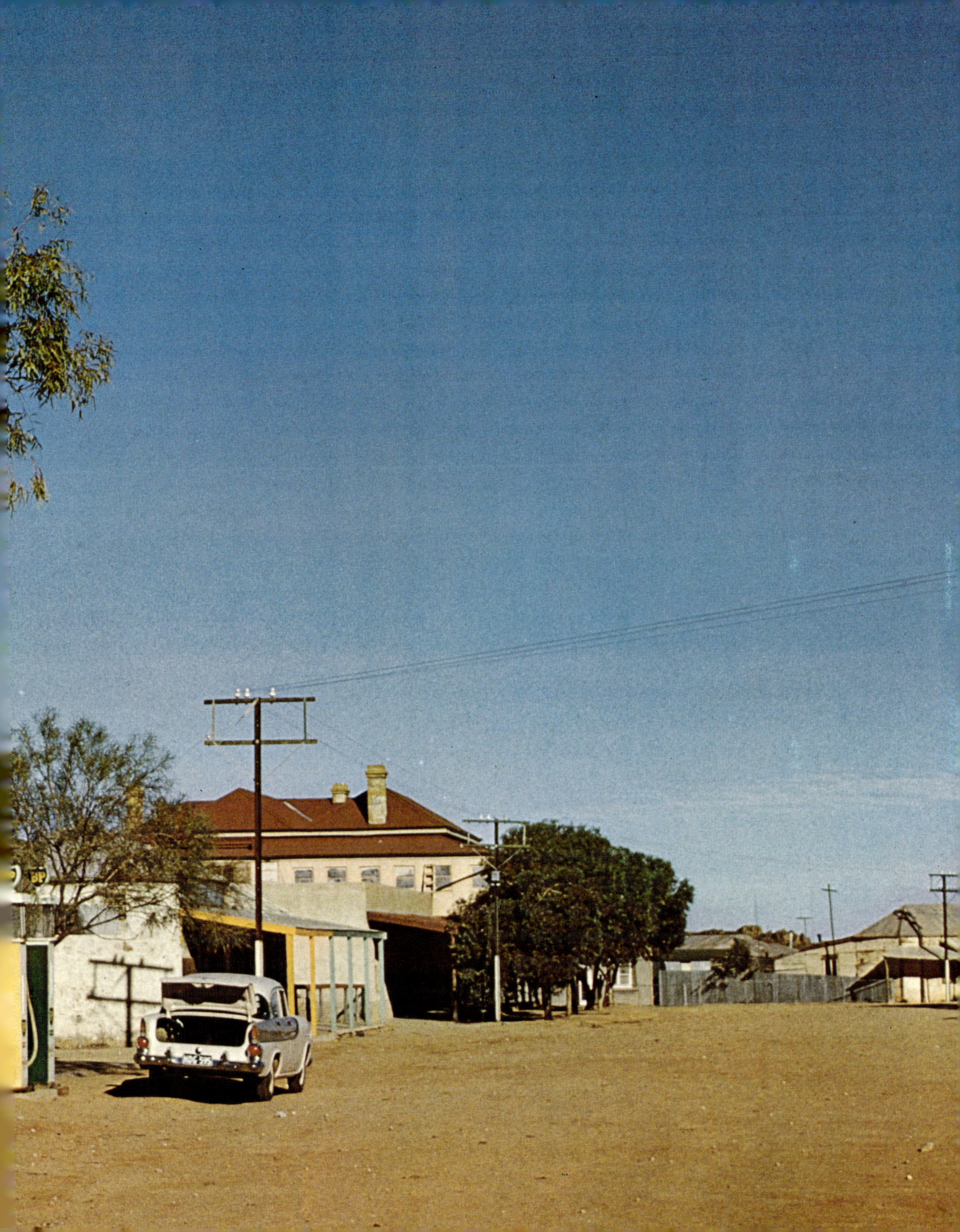

that have come to trouble him and his friends. A few miles away Mt. Isa Mines Ltd. has discovered a rich deposit of zinc. Within five years Borroloola is expected to lie midway between two towns serving the new field. Ten thousand people will be there. And a railway. And perhaps a hydrofoil service. Certainly lack of peace.

"We are being pushed out," Blumantels complains. "Beachcombers have nowhere to go. The bush is disappearing. Australia is becoming a factory and a quarry." His recipe for the future is a mixture of solitude and anti-progress, of support for anything that will deter the bulldozers, the hoardings, the service stations, the hot dog stands, the no-parkers, the desecrators, the speculators who would lease chains of waterholes. He would boil them in oil, and he has many in his team, myself included, who would gladly stoke the fires.

There are others like him. Roger Jose was one. Until the day he died he carried his water buckets on a yoke across his shoulders and lived on such food as crows, hawks ("uninteresting if not fat"), lizards, lily roots, turtles and brolgas. He barred pelicans. Sandals he made himself were tied to his feet with rags. A tea cosy sat on his head as a fez. He looked like Moses with long grey hair and beard, leaning on a stick he called a staff. He tended the grave of his fullblood aboriginal first wife, Maggie, and when he re-married it was to her sister, Biddy. Jose and Bill Harney both read through the hundreds of volumes in a library established at Borroloola (of all places!) by the Andrew Carnegie Trust. Both had photographic memories and competed in quoting the Bible, Shakespeare, Plato, Aristotle, Tolstoy and Goethe. Fortunately, they absorbed their knowledge before termites got to work on the wooden shelves and the precious pages. The tatters they left were scattered by trade winds until all traces of the library disappeared. Jose loved literature, especially the Bible. When I asked him about the New Version he said: "Like many of his kind, this salty, uninhibited, utterly hopeless old recluse is a dyed-in-the-wool paranoic. His current obsession is the cremation while still alive of those reptiles who would fain interfere with The Book."

Having been in The Bush for so long myself, I am able to understand these cries from the hearts of men like Blumantels and Jose. I am not entirely against the idea of anti-progress, or at least of the idea of preserving what remains unspoilt. Soon it may be too late. The superhighways are reaching out. A Sunday drive in the country near the major cities is already a bumper-to-bumper agony. Before long we may have elevated roads with concrete walls scarring across the landscape. Then you'll see only the car ahead and the cars around you and the uniform green and white signs announcing: "Next exit for Coober Pedy."

It is idle to hope that we might become as backwardly enlightened as Britain in preserving country lanes and perpetuating green belts. We are not likely to legislate for man's right to live in solitude, nor to protect the race of drovers and bullockies. Most of them have gone from the far outback already and will soon be a dimming

Facade, Albury, N.S.W.
34, 35) High country, N.S.W.

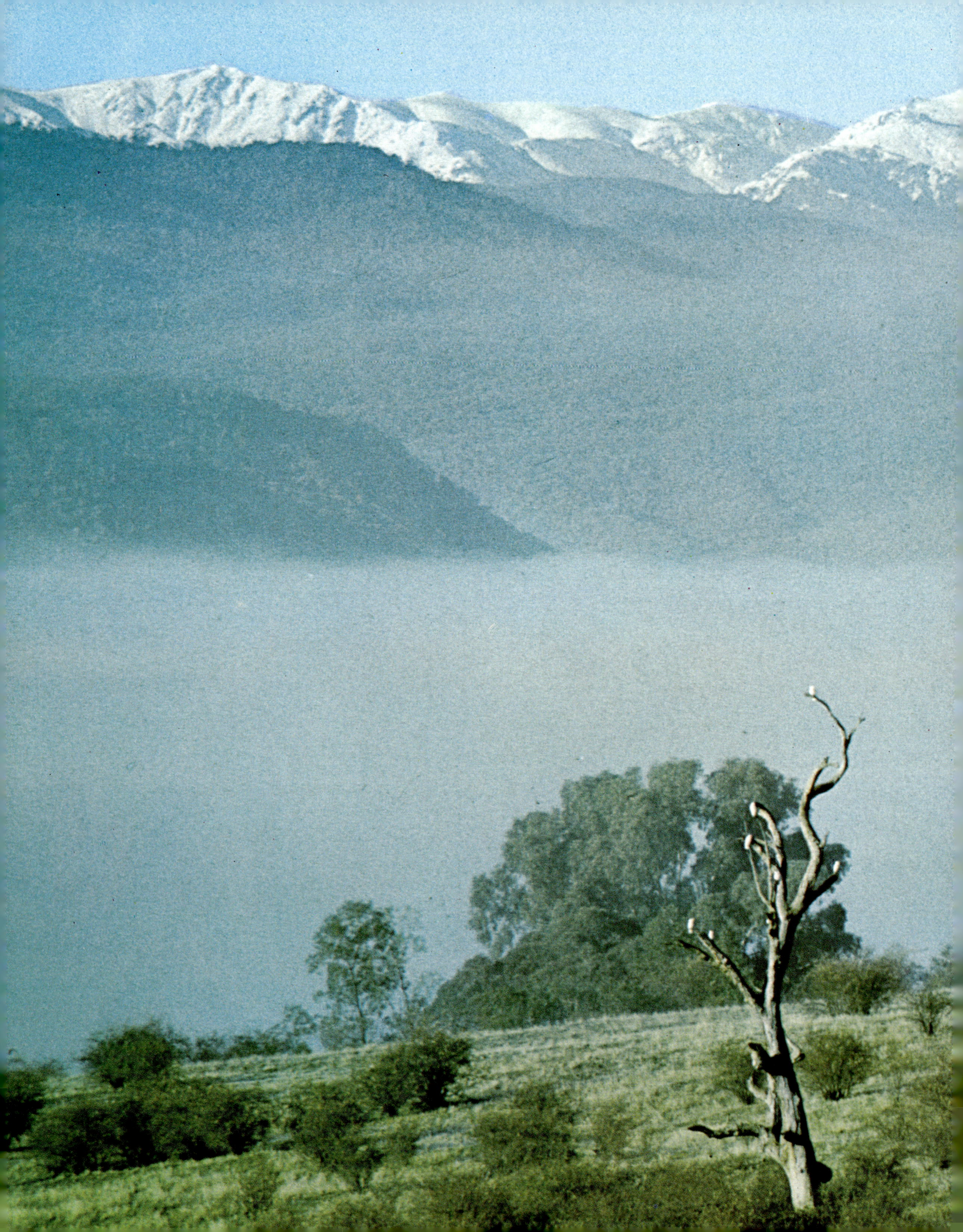

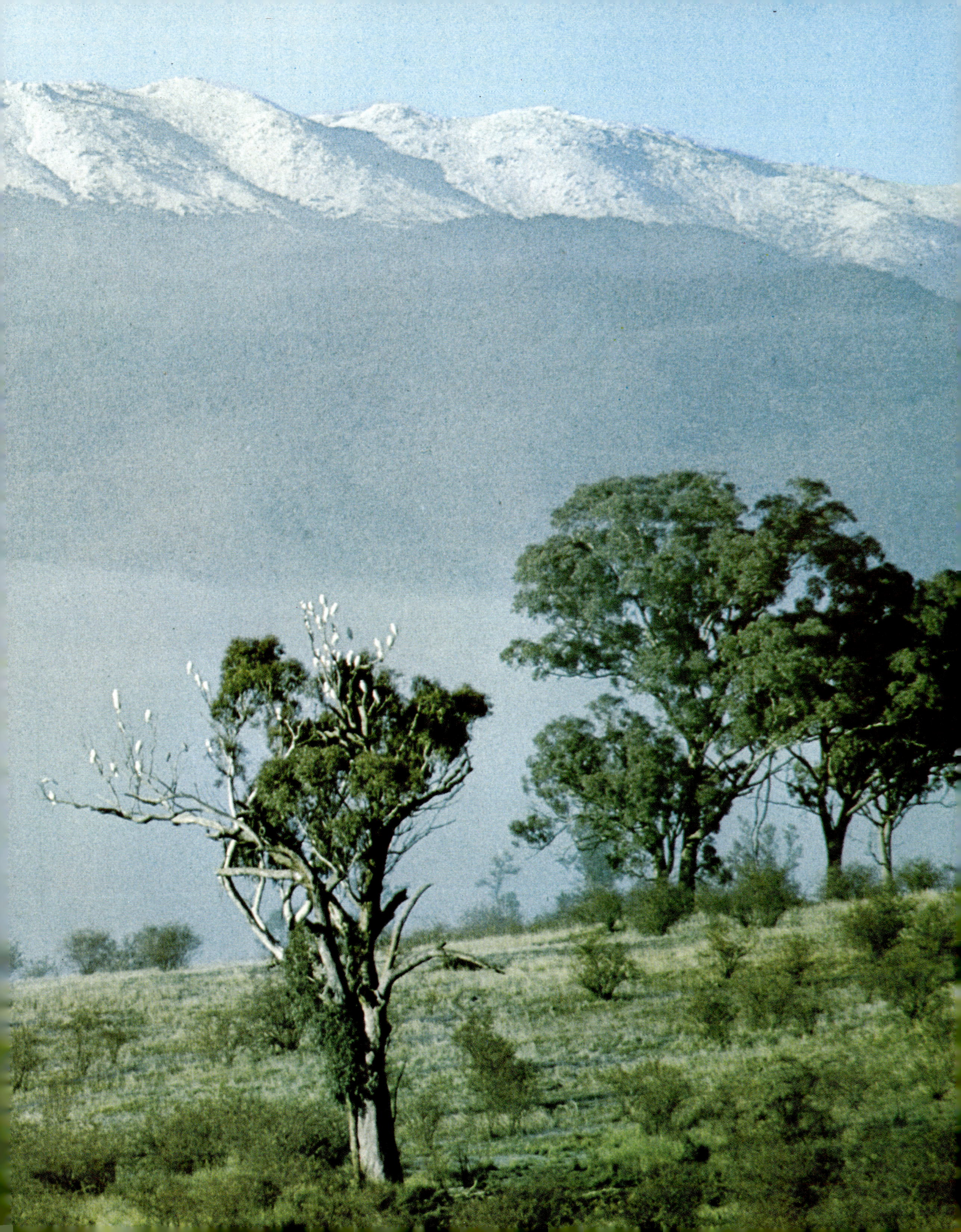

memory. There has been a transformation on the Barkly Tableland and the Murranji stockroutes, where a hundred thousand cattle once tramped annually to market two or three months away. Among the most enchanted evenings of my life are those I spent around drovers' campfires while aboriginal stockmen sang to the huge mobs of 1500 cattle. But now the drover is a driver, and he carries a spare. He sleeps not in a swag but in a bunk in the cabin of a truck while his mate drives. The cattle come along behind, trapped in mobile cages, hauled to their miserable fates.

Similar changes have occurred in human travel through The Bush. I remember the days when we rode and were welcome. That did not alter in the era of the first cars and the first wheel tracks. But highways have caused the signs to be replaced. The entrance to one homestead on the Barkly Tableland has a notice which says simply, "Keep going." Another proclaims, "This is *not* a roadhouse." A few years ago those settlers were glad to see visitors. Now they are regarded as pests.

Air travel through the outback used to be an experience. Today it is transportation. My first trip from Adelaide to Darwin was in a 10-seat Lockheed. We landed at Mt. Eba for breakfast in a shed, with the station owner and his wife waiting on us. We had lunch on the ground at Alice Springs and dinner and a bed at Daly Waters. The pilot, Ken Steele, took us along to meet Bill Pearce, the publican, and stayed to have a few drinks with us. He was one of the boys. During the flight he came along to sit on the arm of my seat to chat reassuringly, to point out places of interest. What happens now? The jets fly across the bushland at night. You see nothing, not even the pilot, who remains in his airtight cabin. Occasionally the loudspeaker crackles impersonally. "This is your Captain on the flight deck." *Your* captain, as though you are his corporal. "We are at thirty thousand feet. Our ground speed is five hundred and seventy miles an hour. Our flying time from Darwin to Alice Springs will be ninety minutes." You are unaware even of the speed. You might as well be deep-frozen—and give them time; they'll get around to that, too.

It used to be different. When the Buchanans and the Duracks, the Bathems and the Bostocks, the Farrars and the Gunns first took their women into the Deep Outside they knew the only way to get back with a broken leg would be to ride. Mrs. Phoebe Farrar was one of them. I knew her as The Bush Mother, a slight, grey-haired lady who felt undressed without spurs at her heels when she was 75. Riding trousers and a big felt hat were as important in her life as nylons and lipstick to others. She was the most courageous woman I have known, and one of the nation's greatest stockmen. It would be unfitting to call her a stockwoman. When she died, aged 92, I hoped they might have hung spurs on her headstone to give her a good ride through the unknown.

In 1882, when she was only 14, she rode with new settlers from Normanton to the Limmen River, in the south-west corner of the

Gulf country. They were four months on the road. She married Robert Farrar, son of one of the settlers who brought her to the wilderness. When her husband became ill, Phoebe Farrar did all the station mustering, branding and droving. She once took 300 cattle for 400 miles with only one half-caste stockman and a dog to help her. At 60, her pelvis was broken when she was knocked down by a bullock. "You'll never ride again," the doctors told her. And it seemed that would be so. The accident prevented her reaching a stirrup iron with her foot. So The Bush Mother mounted from stumps, from trees, from stockyard fences, and sometimes with human help—but she mounted, and stayed riding until she was 75. Then she had to stop because her eyesight failed.

That was the sort of stuff the bush pioneers were made of. And these days there are still people like them, because even though the Bush is changing fast, becoming civilised, you can always pick some tough, remote part of it to test your strength against. In 1947 Constable Bill Waudby left the N.T. police force and selected 1200 square miles of semi-desert 150 miles west of The Alice. He found water by boring, used his RAAF deferred pay for a grubstake and camp gear, and borrowed $400 to marry Patricia Rugless in Adelaide. He brought her back to a bough shed on Central Mt. Wedge station. Waudby carted an army hut 800 miles and re-erected it as his homestead. In 1952 his first cattle were ready for market. He drove them towards Alice Springs with his wife and infant son, James, sleeping in swags beside him. One night Pat Waudby said, "I can't move my legs." She had not been near civilisation for two months, yet she had polio and spent the next nine months in an iron lung. Their homestead was burnt down. They struggled through eight years of drought, with the raingauge good only as a dustgauge. Then it was carried away in a flood and the new homestead was isolated for three weeks by mud and water. Waudby walked cattle 500 miles from the south Kimberleys, and walked much of it with them, to help restock his depleted property.

His young neighbour, David ("Diddy") Smith, was a small teenager when he left college to establish Mount Allan station. For eleven years, while he built fences and dams and a homestead, his only bed was a swag. Like thousands of other stockmen whose interest is in horses, he relaxed at bush rodeos and race meetings, seldom drove the 180 miles to Alice Springs. And a few years ago the Coppock family drove stock west from Alice Springs, towards the sunset, until they found pasture at Newhaven, more than 200 miles out. Just like that.

But the sort of pioneering which our forefathers faced, pioneering accompanied by the danger of utter and absolute remoteness from any other human contact—that's gone. Young settlers taking up former desert land in South Australia's south-east, in Victoria's north-west, in Western Australia's south-west, in Queensland's north, have the advantage of adequate communications, of refrigeration, of bottled gas, of radio that keeps even the most isolated of them within

38, 39) Cattle crossing, Hunter Valley, N.S.W.

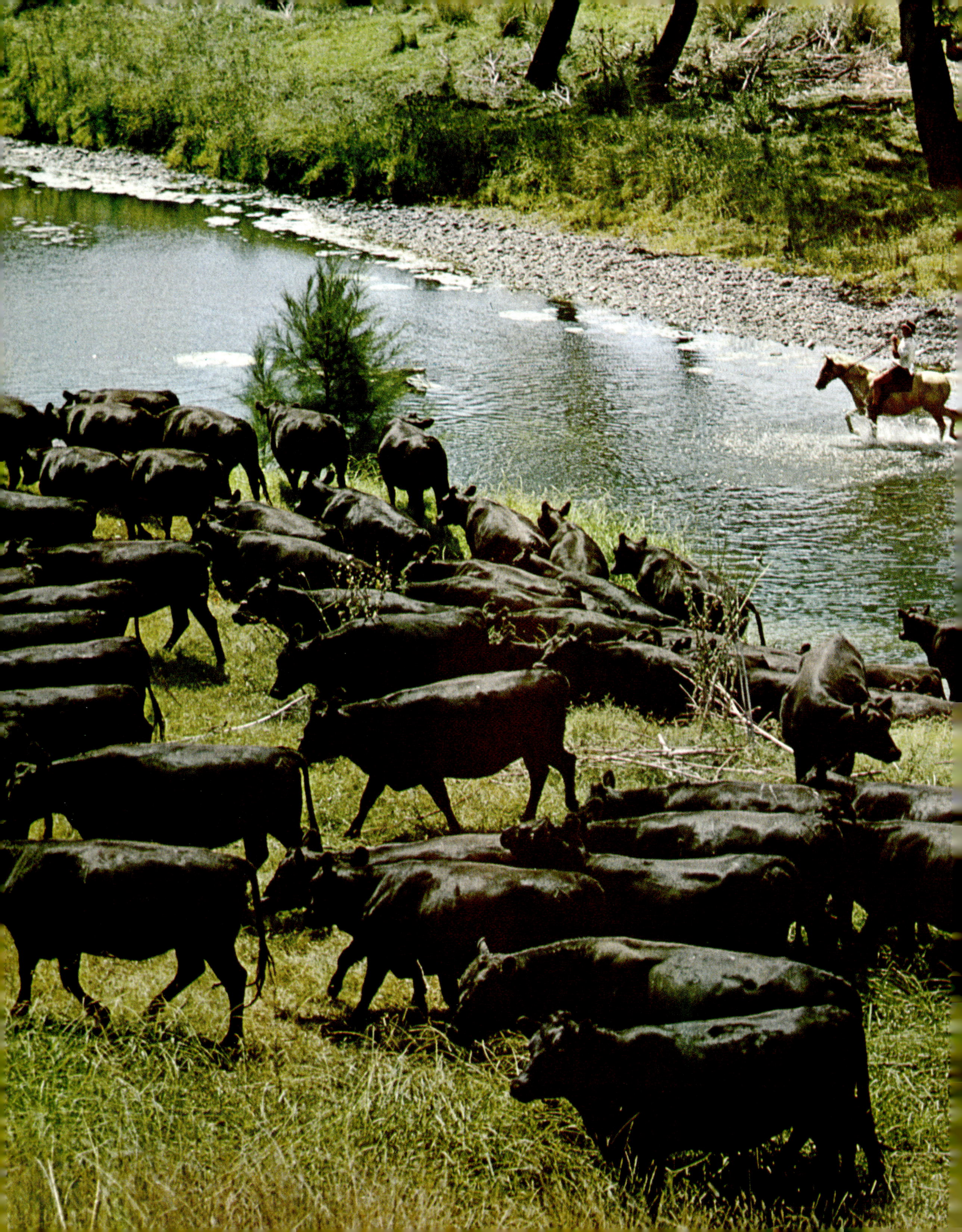

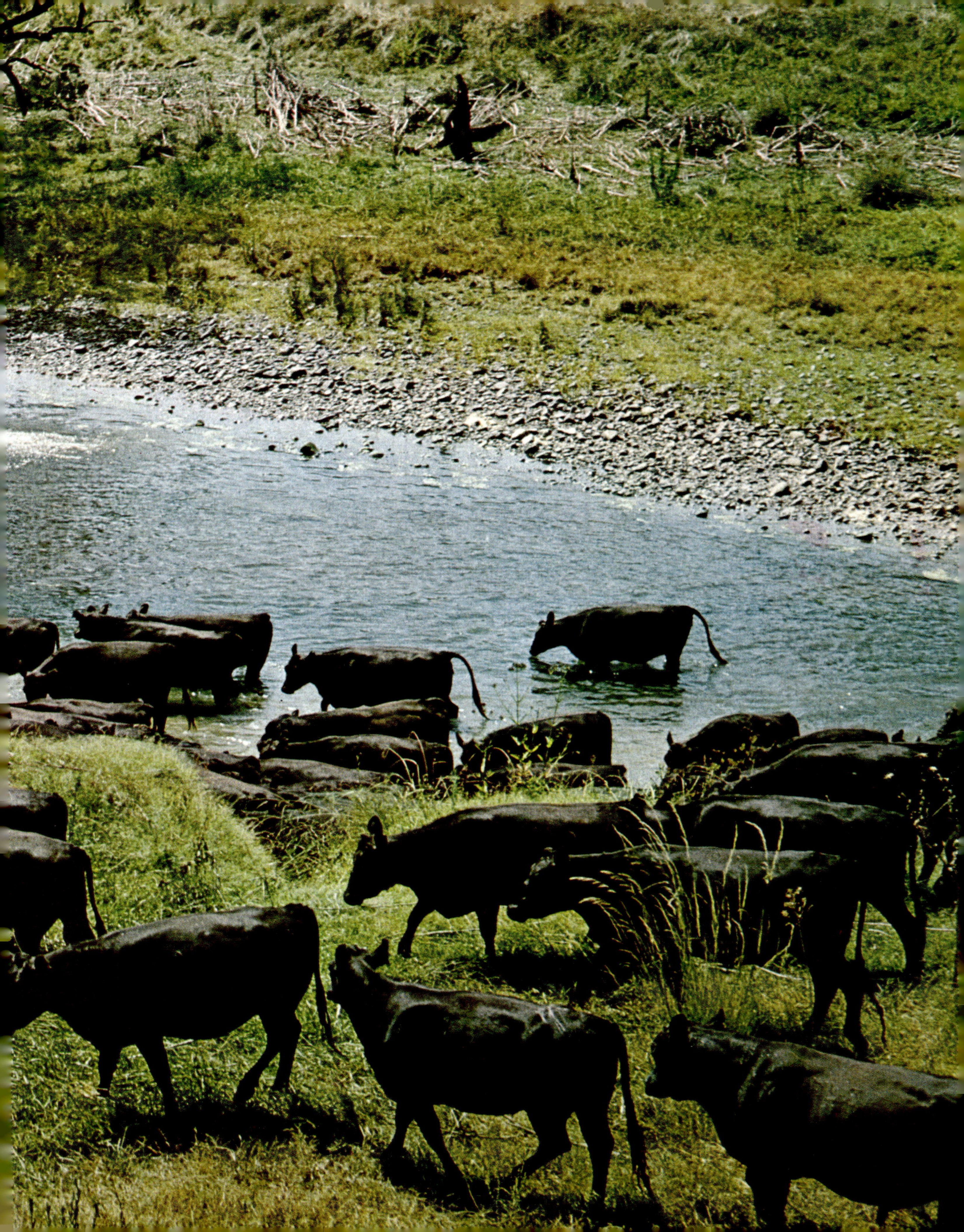

immediate reach of emergency aid. That is equally true of the cattle stations in Central Australia, in the Kimberleys, in the Victoria River district, and around the Gulf of Carpentaria. White women of the west need no longer fear approaching confinements. Most of them are on scheduled airline services, or within easy distance. Connellan Airways, alone, lands at more than 100 missions, settlements and stations in north and central Australia. The Commonwealth Aerial Medical Service and the Royal Flying Doctor Service make routine and emergency visits to hundreds of properties. Treatment is available within hours for anyone, down to the lowliest aboriginal baby. In fact, aboriginal patients predominate. A doctor speaks by radio, successor of Traeger's pedal wireless, to a mission nurse or a station manager's wife. A diagnosis is made and treatment may be prescribed. If the symptons are serious the patient is flown to the nearest hospital. Doctors and nurses visit all centres about once a month, checking on everything from leprosy to a cut finger, and suggesting when pregnant women should fly in to hospital.

There are people who have devoted their lives to this service. Captain Jack Slade, A.F.C., M.B.E., has been flying for the Aerial Medical Service since 1946. A number of Flying Sisters have been at it for years. But they could not operate without dedicated men and women at the other end who run the missions and settlements caring for aborigines; and of these none is less famous, except to the natives, than Mrs. Harold Shepherdson, wife of the Methodist Missionary at Elcho Island.

She has been with her husband in Arnhem Land since 1928. When the north coast was threatened by Japanese invasion she refused to be evacuated. From 1942 until the end of the war she was the only white woman civilian on the coast between Wyndham and the Gulf. At the height of the danger she was "bushed" for two months by her husband. She lived in a small shack a few miles inland from Milingimbi, accompanied by twenty natives and a herd of goats. She ate wallaby, crabs and turtles caught by her guardians. She had a battery-driven radio. The situation was such that she couldn't converse but every day she sent a brief message in code saying she was all right.

Her husband, the Rev. Harold Shepherdson, is equally remarkable. He fought isolation by building his own aeroplane so that he might fly to the aid of the Stone Age people then living in Arnhem Land. Although now over 60, he still flies to eight unlicensed strips on the coast and in the unknown interior. He builds and maintains these strips himself with native help. He has survived a crash or two, has had six planes, and will go on doing unpretentiously what he has been doing for forty years.

These are some of the people, the pioneers and heroes and battlers and eccentrics, who live in The Bush today. But The Bush has become a wide generality since the Hentys landed at Portland, since the Manifolds pushed out into the Western District of Victoria, since Blaxland, Lawson and Wentworth crossed the Blue Mountains, since

Leichhardt made his crossing from Brisbane to Port Essington in 1845, since Eyre and Sturt and Giles and Stuart were laying the tracks for others to follow. Much of what was then The Bush has since become urban, throbbing with heavy and primary industry. Once it was kangaroos and koalas, with wild aborigines to contend with. Today it is sheep and cattle, wheat and wool, rice and cotton, silver, lead, zinc, gold, iron ore, uranium—and white people. The archetypal Australian was once supposed to be a lantern-jawed, digger-hatted, sun-bronzed stockman in elastic-sided boots, rolling his own cigarette. His name was Mate or Pal or Cobber. But now the big-hatted stockman is one in ten thousand. Like the steam engine, he has been replaced, and the man in his boots is more likely to be named Maddalozzo or Papandonikis, Faustmann or Mihailovitch, Hjasek or Van Eck, Featherstonehaugh or J. Marlon ("Bud") Denver, jnr. Greeks and Italians are building the new outback towns. Yugoslavs are driving dump trucks and gouging opals, some living underground at Coober Pedy to escape heat on the treeless plains. Finns are working in the mines at Mt. Isa. The office telephones in roadhouses across the nation are likely to be answered in a Cockney accent. Americans are acquiring land. Every plane flying north and west has its complement of Texans or Californians come to inspect the new frontiers. They include the Art Linkletters, who are absentee owners at Esperance, Western Australia, and in the Northern Territory, but they also include the Asa Townsends who have disturbed the roots of generations in their native Florida and come to live— grandparents, children and grandchildren—at Stapleton station, near Adelaide River in the Northern Territory. Hot cakes and maple syrup instead of salt beef and damper for breakfast. A bunkhouse instead of a swag in a shed. A corral instead of a horse yard. And aeroplanes in the stable.

When I first knew it in the Victorian Wimmera, The Bush was a place where a man worked with his hands. As a youth, I helped drive 8-horse teams in ploughs, harvesters and huge wagons that carried 100 bags of wheat to the railway yard stacks around Horsham. Feeding the reins through my fingers, ribbons that controlled fine teams of Clydesdales; the harnessing and unhitching on winter mornings and summer evenings; and feeding them chaff and oats in stables whose thatched roofs were pocked with sparrows' nests—these are memories that I, at 52, cannot adequately communicate to my son. He has grown up in bush disturbed by machines. Sputtering tractors pull the ploughs. The wheat is not even bagged, let alone stacked; it goes in bulk trucks to the hungry traps of a silo, to be hidden behind concrete. Thus it is with the earth-movers shifting overburden from manganese on Groote Eylandt, from bauxite at Weipa and Gove, from Pilbara iron ore, from Queensland open cuts, or with the machines that cultivate cotton at Kununurra and rice along the Murrumbidgee.

Fullblood Andilyagua tribesmen at Groote Eylandt are driving D8 bulldozers for Broken Hill Proprietary Co. Ltd. and being paid award wages to do so. In that respect, at least, the change amounts to

42, 43) Sugar farm, Mt. Dryander, Queensland

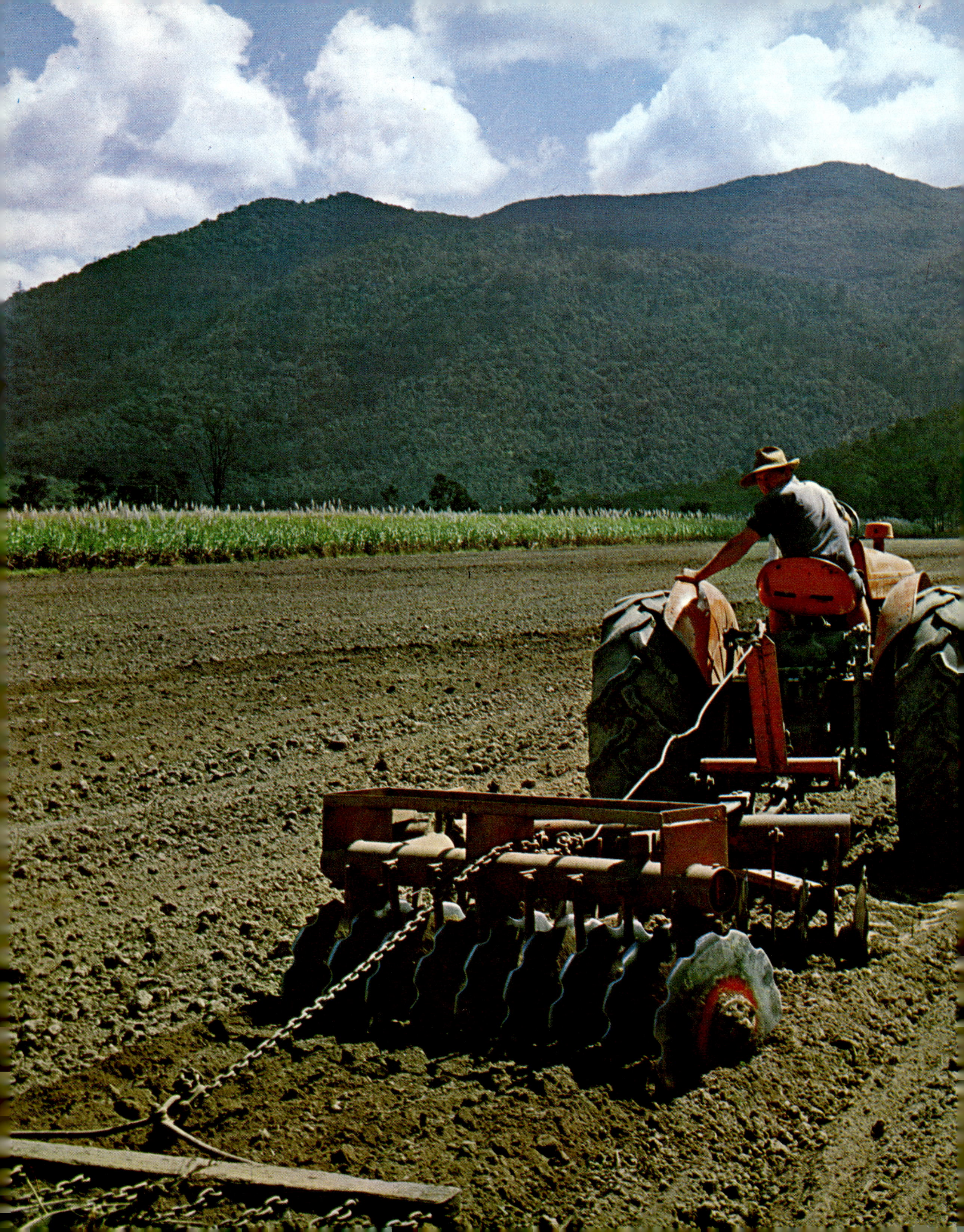

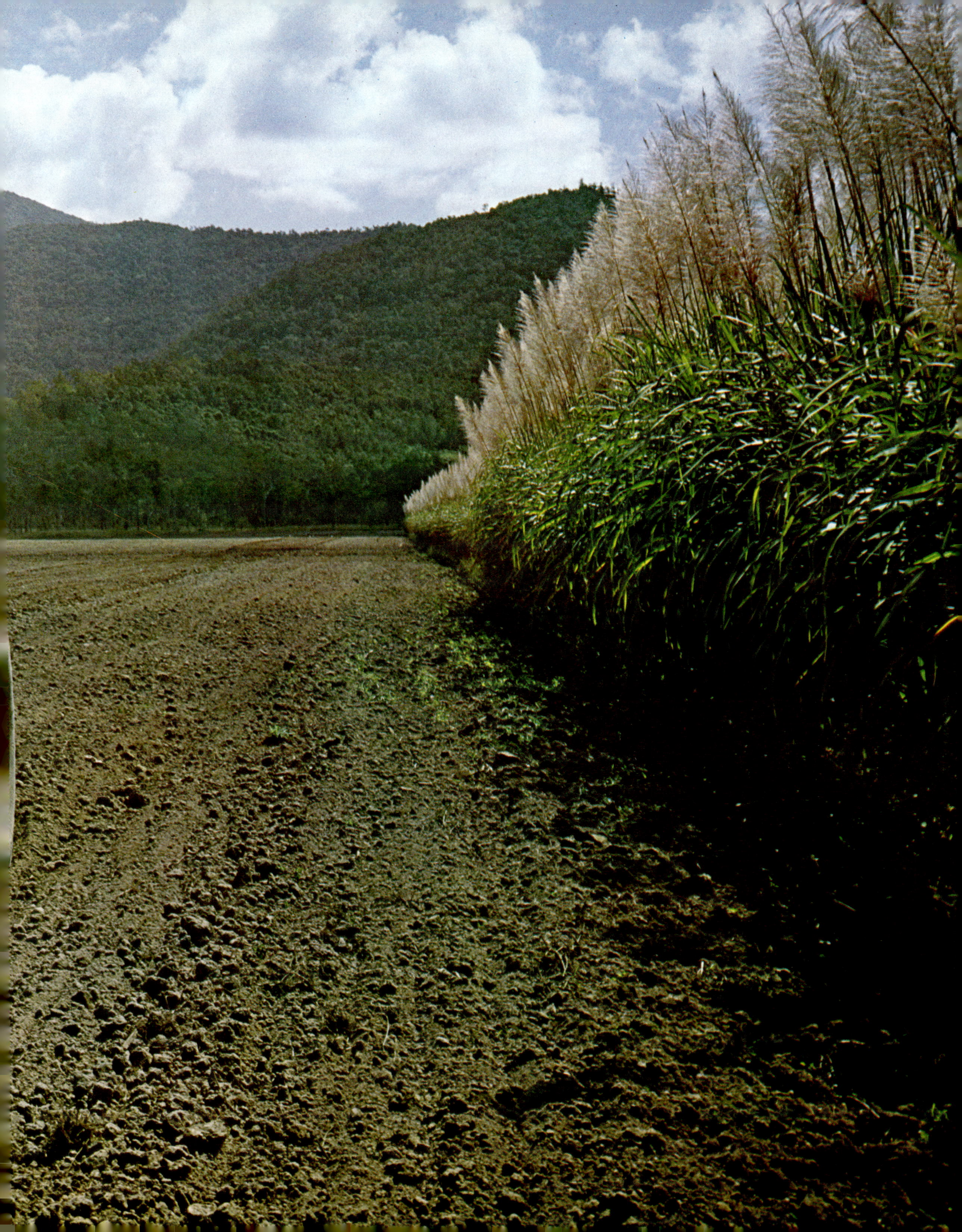

revolution. Chineses carriers once hauled firewood along Darwin's main streets in buffalo carts. Having outlived the market for their hides, and being no longer practical as beasts of burden, the buffalo are shot for their flesh. Perhaps half a million remain on the flood plains south and east of Darwin, the descendants of half a dozen survivors from the death of the north's earliest settlements at Fort Dundas, Raffles Bay and Port Essington. I saw Italians cutting cane at Innisfail and Ingham and believed they would always be there, going in behind the fires with the broad-bladed knives. Sugar cane, it seemed, would defy automation. But I have since seen it spewing, tons at a time, in uniform lengths from the bowels of yet another monstrous machine. So it is with most of our primary products. Men's hands are used to tally the crops instead of harvesting them.

I am not deploring any of this, except that it destroys the beauty of The Bush. Modern comforts and gadgetry, perhaps more than anything, will bring people away from the ugly cities into the softer, kinder life of The Bush. New towns are growing back of beyond. Port Hedland and Dampier, plastered with the red ochre the aborigines used for corroboree daubs, will be as important as Geelong, the city of wheat and wool. Ballarat and Bendigo, Bathurst and Kalgoorlie, the provincial cities founded on gold, will have 20th century contemporaries built on non-precious metals. The ghost towns will live again. Borroloola, God help us, will have laundromats and parking meters. Normanton is already at the end of a sealed beef road and has become the centre for Gulf traders freighting stock to Julia Creek and to the railway to Townsville. Alice Springs is the darling of tourism, attracting 20,000 a year (three times its own population) to the harsh scenery at Ayers Rock, Palm Valley, Standley Chasm, and any other valley or rock or chasm the brochures can boast about.

Even the Gibson Desert is no longer deserted. Len Beadell and his grader drivers have pushed and sliced through the red earth a long way west of Alice, creating the roads which will bring men. The Gun Barrel Highway, straight as its name, leads to Giles . . . and Sandy Blight Junction . . . and Jupiter Well . . . and finally to the Canning stockroute in Western Australia. At that point you are deep in the tribal lands of the Pintubi nomads and closer to the western coast of this huge continent than to Alice Springs.

It was there, on a 1963 government patrol, that I first met an Australian who had never heard the word "Australia." He had never seen a white skin, nor a shirt, nor a tin of bully beef. He and his tribesmen had no knowledge of world wars, of oceans, of sheep, of houses, even of safety matches which produced instant fire. These men had been terrified of aeroplanes that occasionally flew over their lands, not knowing what they were, believing them to be monstrous devils. They buried themselves in the sand, or hid under the spinifex—as they did when Len Beadell's blades of steel, mechanical dinosaurs, ate huge chunks of earth as they wheeled across the desert and left behind the biggest tracks any of these professional trackers

Excavating iron ore, Koolanooka, Western Australia
46, 47) Ayers Rock, Northern Territory

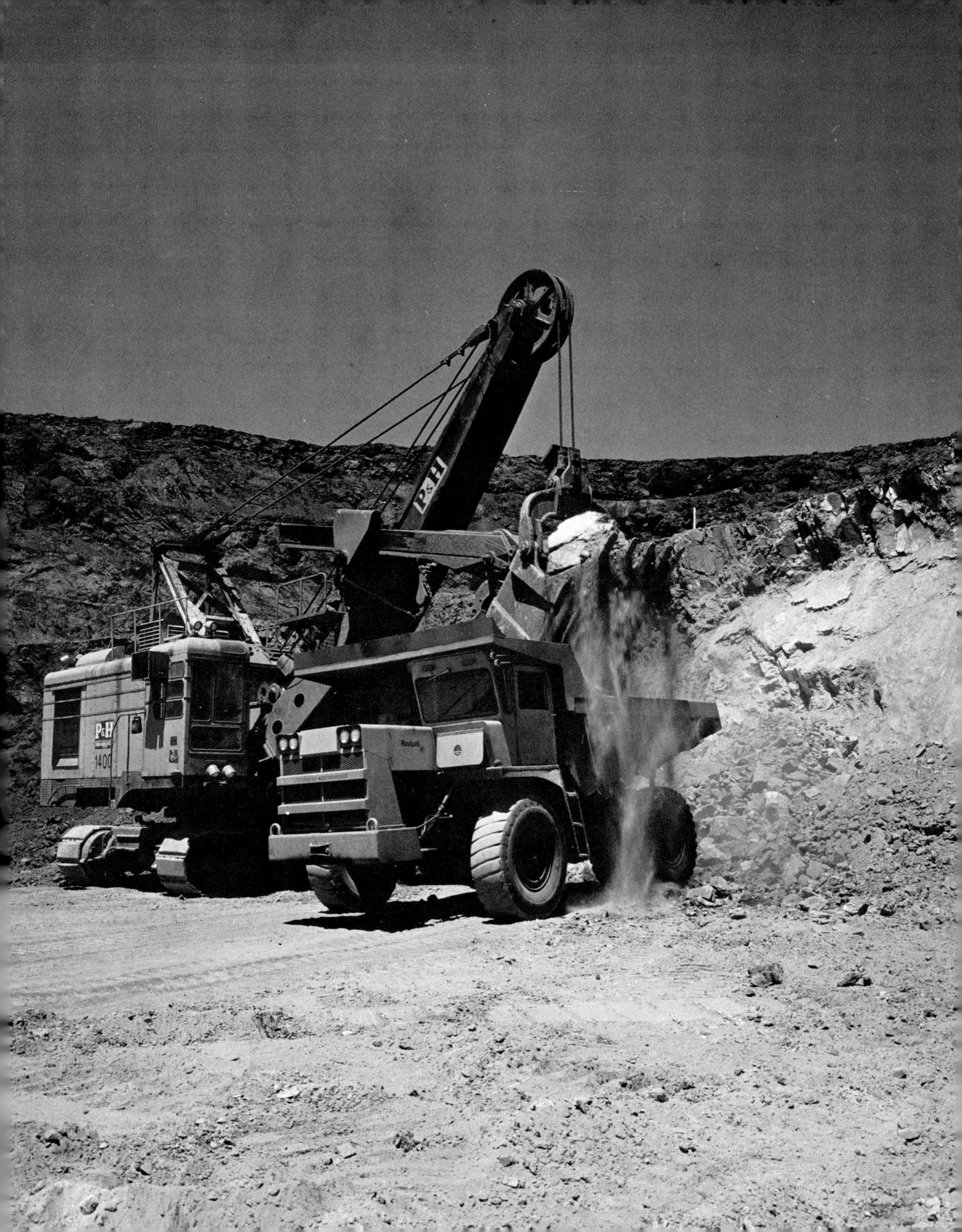
P&H
P&H
1400
Haulpak

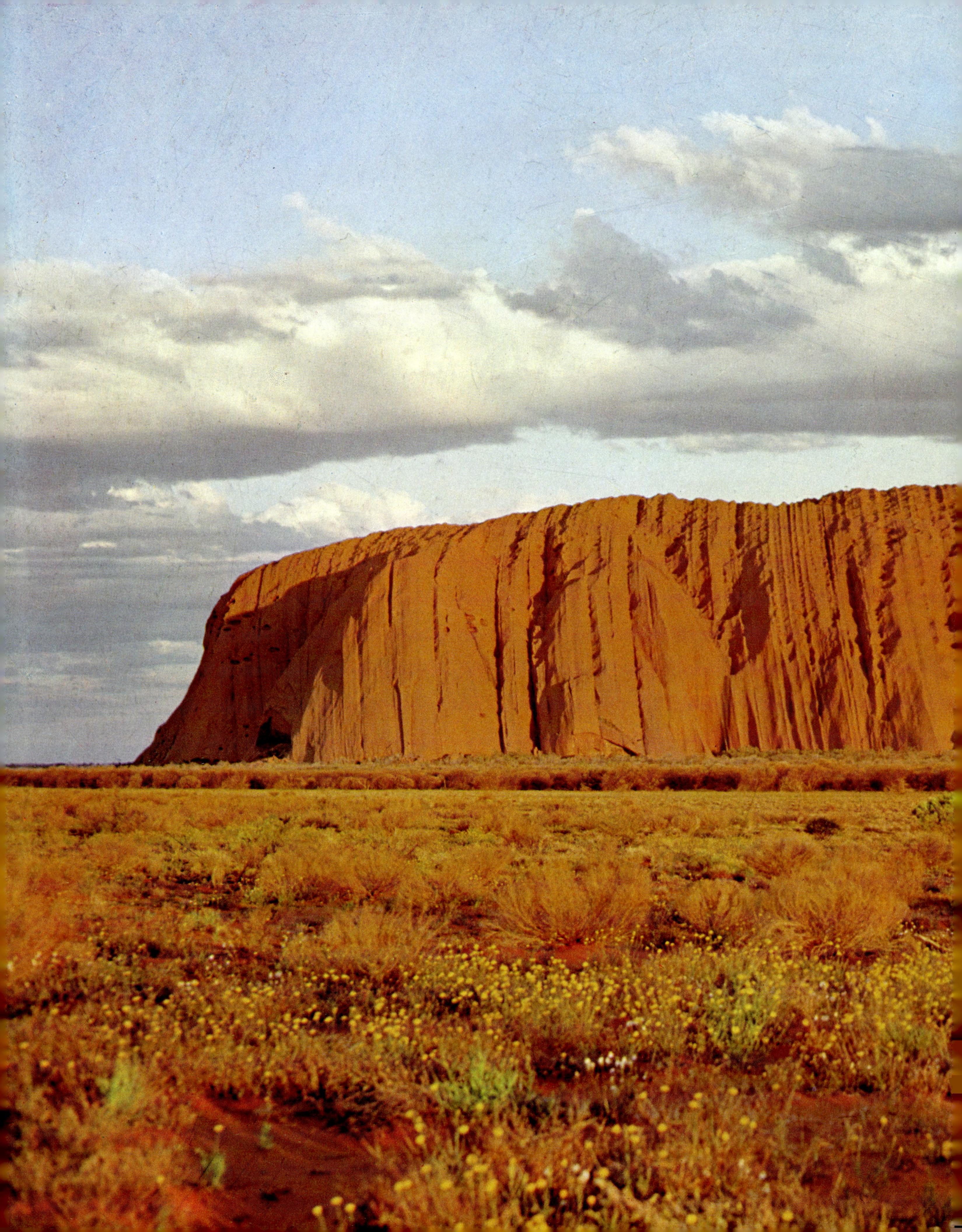

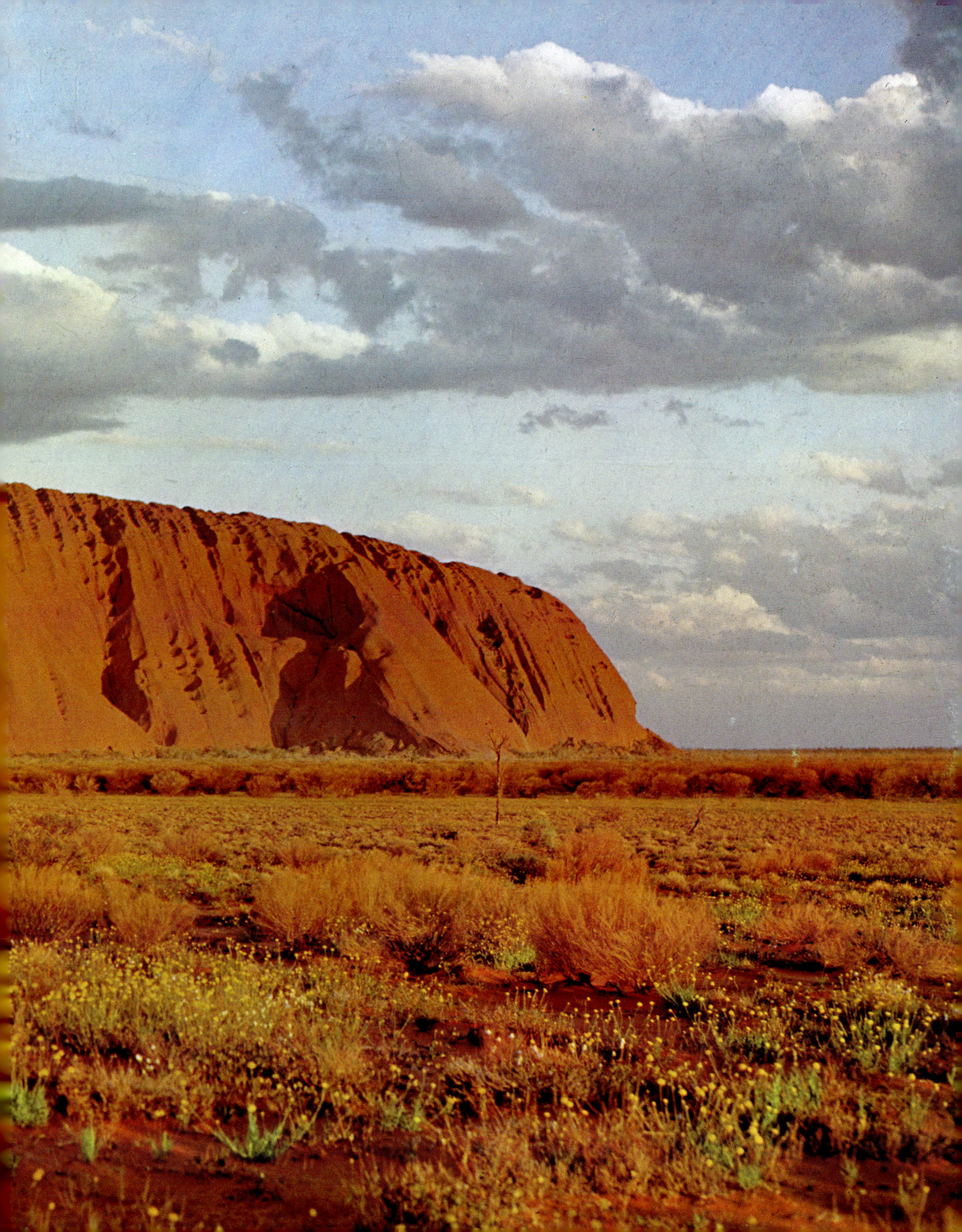

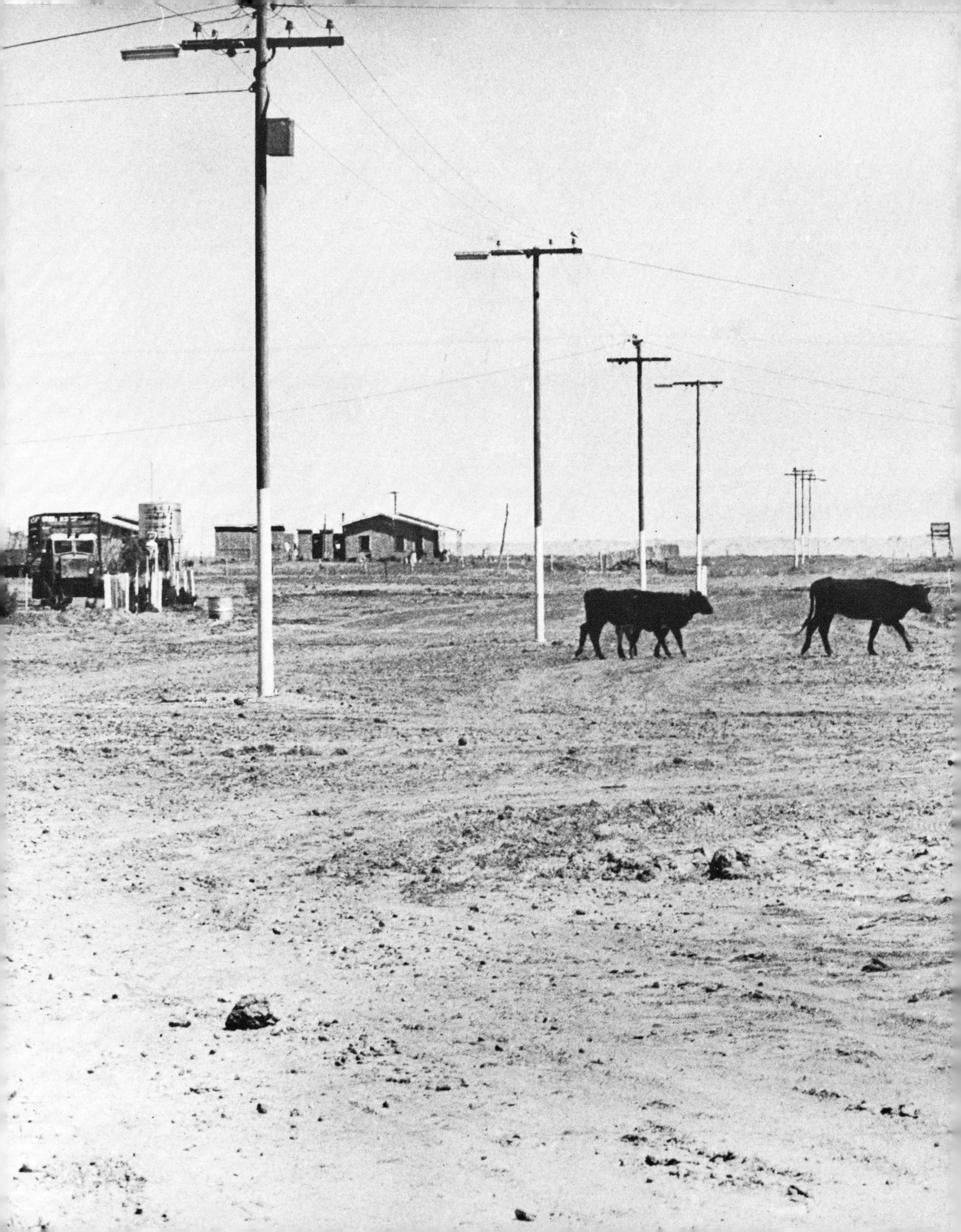

Main street, Birdsville, Queensland

50, 51) Autumn, Bright, Victoria
Outback family, Clifton Hill station, South Australia

49

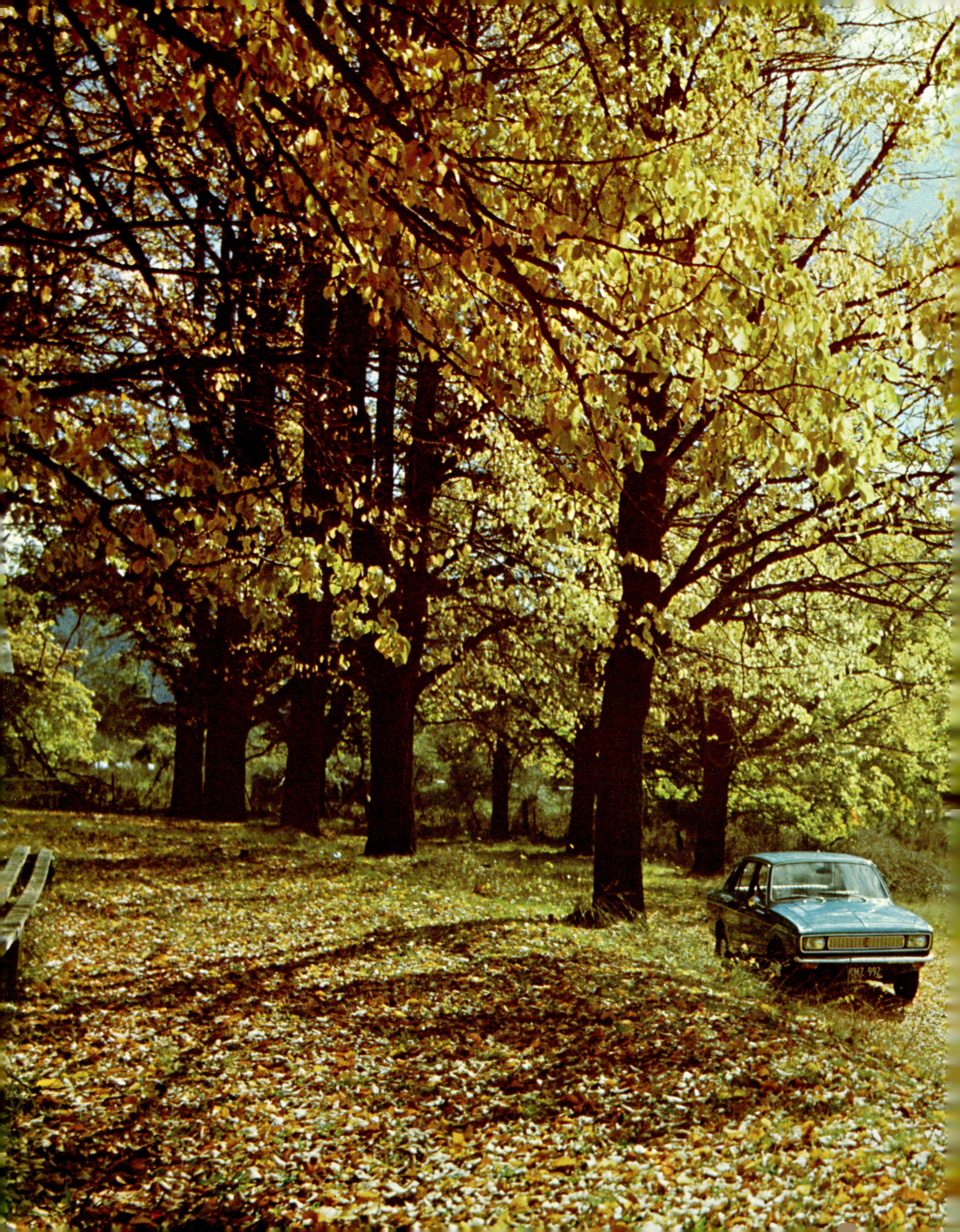

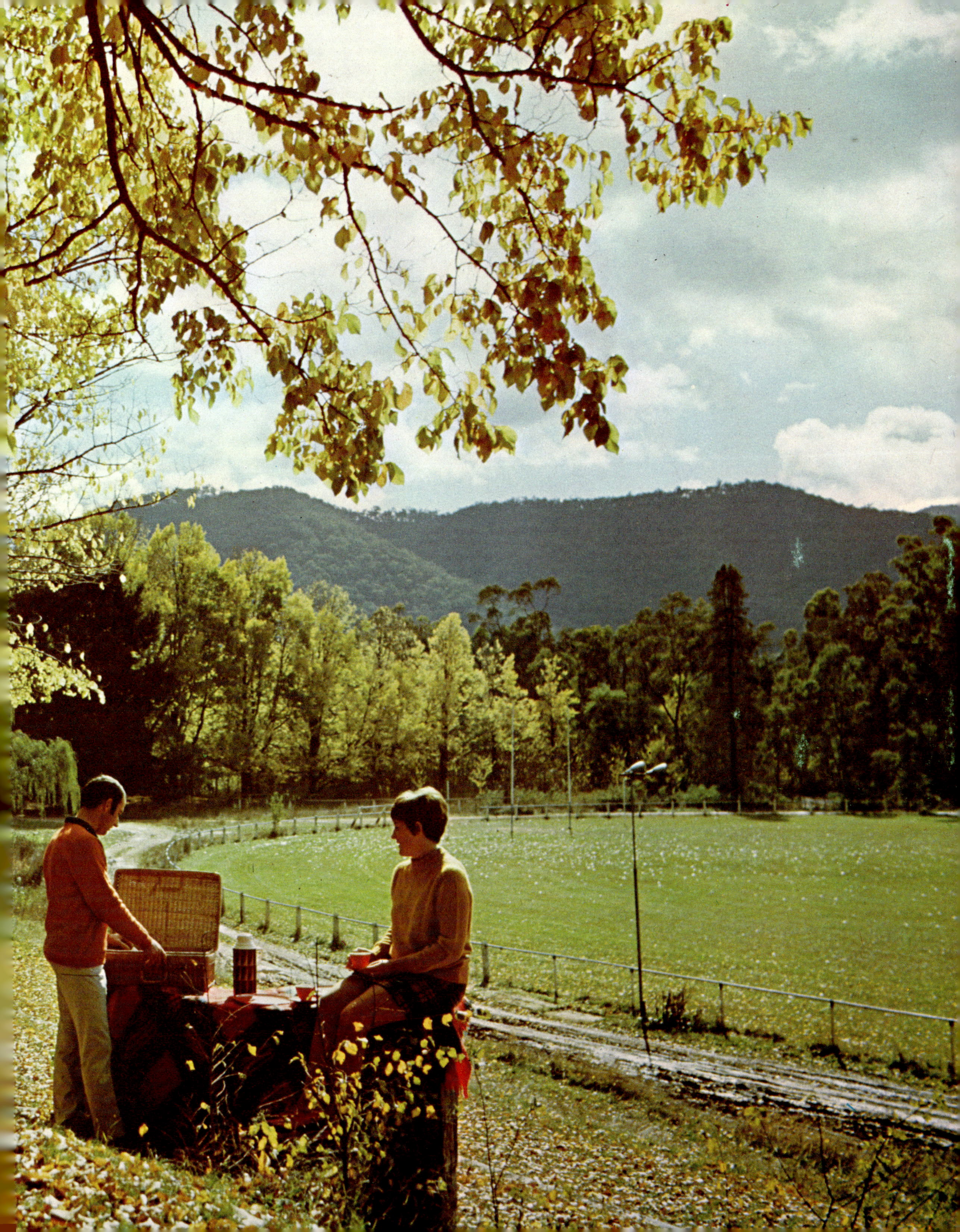

Aboriginal stockman, Coopers Creek, Queensland

had seen. Their terror must have matched that of their grandfathers, some of whom *had* seen a white skin. It belonged to the Hon. David Carnegie, who had chased and roped them in 1896, and kept them roped until they were forced to lead him to their sparse desert soaks. Only in that way could Carnegie survive. He could not carry enough water on camels while riding from the fringes of the Nullarbor to Hall's Creek.

But we could. We established water and fuel dumps. At Sandy Blight Junction and elsewhere we called Alice Springs daily to report our progress. When a truck broke down we asked for help. We had wheels, tools, radios, as much water as we needed, cool martinis to quench the thirst the water wouldn't, olives on toothpicks, steak for dinner . . . and everything else a man might need to follow the highway westwards from Alice to where the sun disappears behind spinifex. The Bush has changed. But the men and women who've done the changing, I hope they don't disappear along with the Chinese carriers and eight-horse teams and battered Lockheeds which progress has shoved back into the history books. We need people like them. The Bush will always need them.

Marree, South Australia

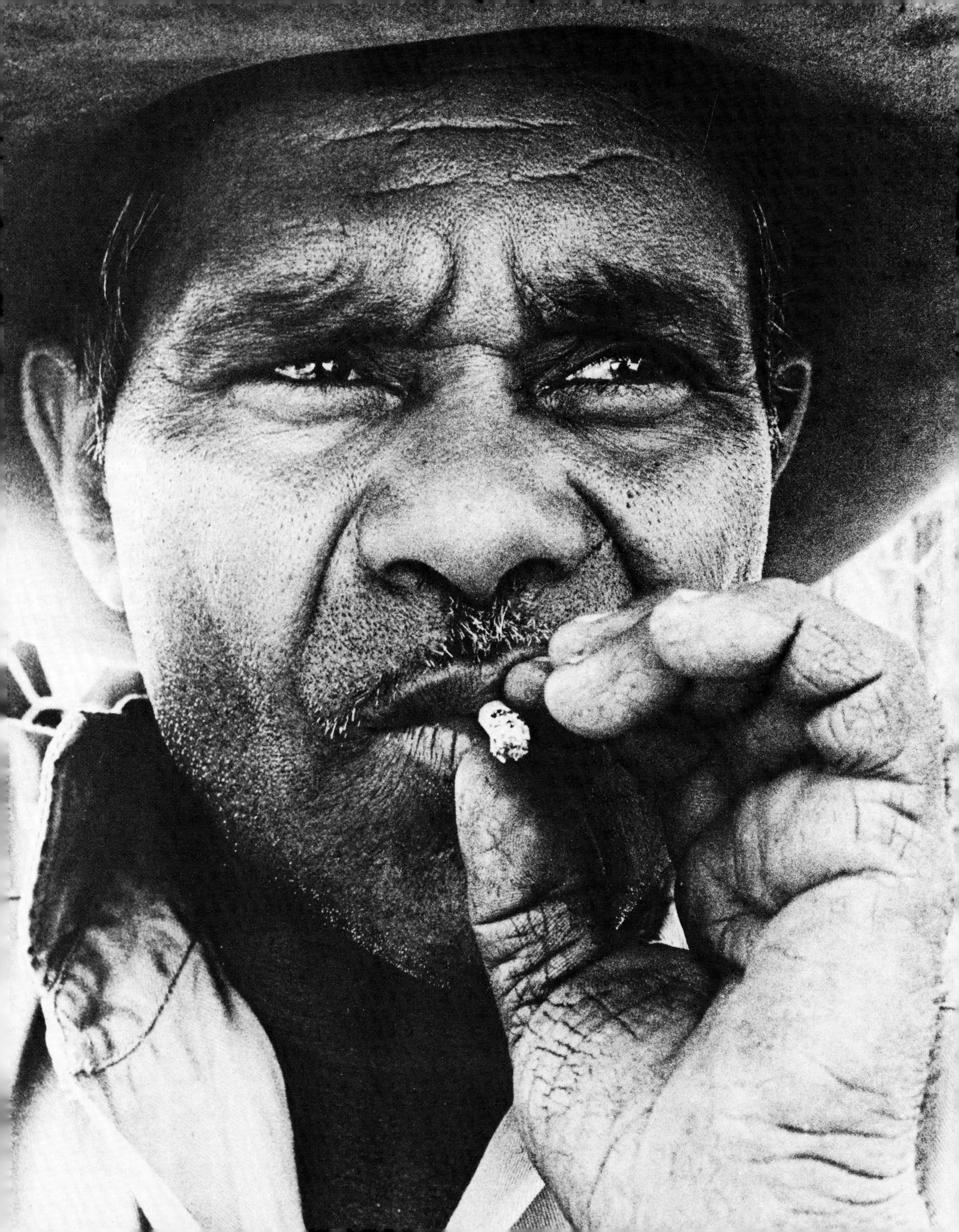

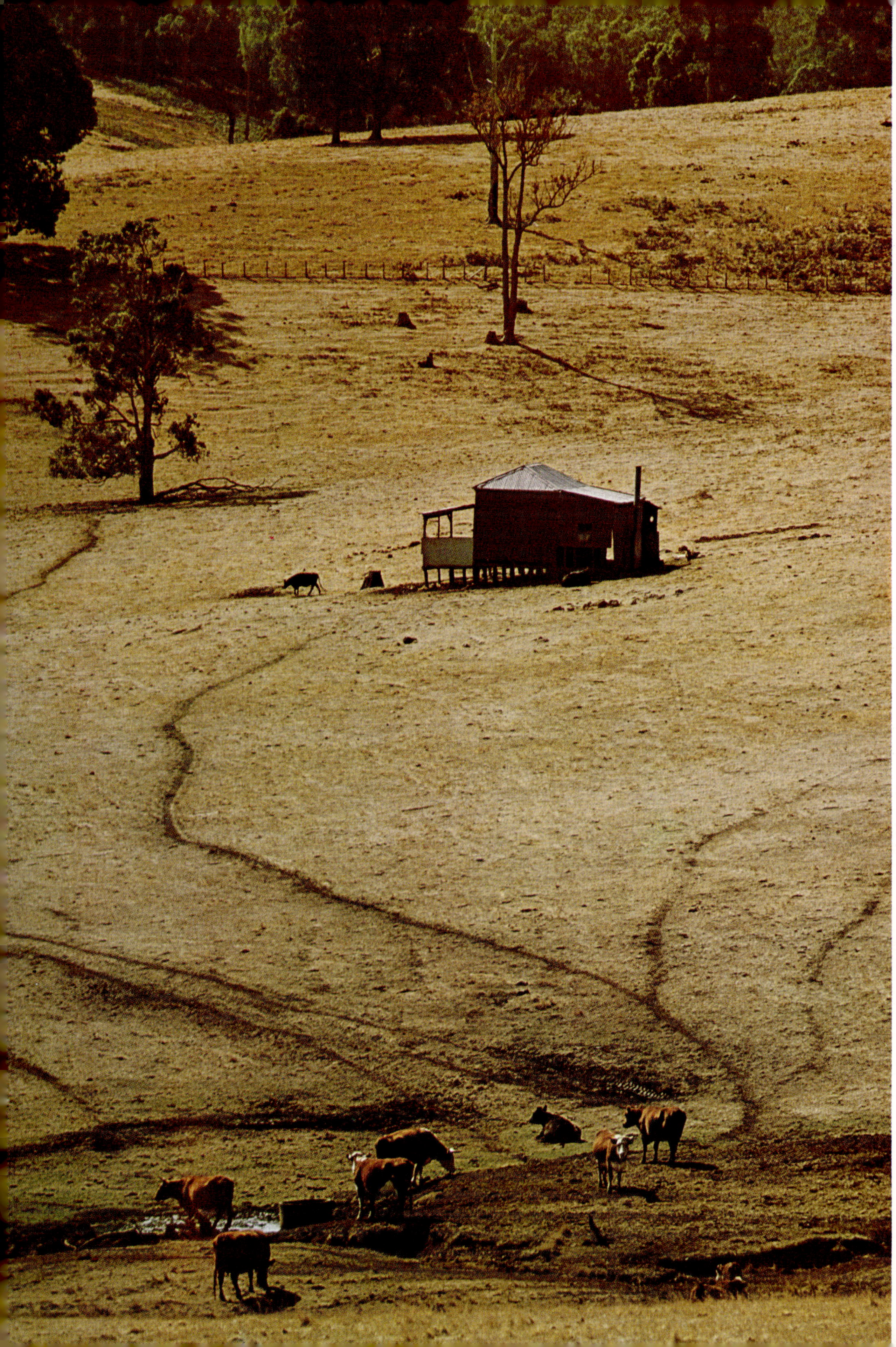

Bella Vista township, N.S.W.

Left) Upland farm, N.S.W.
56, 57) Sydney from Cremorne Point

55

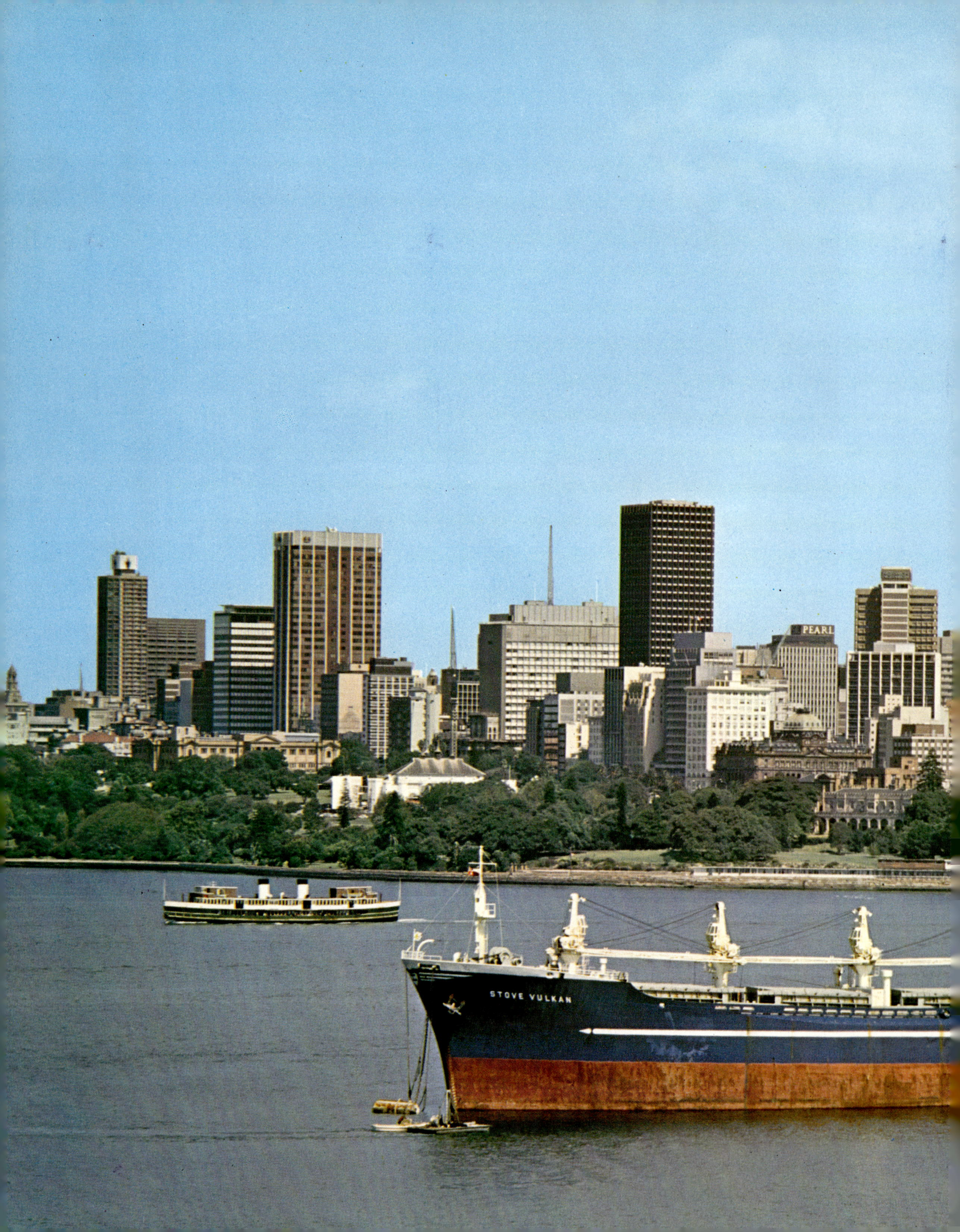
PEARL
STOVE VULKAN

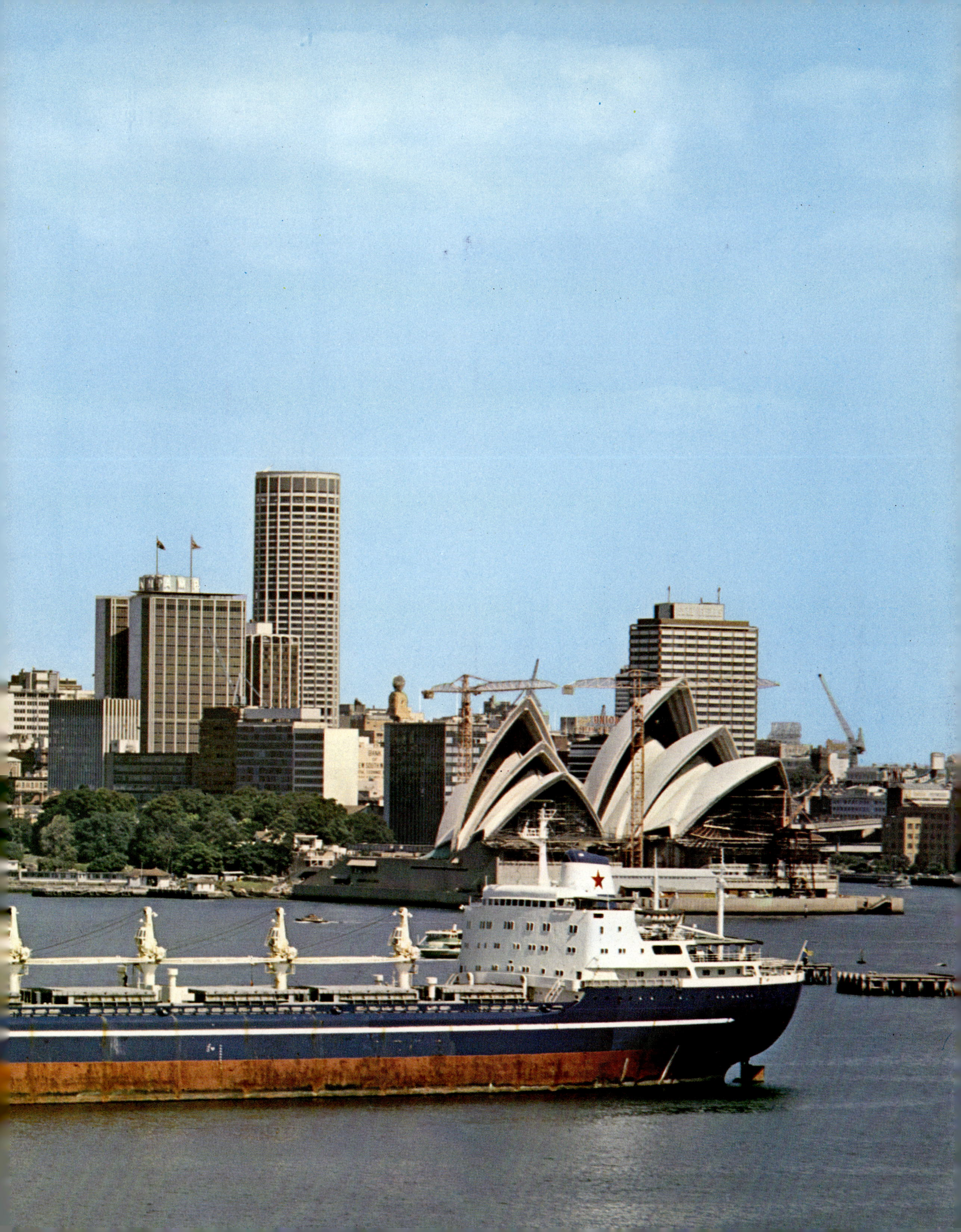

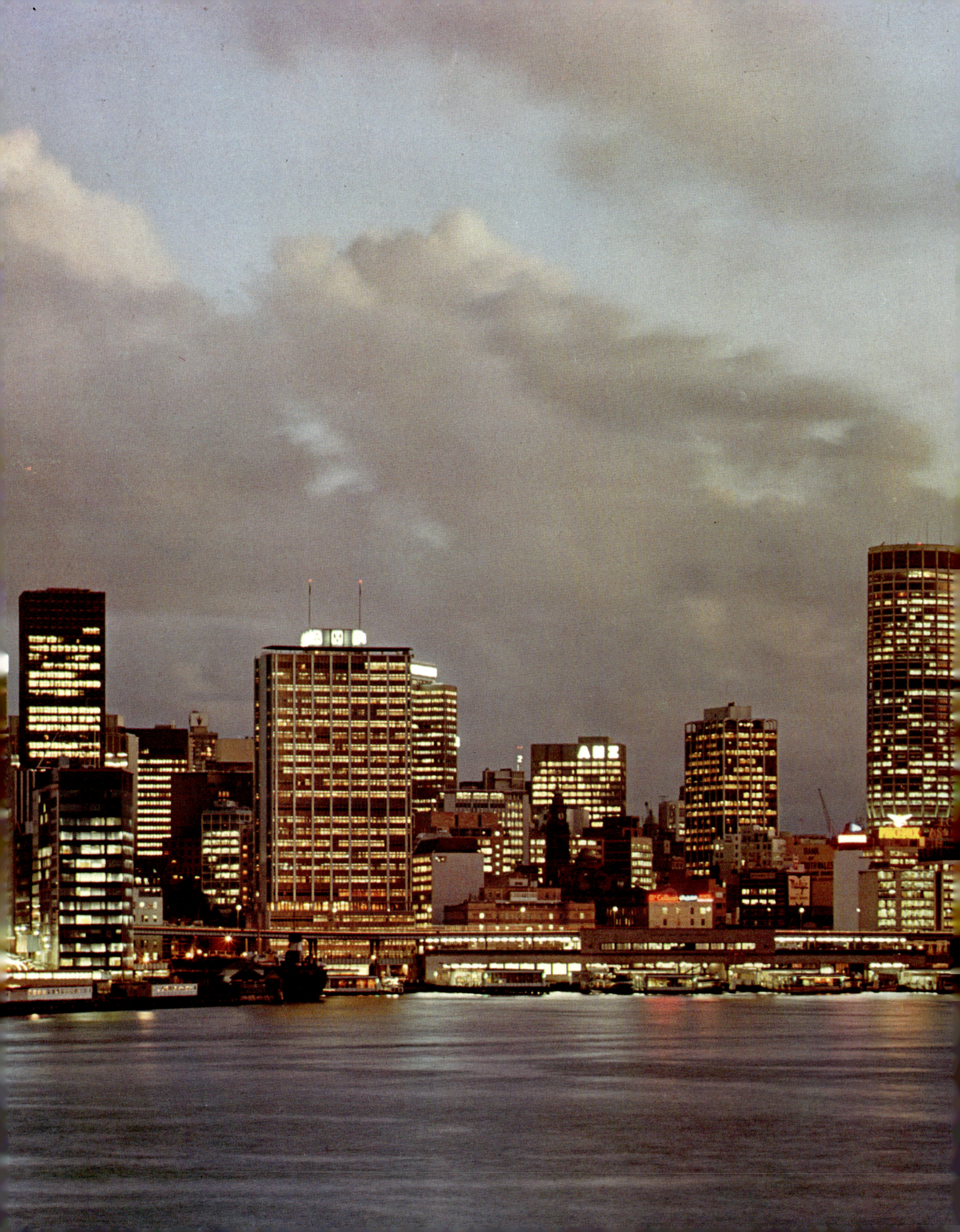
ANZ

THE CITIES

TEN SHADES OF DIFFERENCE

Gavin Souter

Night skyline, Sydney
60, 61) Melbourne at night

There is no mystery about the happy knack which so many writers on Australia have of regarding our cities as being invisible, or at least transparent. Their business is to detect differences, and the sad fact about the ten cities which contain two-thirds of Australia's population is that they are not strikingly different, either one from the other or collectively from the average American or English city. In such a predicament, one is tempted to look past or through the cities to the country, where differences of landscape and life are a penny a dozen. But this is altogether too easy. The dead heart is not the heart of the matter; to see Australia whole one must first acknowledge that its cities exist, and then search for differences beneath that disheartening sameness. Subtle though the differences may be, they too indubitably exist.

So let us forget the outback, with all its fascinating paraphernalia, and admit that Australia is the most urban continent in the world. Nearly half of its population of 12,700,000 lives in four cities, the most distant of which are little more than 500 miles apart: Sydney, Melbourne, Newcastle and Wollongong. One out of every four Australians may be found along 120 miles of coastline which is fast developing into the one swarming conurbation of Sydney-Newcastle-Wollongong, and four out of every ten live at the two opposing poles of urban Australia—Sydney and Melbourne.

Because the polarity of Sydney and Melbourne will be basic to this view of the Australian cities, I must confess my own firm preference for Sydney, the positive pole, and my rather tepid attitude towards Melbourne, the negative pole. This flies in the face of popular assumptions that Melbourne is positive, enthusiastic, tidy and upright, while Sydney is negative, cynical, untidy and corrupt; yet my bias is not quite as unreasonable as it may seem, and I shall try to justify it.

The other day I flew to Sydney from Melbourne, and rode into town on the airline coach which runs past the glue factories, boiling down works and scouring plants of Alexandria. After being in municipally proud Melbourne, and after being driven along the wide, odourless road to Essendon airport, I had to admit that this noisome entry to Sydney was an offence against all civic pride. So why, I asked myself, did it seem like a wedge of tangy cheese after three courses of good, wholesome food? Like a dry martini after lemonade?

Let us look for the answer in some other contrasts between the two cities. While Billy Graham has called Melbourne the most moral city in the world, a New Zealand evangelist whose names escapes me for the moment has likened Sydney to Gomorrah. The Lord Mayor of Melbourne is invariably a knighted millionaire, and his official car is a Rolls Royce Phantom; the Lord Mayor of Sydney is usually a Labor politician, and his car a Cadillac. Melbourne yearns for its population (2,425,300) to overtake that of Sydney (2,780,310); Sydney would not care if it fell behind, yet consistently it stays ahead. Melbourne's artists tend to be figurative rather than

abstract; Sydney's have thrown tradition to the wind. Melbourne is building an Arts Centre of conventional design and reasonable cost; Sydney is building an Opera House of wildly unreasonable cost and superb eccentricity.

Melbourne is conservative (even its Communist Party is conservative, in the sense that it believes in conserving Marx rather than revising him); Sydney is radical (even some of its Liberals are liberal). I use these terms in more than their political sense. For all its obsession with industrial growth and material change, Melbourne remains wedded to the tried and true. Unlike Sydney, it has a clearly defined Establishment—a tight-knit, powerful group of businessmen and politicians which Donald Horne has suggested is mainly responsible for the perpetuation of Australia's obsolescence. Sydney talks less about progress, but moves ahead with more daring. Its ways may seem crude and nihilistic to the gentlemen of the Melbourne Club, but Sydney is more open to suggestion than Melbourne, its controversies are lustier, and its preoccupations mercifully less earnest. Somehow the pungent smell of Alexandria suits it well.

Sydney can of course afford this preliminary ugliness, for it is also a city of overwhelming natural beauty. Its shapeless suburbs spread inland beyond one's comprehension, but along its 35 miles of beaches and on the northern and southern plateaux of Hawkesbury and Woronora sandstone, the city is clearly characterised by sea and bush. The Harbour, with its innumerable coves and bays, extends deep into the geography and psychology of Sydney. "It is shaped somewhat like an oak-leaf," wrote Mark Twain, "—a roomy sheet of lovely blue water, with narrow off-shoots of water running up into the country on both sides between long fingers of land, high wooded ridges with sides sloped like graves." Most of these ridges are now clad with red-tiled roofs, but some of the slopes are untouched, and in many a suburb it is still possible to look through a window at the bush or the sea or both—to hear currawongs yodelling, and watch nylon spinnakers straining before a nor'-easter.

My favourite view of the city is from one of the old green ferries which run from Mosman or Taronga to Circular Quay. In the few minutes it takes the ferry to cross the Harbour, Sydney dazzles me afresh: the towers of Darling Point, and at night the lights of King's Cross, one of the most densely populated and convivial square miles in the world; Pinchgut, the convict-built Martello tower which seems to float in the Harbour like a sandstone submarine, an unashamed reminder that Australia was born in chains; the green lawns and fig trees of the Botanic Gardens; the thicket of new skyscrapers in the heart of the city; and finally the outstanding white convexities of the Opera House, which now catch one's eye even before the Harbour Bridge. Sydney has gone one better than the Bridge, and such a dash does this city unselfconsciously cut that I should not be at all surprised if some day it goes one better than the Opera House.

Lack of selfconsciousness and a lordly indifference to the opinion of others are two prime characteristics which distinguish Sydney from

Melbourne. One could never imagine Sydney, for example, publishing an official self-portrait with a title like *Melbourne: Big, Rich, Beautiful*. Yet this is exactly what Melbourne City Council has done. Melbourne believes in blowing its own trumpet—with dignity, but quite audibly just the same.

I once wrote an article about Big, Rich, Beautiful Melbourne in which I likened the voice of the city to that of big, booming Honest Jim Blausser in Sinclair Lewis's *Main Street*. "They say we can't make Gopher Prairie, God bless her! just as big as Minneapolis or St Paul or Duluth," roared Honest Jim, Gopher Prairie's staunchest booster, in a speech at the Commercial Club. "But lemme tell you right here and now that there ain't a town under the blue canopy of heaven that's got a better chance to take a running jump and go scooting right up into the two-hundred-thousand class than little old G.P.!" In Melbourne at the time it was also a matter of "Boost, boys, and boost together—put Gopher Prairie on the map." The City Development Association signed its correspondence "Melbourne's On the Move" instead of "Yours faithfully," the Victorian Chamber of Manufacturers issued match-books embossed with "The Largest Employer Organisation in The Southern Hemisphere," and 12 of Melbourne's most enthusiastic boosters were then on a promotion tour of the United States. Perhaps the analogy was unfair, for the typical Melbourne booster is likely to be more sophisticated than Jim Blausser and to wear a Melbourne Grammar or a Scotch College tie. At any rate the Melbourne newspaper which reprinted my article deleted all the quotes from *Main Street*, leaving only a hotchpotch of uplifting information about Melbourne.

Big, Rich, Beautiful . . . Well, the city is undeniably big and rich. It has scooted right up into the two million class, and has absorbed relatively more New Australians—particularly Italians and Greeks—than any other capital city. Its suburbs sprawl 25 miles around Port Phillip Bay to Frankston, 20 miles along Princes Highway to Dandenong, and another 20-odd miles to Boronia, at the foot of the Dandenong Ranges. Seven of Australia's ten biggest companies have their headquarters in Melbourne, the Melbourne Stock Exchange is regarded overseas as Australia's financial index, and Toorak is the "best" suburb in Australia.

Melbourne is Beautiful too, though its beauty is man-made. Although neither the Yarra nor the Bay can compare with Sydney Harbour, the city is justifiably proud of its 1700 acres of parks and gardens (Sydney has only 665 acres), the majesty of its main streets, and the quality of its architecture. There is not a city scene in Australia to match Collins Street as it sweeps down past the steeple of Scots Kirk towards Swanston Street; there is not a retail store to match Myers; and not a suburban scene to match some of the better streets in Toorak, Kew and St. Kilda.

To Big, Rich and Beautiful one must regretfully add Provincial. The city's obsession with "footy," its ponderously gay Moomba

Beer-garden, Surfers Paradise

Race meeting, Adelaide

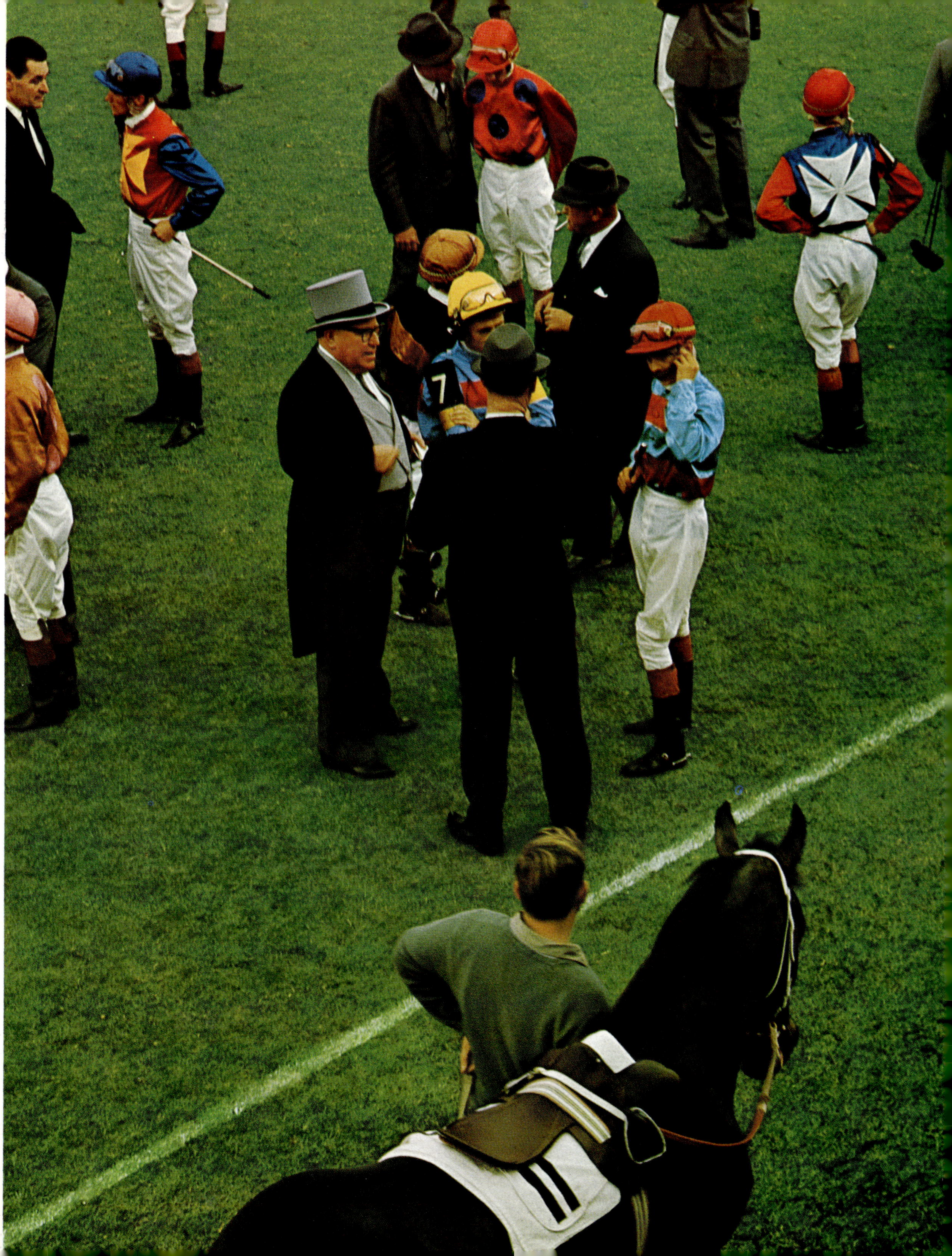

Festival, its stern disapproval of "knockers," and its grim determination to Get On The Map all bespeak a state of mind less metropolitan than Sydney's. I know these generalisations are grossly unfair to Melbourne. I know too that I have left many of its virtues unrecorded. Melbourne's civic mindedness has produced such admirable institutions as the Myer music bowl and the Felton Bequest, and for all its conservatism the city has both a vigorous political Left Wing and an intelligent Roman Catholic "left." With cities as homogeneous as Australia's, however, one can only differentiate by being unfair. Inside the hyperbole, there is a grain of truth.

Brisbane, the third largest city in Australia, takes after Sydney rather than Melbourne. Could this be because Brisbane, like Sydney, started its life in chains? I doubt it, just as I doubt that the character of Sydney today has been influenced, except in so far as its inhabitants' view of themselves may have been influenced, by the fact that between 1788 and 1849 approximately 80,000 convicts were transported to New South Wales, which for part of that time included Moreton Bay as well as the penal settlements at Sydney, Newcastle and Port Macquarie. Brisbane, like Sydney, is a lusty city. Its hotels have been trading late at night since who knows when, and its notorious red light district, like that of Sydney, has only recently, and perhaps only temporarily, lost its semi-official status. Brisbane is also ruled by Labor aldermen, and like Sydney it has no clearly defined Establishment.

But there, of course, the similarity ends. Brisbane is a sub-tropical city, much smaller in population (853,000) and far slower in pace than either of its southern sisters. Many of its wide verandahed houses are built on high posts for the sake of coolness; its streets are fragrant with bauhinia, and vivid with bougainvilia; and life seems no more urgent than the lazy Brisbane River which coils and winds its way through the city into Moreton Bay.

Adelaide, on the other hand, takes after Melbourne. This city which fits snugly between the Mt. Lofty Ranges and the blue waters of Gulf St. Vincent was described in its infancy as a "farinaceous village" because the main product of its hinterland was wheat. Nowadays the hinterland produces wine and wool, washing machines and Chrysler cars, and the village has grown into a city of 825,000 people; but "farinaceous" is still an apt enough adjective. There is something solid, wholesome and just a little starchy about Adelaide.

The city's old bluestone and freestone houses, with their high ceilings and deep wine cellars, seem far more substantial than brick or timber; its 40 statues and memorials are heavy with Victorian dignity; and its inner square mile of wide streets surrounded by parkland—a plan drawn up by Colonel William Light in 1837, and adhered to ever since—is both sensible and stately. Like Melbourne, it has no leg irons on its escutcheon; a plaque on Parliament House reminds visitors that "the Province of South Australia was founded by free settlers with freehold lands." The Old Adelaide Families—OAFs as the disrespectful sometimes call them—are still the sturdy weft and warp of the city's social fabric. Each generation the same names (Barr-Smiths, Grosses, Bonythons, Ayers) recur in business, society and public affairs, and the green shuttered Adelaide Club diagonally opposite Parliament House can still afford to be choosey.

One should not be too hard on Adelaide, for times are undeniably changing. The Adelaide Festival lets in a lot of fresh air once every two years; a Labor Government is now in office—briefly, one suspects—after more than a quarter of a century of Liberal-Country League rule under Sir Thomas Playford; and the cultural landscape is enlivened by such atypical figures as the poet and publisher Geoffrey Dutton, the bookseller and writer Max Harris, and entrepreneur and art collector Kym Bonython.

Perth, the fifth city of Australia (663,000), resembles Brisbane more than any other capital, and so belongs to the Sydney rather than the Melbourne group. It has a warm Mediterranean climate, a touch of convictism in its past, and a sense of alienation from the larger Australian cities. Like Brisbane (which holds 40 per cent of Queensland's population), Perth (50 per cent of West Australia's population) feels more akin to the rest of its own vast State than to its fellow cities elsewhere on the Australian coast. Both of them doubt the goodwill of their distant sisters: Brisbane remembers the strategic betrayal in the "Brisbane Line" of World War II, and Perth regards as both a strategic and economic betrayal the Federal Government's reluctance to subsidise the development of north-western Australia.

If the Ord River agricultural project has not moved ahead with the speed which Perth would have liked, the exploitation of West Australian minerals—notably iron ore and oil—has outstripped all expectations. This boom is reflected in the handsome, sun-burnt face of Perth, where some $50 million has been spent on new construction in the past ten years. The most striking symbol of the city's progress is the Narrows Bridge across the Swan River. On one side there are clover-leaf exits and on the other a freeway which joins the city to the great oil refinery at Kwinana. In spite of progress, however, Perth remains essentially an easy-going city. It has hitched its wagon to the stars of mineral and industrial development, but has not foregone the joys of sipping beer, strolling through King's Park, and surfing at Cottesloe.

The two next largest cities in Australia are not State capitals but the industrial complexes of Newcastle and Wollongong. These smog-laden giants on either side of Sydney are growing relentlessly, but neither of them has yet developed much in the way of a metropolitan ethos. The statistical district of Newcastle (which also includes Maitland, Cessnock and Lake Macquarie Shire) has a population of 344,900 and the statistical district of Wollongong (including Kiama, Shellharbour and Port Kembla) has 203,110. Newcastle, the older of the two, has acquired a modicum of gentility in one or two suburbs far removed from its coal mines and steel mills, but

'Blessing the Fleet', Fremantle, Western Australia
69) Victoria Square, Adelaide

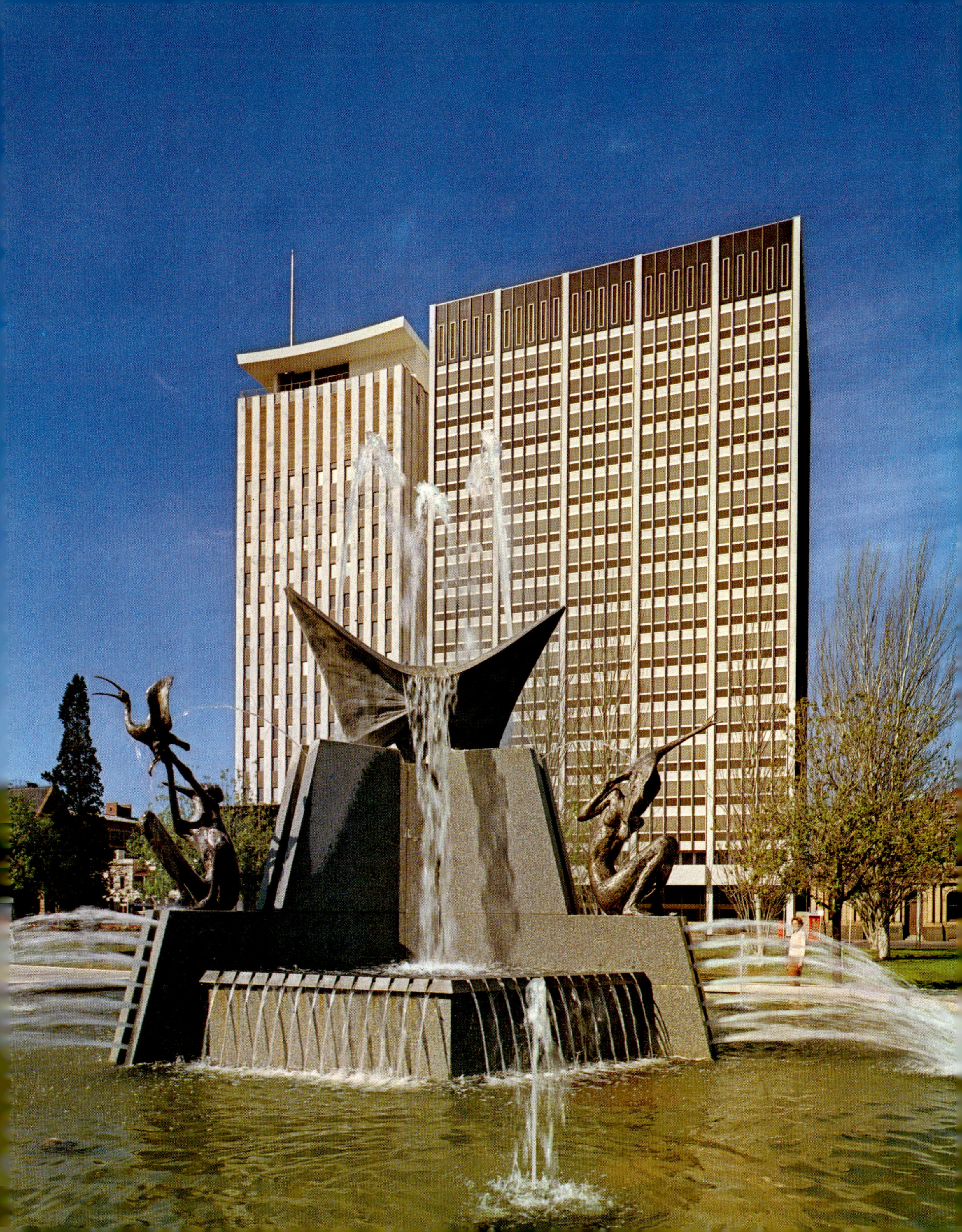

Wollongong is still too busy to worry about appearances. Its one saving grace is the natural beauty of hillside and sea which rapid, unplanned expansion has not yet quite effaced.

Hobart (150,910) resembles Melbourne rather than Sydney. This breaks the convict rule of thumb, for Tasmania was once a penal colony; but it would be ludicrous to speak of Hobart in the same breath as Sydney. It is a comely, insular, utterly respectable little city nestling between Mt. Wellington and the Derwent River. Its Establishment is smaller and tighter than Melbourne's, and almost as starchy as Adelaide's.

Hobart regards the Australian mainland with a suspicion reminiscent of that with which Brisbane looks south and Perth looks east, but for its dreamtime Mother Country on the far side of the world it feels nothing but loyal devotion. A recent Lord Mayor's report opened with a section entitled OUR ROYAL GUESTS. "I am sure I speak for all," writes the Lord Mayor, "when I say that this visit [by the Duke and Duchess of Gloucester] further cemented the strong ties that we have with the Mother Country." The next section, entitled OUR GOVERNORS GENERAL, described a farewell visit by Lord De L'Isle, and an inaugural one by Lord Casey. It recorded with satisfaction the following promise by Lord Casey: "I will take the earliest opportunity to inform Her Majesty the Queen of your loyalty and devotion which I know will be a great satisfaction to her." Hobart may well be the last Australian city to emerge from the trance of fealty.

Finally we come to two cities, or rather a city and a town, which are quite remote from the Sydney-Melbourne polarity. Canberra (146,450) and Darwin (32,943) are artificial communities which defy comparison with the other capitals.

Canberra derives its character largely from the Public Service, Parliament, the Australian National University and the Diplomatic Corps. Burley Griffin's spacious plan, with its lake and deciduous trees, has diluted the city so effectively that often Canberra seems almost rural. The effect is a happy one: Canberra is no longer a bush capital, but the visitor may still look forward with joy to a leisurely drive from Canberra airport past tawny paddocks where sheep browse, and where in the right season wattle trees burst into gold.

Darwin is a very different proposition. It too is an administrative capital, peopled to an even larger degree than Canberra by public service transients. Although more a town than a city, Darwin deserves its place among our first ten communities. This tropical, free-wheeling, beery town is the only Australian community to have suffered war (Sydney was shelled briefly and inefficiently by a Japanese submarine, but Darwin was well and truly bombed), and the only large Australian community with a multi-racial population. Darwin is peopled by Asians and aborigines as well as white Australians, and its Mayor is a locally-born Chinese.

An Asian presence of this kind may one day modify the character of urban Australia. It may take time, but considering our growing intimacy with Asia such a development seems inevitable. Apart from Darwin, the only capital in which such a presence may yet be felt to even a minor extent is Sydney, whose universities accept thousands of students from South-East Asia. Perhaps the future course of urban Australia is already being set in the very city where it all began.

British terrace, Paddington, N.S.W.

72, 73) Inner suburb, Sydney

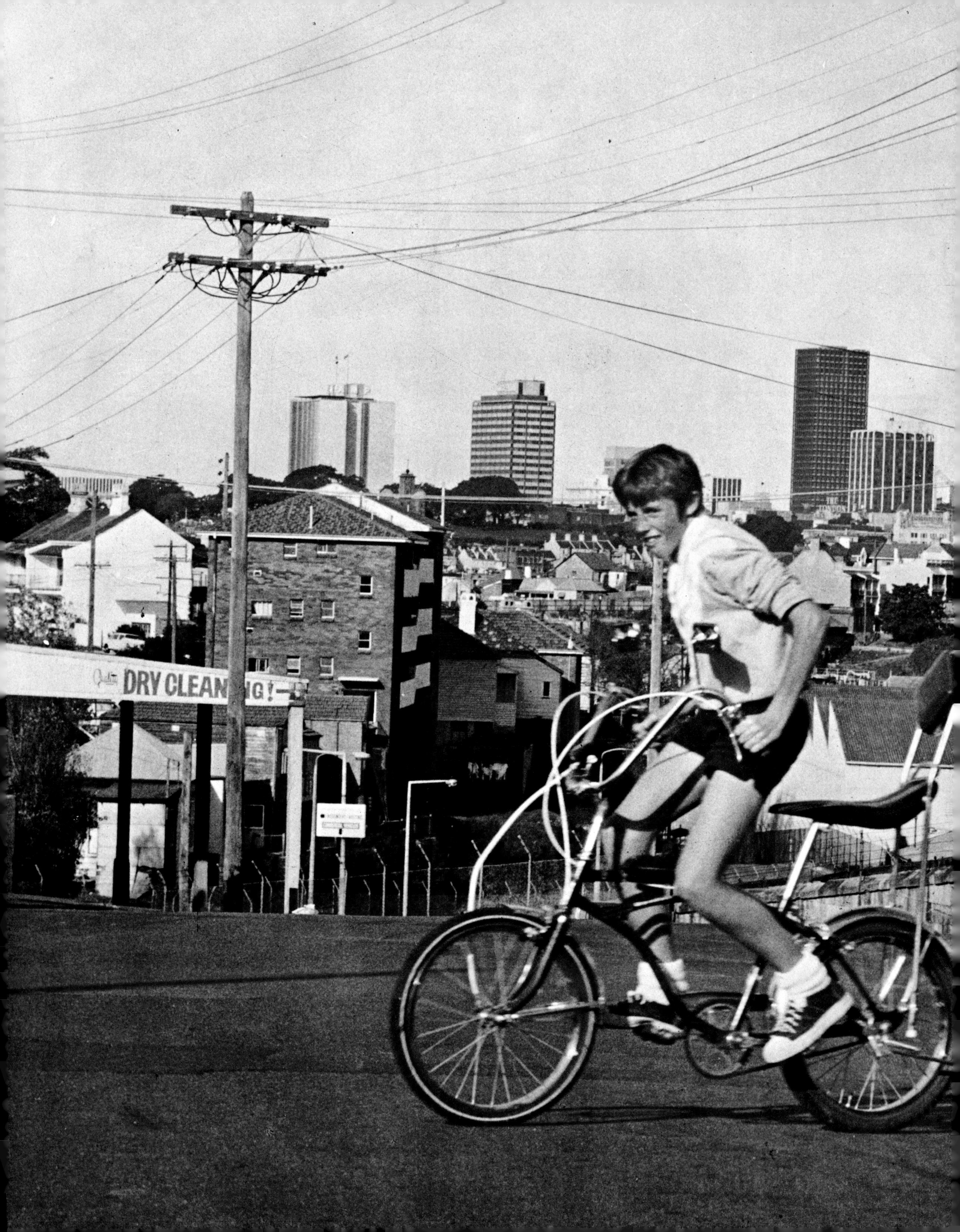
DRY CLEAN

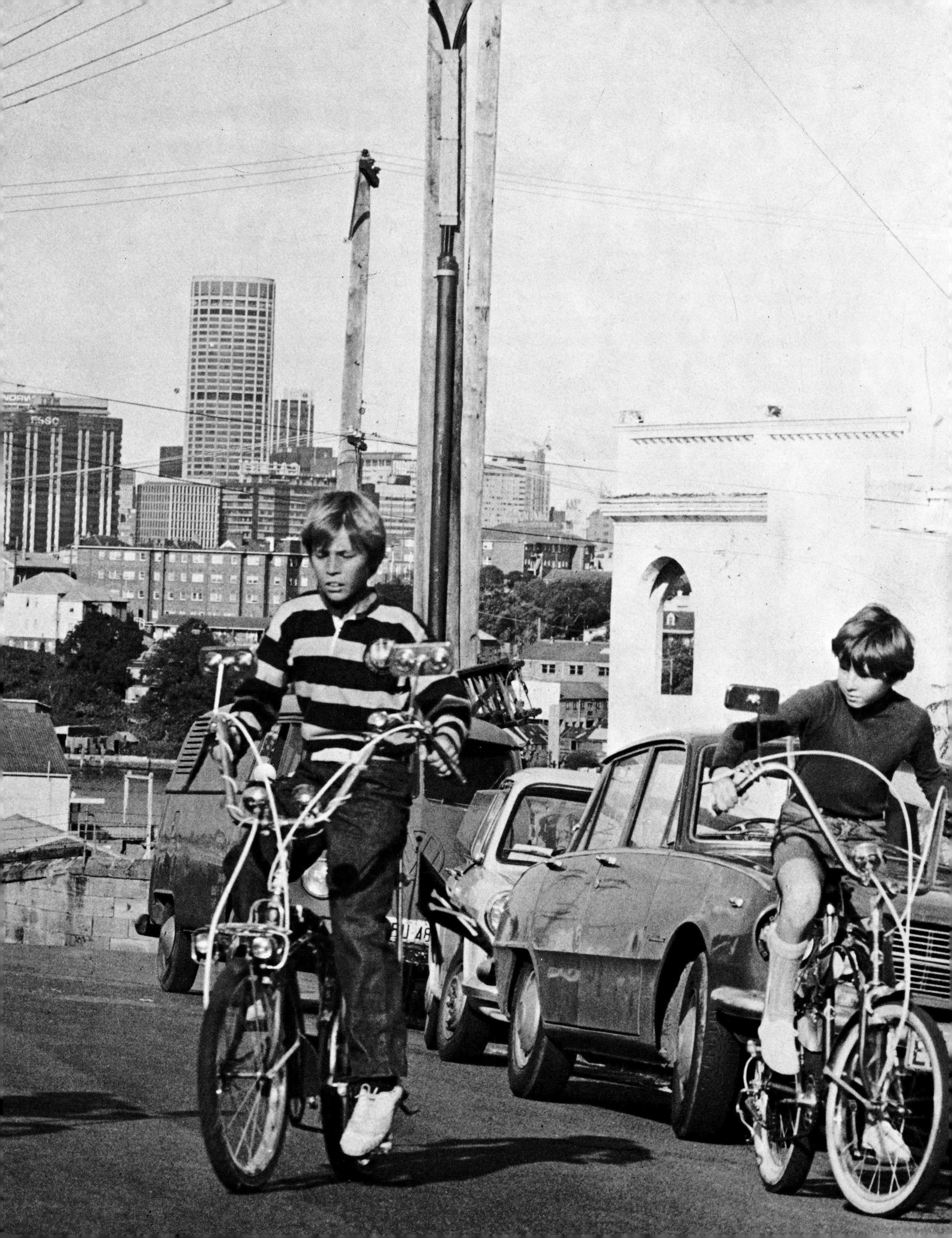

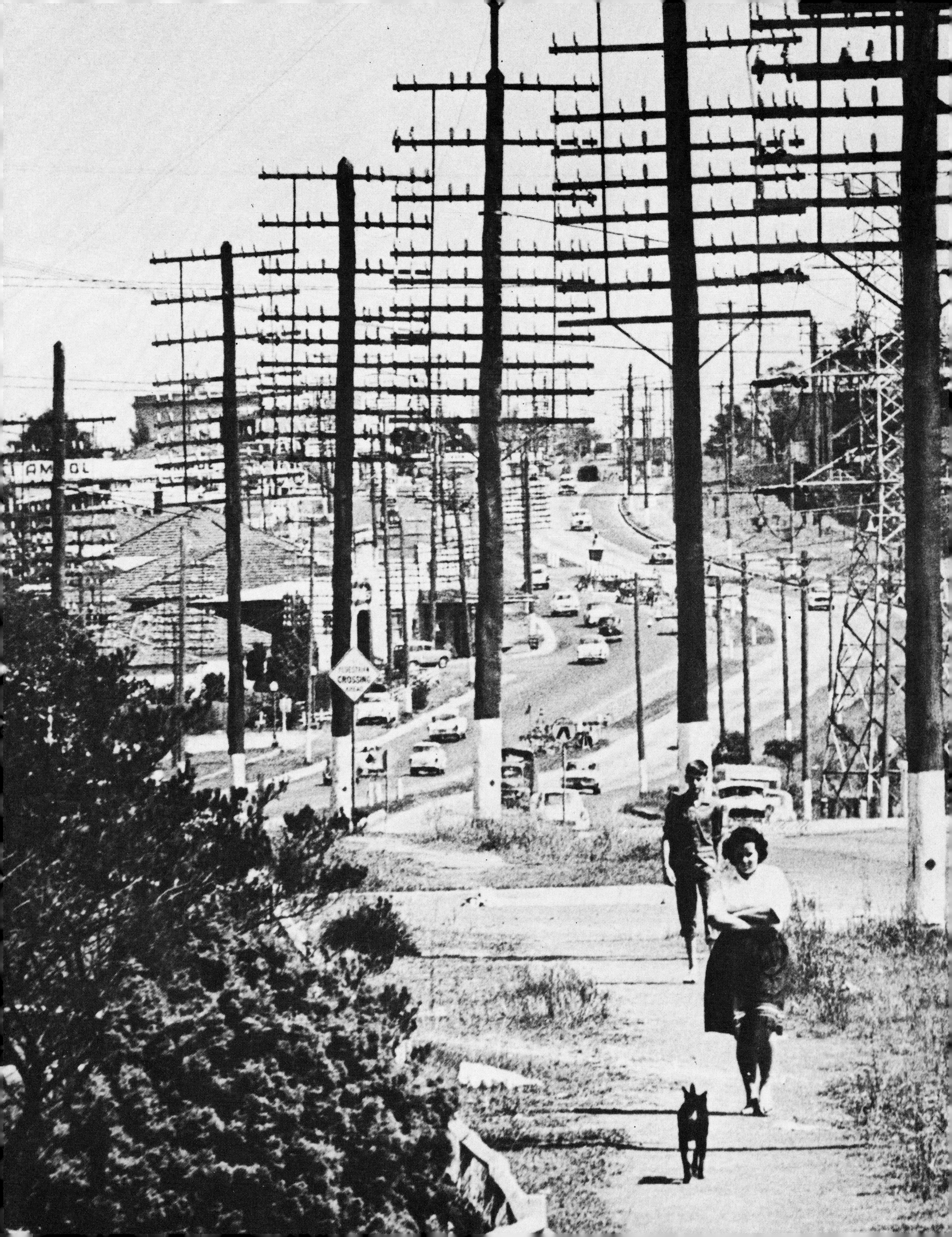
CROSSING

Confusion of progress

Melbourne

Sydney

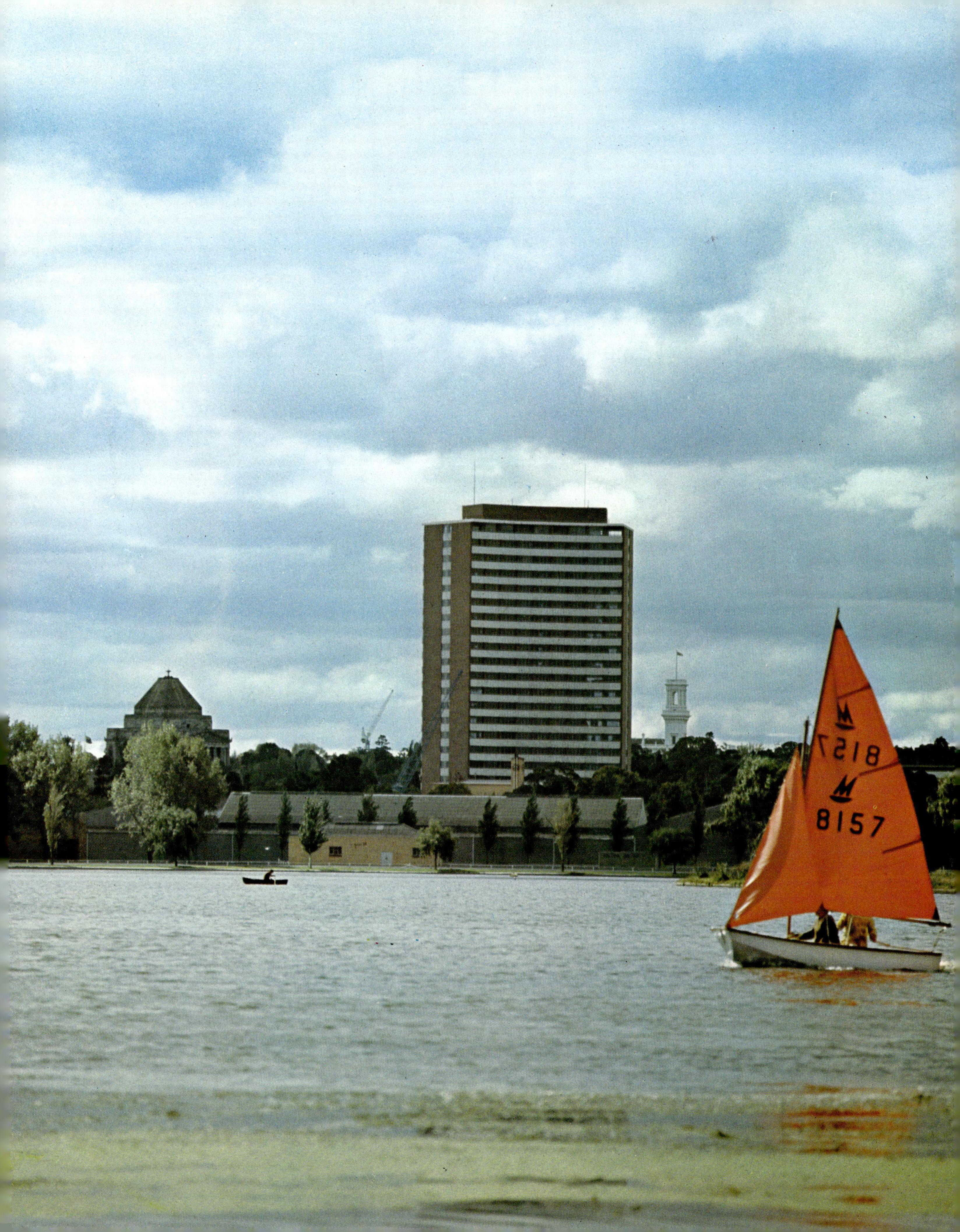
8157

Shop front, Paddington

Traffic policeman, Sydney

Self-service barbecue, bistro, Melbourne

78

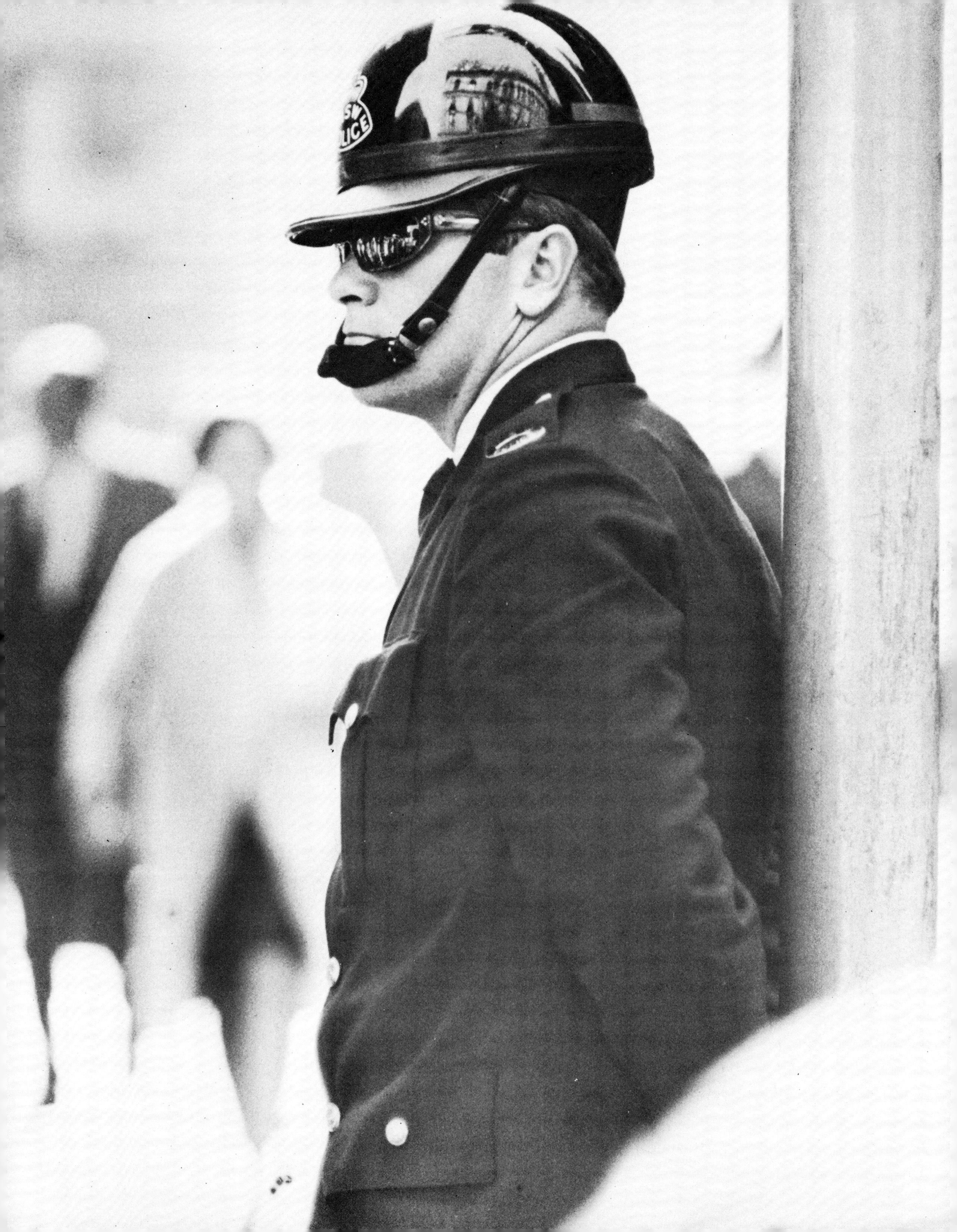

THE PEOPLE

IN SEARCH OF A DREAM

Ian Moffitt

The lit tankers sat solidly in the dusk at Botany Bay, the chimneys at Kurnell smudging the pink sky above the Captain Cook monument, the grey water where the First Fleet aired its foetid convict hatches. Here were the cold shores of Australia's history: a drear slice of Sydney beyond Long Bay Gaol, where curious aborigines first watched Englishmen in buckled shoes begin blandly, in all Christian charity, to destroy them.

Botany Bay was still the shabby tourist attraction I had remembered. Cook found it in 1770, and Phillip and his convicts returned there in 1788 and abandoned it quickly for Port Jackson—just as Jean-Francois de Galaup La Perouse arrived to lick his wounds following a Samoan attack. And now, in 1967, Kurnell sprouted monster metal plants which Banks had never classified, and La Perouse was merely a withered thumb thrust like a convict gesture into the Bay. "Hey mister. Got sixpence?" a small aboriginal boy asked cockily.

The bitterness of Australia's origins still lingered in the convict-coloured water, the gentle resentment of aborigines huddled now in the reserve ("Some of the white people are always pickin' on us—they hurt a man's dig"). Tourists stepped around the Bay carefully, seeking pride in this clumsy attempt to exalt an historic, human garbage dump into an object of reverence. But then a big white Australian loomed out of the last strange light of the day and called to heel his young blue cattle dog, which was nipping his dusky daughter and my children as they screamed together in delicious terror on Frenchman's Beach. "These are the things," he said, "that children remember. . . ."

His operatic materialisation seemed too good to be true, and I eyed him warily as he stood there with his clown of a dog, its red tongue lolling; behind him a wind-twisted apple tree and dwarf palms which seemed to blend Samoa, France and England in a wild Australian melange. And yet there he was above the small white crescent of sand—the allegorical Australian figure returning to his origins. A bushman, a drover and an Anzac who had become a security guard in the city. A man of Scottish descent who had married a part-aboriginal woman, now dead. "You say good-day to people these days," he said, "and they seem like they're in a trance, with all these computers. They can't break the circle of living. . . ."

He had broken the circle of living to go down to Botany Bay—after visiting a cousin in a nearby hospital, and before driving his Kombi van (and wombat-headed bush dog) back to his present home in an industrial suburb. And he proved, at 51, to be the best bush brand of Old Australian: patient, tough, cheerful, sanguine. The cousin of an officer who led a unit each year in the Anzac marches, and the father of four dark children whose distant ancestors had fled when Phillip's officers stepped ashore, their buttons tarnished from the stench in the bilges. "Funny," he said. "Time was, we Australians thought all the knowledge we possessed other people had to learn. But the young Australian today is a vitally different proposition. . . ."

This Old Australian never went to school in his life. At 12 he was delivering cattle in Queensland for his father; a lone white boy amid aboriginal stockmen for anything from five to nine months on the track. At 25 he was a sergeant fighting a losing rearguard action with the A.I.F. 6th Division on Crete, escaping in a British submarine with one arm smashed in a Stuka attack in Greece. And at 29 he was back in Queensland, courting a part-aboriginal girl whom he first saw wheeling a bay horse, while she was rounding up cattle on a Presbyterian mission property. . . .

"I didn't think very much of the average aboriginal until I married Margaret, but she had a spiritual quality," he said. "She was educated on the mission, and she had a grace and charm that great scholars commented on when they visited there. And she had a great sense of humour, too—I used to tell people I found her in a hollow log, and she'd throw a punch. . . . She was a Sunday school teacher, Margaret, and she had a very musical voice—at one time she could quote whole slabs of Lawson and Kendall. And I always respected her sense of intuition later on in the carrying business, when she didn't want to stop the night in some ominous part of the bush. I'd joke and tell her to get out her boomerangs if she was frightened, but I'd always move on. She might have known something I didn't. . . ."

This man's life spans the Australian legend. He was reared in the bush, where he broke brumbies ("There's a vast difference between a bushman and a country fella, you know"). While drowsy boys his age were dissecting English poets in classrooms, beneath peppercorn trees electric with cicadas, he was learning to await cattle stampedes after dry stretches on the track ("They dream, you know. They dream of dogs or a snake, or anything, and when one is about at the end of his endurance, he'll jump up . . .").

He bought a meccano set once, studied it, and then built his own crane. He has been through seven droughts, four floods and three fires. The banks foreclosed on his father's mortgage after one bitter dry spell (the father died nine months later), and he himself lost most of his money in the carrying business. And then his wife died two years ago with an unsuspected heart complaint.

"I'd like to start a butchery business with the kids in a country town so we can stay together," he said. "My three boys are in a Salvation Army home until I can get on my feet again, and they're great kids for work. . . . But why talk to me? My life's a chapter of failures right along the line. About all I've got left is something that Margaret helped teach me—a great amount of knowledge will get you down in the gutter if you haven't the wisdom of the Scriptures behind you. . . ."

This man, stepping from the past at Botany Bay, has more than the wisdom of the Scriptures behind him. He is one of the better end-products of this nation's seamy history since 1788. Behind him is a heritage which Australians strive so hard to cherish: the story of a nation founded, largely, because the rebellious American colonists refused to accept more British convicts. A nation whose first policemen were convicts (nobody else volunteered), and whose biggest heroes are still bushrangers; a nation which raised the Union Jack (before it became a perfect op art symbol) over prostitution, drunkenness, brutality, illegitimacy, and scornful Irishmen, and obediently honours the event each Australia Day; a nation which shot, poisoned and infected its aborigines, and then built a wall against Asians; a land with half-officially-suppressed memory of its one minor rebellion against authority—the Eureka Stockade, the only battle fought so far on its soil.

Spawned in the effluent of the Industrial Revolution, Australia has grown from a huddle of city working class radicals (with a bitter hatred for the upper classes who kept them down) into a fringe-sprawl of largely urban middle-class conservatives (with a cheerful contempt for the upper classes they finally thrust aside). This radicalism, which burst into brief national bloom late last century, withered long ago under Britain's beneficent shade—for the British Colonial Office, singed once in America, applied reforms here more promptly. And so we have the Australian people today: international children with no common suffering for a cause—and no real dream—to sustain them. A second-class race with ambivalent, unresolved loyalties, comforting itself (in this ruthless technological-atomic era) with tattered little myths celebrating Australian egalitarianism, courage, shrewdness, independence, improvisation. . . .

The mirror lies. It is closer to the truth that Australians have become dull reactionaries in a perpetual province—people who will put up with any abuse as long as they are allowed minimum comforts. The bushman on Frenchman's Beach was genuine; so many other Australians are not, and the world is about to find out. All most Australians really want now is the good fat life—and there is no guilt on the gingerbread.

About 80 per cent of Australians are of British stock, though migration (about 140,000 a year) is fast diluting this. Most are white collar workers putting in 40-hour weeks. The women, while the Government cries out for population, are the world's heaviest users of The Pill. The men (one in four has a vehicle) suppress the population more openly. They drive big American cars heedlessly on narrow Australian roads, slaughtering 3,800 people each year—for a casualty list twice as long as Australia's total in all wars.

Australia is still the most egalitarian of the world's democracies (though about the last of the colonial powers), but somehow egalitarianism doesn't include the aborigines. They have dwindled from perhaps 350,000 in Phillip's time to about 100,000 today. Australian history begins with the whites, New Zealand's with the Maoris, and only now are Australian whites slowly beginning to atone for stealing the aboriginal's campfire and bleaching his essence, leaving him flitting faintly through the trees at the edges of white consciousness.

Aboriginal children, Ernabella Mission, South Australia

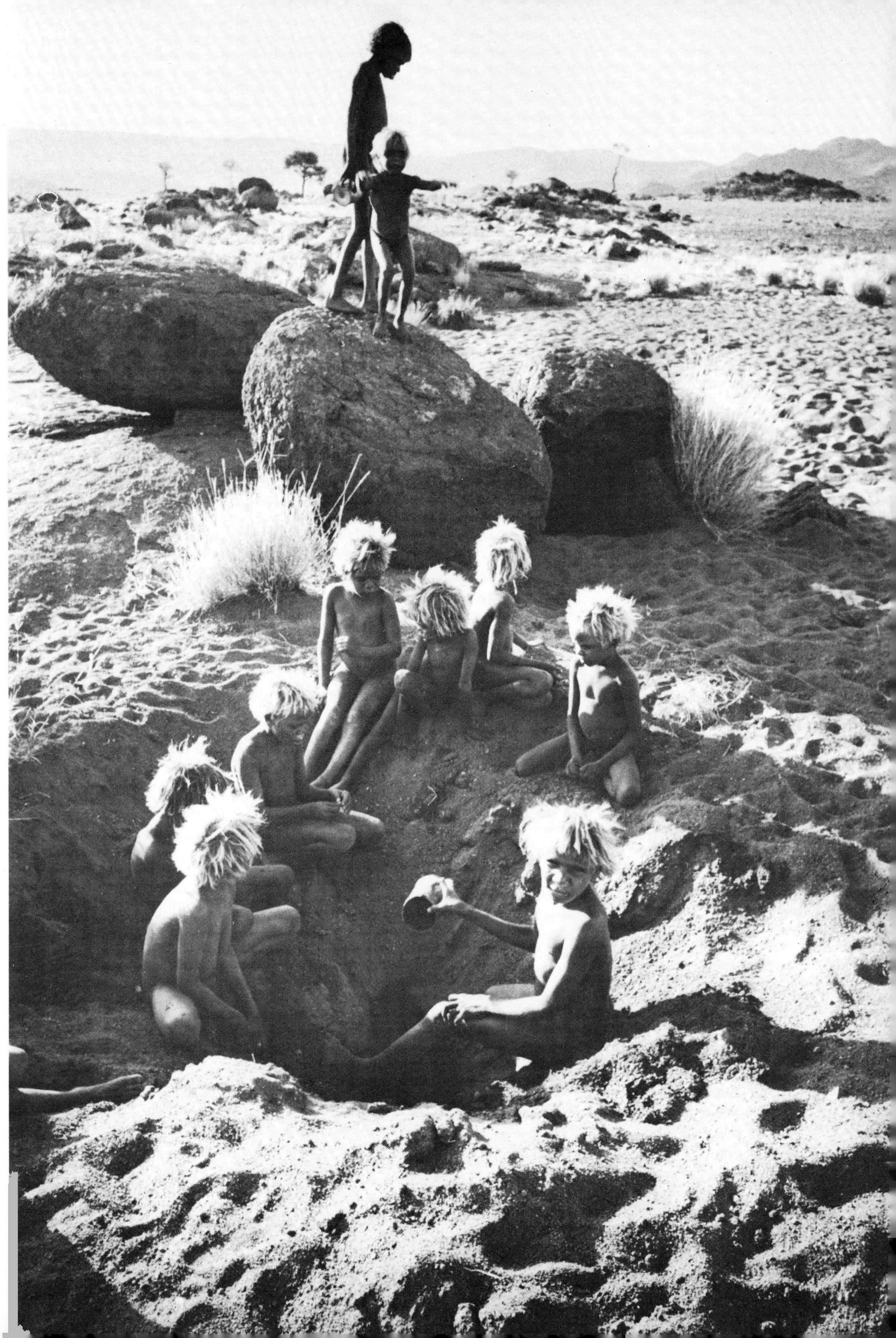

The aboriginal for years has been sunk in apathy on the fringes of country towns, filing obediently into the roped-off front stalls at the local cinemas, swigging forbidden wine in the river mangroves behind the pub, while white Australians paraded their egalitarianism abroad. The schools, which once believed an aboriginal's ceiling to be fourth class primary, have not encouraged him to be proud of his rich heritage—any alien dynasty has always been more important than the Dreamtime, and the school's main concern, anyway, is to produce cogs for a white machine. And so the aboriginal has fallen between two worlds: his height of attainment to make the wing in a Country Rugby League team, or get a fight at the stadium. White Australians cheered Ron Richards as a hero in the ring, but the aboriginal middleweight's faded scrapbook did not match a diploma. And thousands of Australian aborigines today still live in worse "kennels" than the greyhounds at city tracks, for they are the most badly-treated aboriginal people in the world.

Many white Australians do not care about this—or, indeed, about anything much. They stand in the arid deserts of public bars, discussing the big ends of automobiles, the comparative qualities of beer, and the delicate art of spreading cement. They shake their heads over injured Kangaroos in Test teams abroad, but ignore the slaughter of the real ones at home (genuine slabs of Australia at 30 cents a pound in the pet shops; the soft eye, the delicate ear, crushed into cardboard boxes for pekingese). They have become quiet accomplices to this stealthy mass-murder for short-term profit—part of their nation seems to be draining silently to extinction in the suburbs (beneath the Marigny cold waves and the cake shops, the dark steps leading up to the dentist's), but it does not disturb them. Their God is a Great White Holden; their spiritual cleansing a sauna bath at the Leagues' Club. George Moore's in his saddle, and all's wrong with their world.

Civil protests against despoliation are growing in Australia, but many urban Australians kill what is wild and free around their homes (from the ants up) with a Puritan stolidity. For them beauty is a geometric back yard, a sheet of concrete (Sydney Harbour, perhaps, studded with home units?), an infinity of Ampol stations, a stone dwarf. They live in suburban tombs, secretly despise their neighbours, and buy soft pink toilet paper for their guests. They call racehorses after Greek gods, but read only the afternoon papers, and they place little china angels on their TV sets holding mock copies of the Lord's Prayer and the Ten Commandments.

These Australians profess to love their children, and perhaps they do, but they do not really want to know what goes on in their minds—or in their schools. Laying a lawn for them takes care of most parental responsibility; when that is done, only repeated traffic warnings remain. The men boast of their beer drinking (and are forced by municipal councils to take their own bottles to local tips), and the women—among the first in the world to gain the vote—have become second-class citizens, constantly battling to gain

Birdwatcher, Surfers Paradise

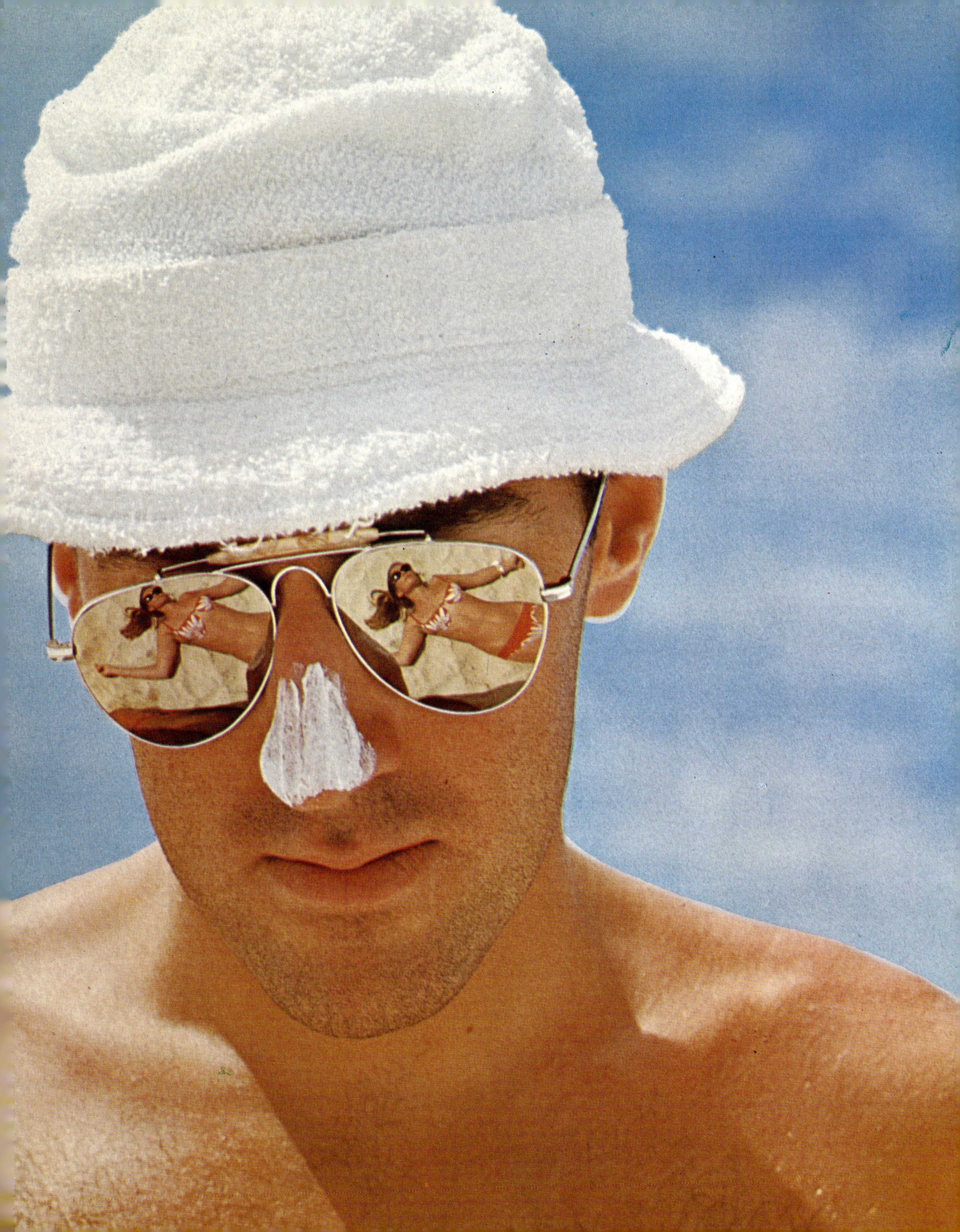

their menfolk's attention. The legend of the sick stockrider has almost disappeared from recognition in their exhaust smoke. They do not gallop into the bush like Ned Kelly, defying authority with a shout and a laugh. Authority is synonymous to them with brute power and corruption, but they do not oppose it. They merely suffer its excesses, sullenly rattling their mental chains. Presented with a challenge, they are often sly and evasive beneath their ruddy commonsense. The pressure is on them not to bung it on, stand up, stand out, make a gig of yourself. They tend to sneer at moral courage and commitment, complimenting themselves on their cleverness in staying out of it while politicians, public servants and big businessmen make capital of their apathy. This fearless Anzac race, in ·fact, is permeated with fear—fear of getting involved, of neighbours' opinions and dishonest policemen; fear of attracting attention, of an expanding Security service; fear even of the waitresses who condescend to serve them in hotel dining rooms. Watch Australians breakfasting in a funereal pink glow in almost-empty Rainbow Rooms heaped with gladioli; see the humble manner in which they consent to crowd in stiffly with strangers, backs to the view, to save the waitresses legs.

So many of them are *sour* people, to whom gaiety is decadent and joy suspect ("You're not the full quid!"). They have driven overseas many other Australians born with a sense of grace and a normal appetite for warmth, which the conformist atmosphere threatens to extinguish. Shallow cynics, whom a destructive selfconsciousness has made impotent, they have imposed their will on society—exulting, like Lichtenstein pop paintings, in the commonplace. Their muttered protests trickle down pub lavatories; they are skilled at detecting bullshit, but too cowardly to confront the bull. Deep in their brains is a vast wasteland of bush marked "No Trespassers"; approach too close and they throw down a brusque triviality, like a barricade. "There you are, my friend!" grates the publican again and again as he slaps down a glass, but "my friend" is not an invitation to intimacy, but a hand pushing the stranger back. They trust their destinies to a curious local superstition, the lottery, and congratulate themselves that they have the game by the throat. But they, of course, are the victims.

Australians no longer initiate: they reflect. They are not only playing Robin to America's Batman in Vietnam, but surrendering so abjectly to foreign investment here that a parody of the perennial Australian newspaper death·notice seems appropriate: "A ray of sunshine came and went, Our darling Aus. was only lent." Business and political leaders laud this swing from brothel to quarry in 180 years as a glowing achievement heralding future greatness but the quality of national life is poor (could Australia produce a John Kennedy?), with little to stimulate the man in the street beyond the current edifice complex over Sydney's crippled "Opera House." Political debate is as thin as Time Magazine, and Canberra, which could be the Geneva of Asia, remains so far a synthetic green graft which has not taken completely on the nation's tawny skin. Politicians place their first loyalty to their parties, not the people, in a Cabinet-cowed Parliament (few of *them* ever resign on principle), and public servants clam up when appointed to office, preferring respectable paid anonymity to public displays of courage. Intellectuals flagellate themselves behind phantom battlements, scorning the populace below, but doffing their hats obediently to the same borrowed anthem. Churches offer special masses to mark the anniversary of the death of Les Darcy, but not for the Vietnamese youngsters burned in the children's war in South-East Asia. Out of sight, out of mind; guard your own flock. . . .

Nations need a dream. The United States has one (though it corrupts it every day), but all Australia really has is the Anzac legend—which is admirable, but not all-embracing. The Australian people still seek their noblest expression and their truest identity in this legend. Gallipoli and France formed a leaden sky which brushed low over the towns and parks in which Australian children played in the twenties and thirties, and this infected their innocence more than the antique horrors in Cole's Funny Picture Book—dimly they became aware of Death. The Second War failed to overlay the awakening of that first conflict: the blue-yellow tones of Tobruk, New Guinea's garish green, smear but lightly the awful sickening grey of the First Great War—the splintered trees and shell-pocked mud, the corpses in craters, the long lines of little men trudging on duckboards to the Front. Middle generation Australians grew up amid the memory, clambering on captured German cannon in the parks, touching the maiden-hair fern flourishing in the pitted Digger helmets, listening to the gassed uncle coughing in the next room.

They remember oval photographs in albums ("Bertie, Killed on the Somme"); hymns sung on hot, cracked asphalt to teachers gathered in the shade of Moreton Bay fig trees; the Menin Gate at midnight rising above school sport trophies in the hall. And on drear days, dark as the Dyson drawings inside, they file through the Australian War Memorial in Canberra, inspecting Death sealed under glass—the bullet-pierced water bottles, a punctured felt hat, some rusted improvised bombs, a muddy money-belt dropped on a sortie from Quinn's Post. The mortars sit around them in vapid, round-mouthed astonishment; soldiers run through a mute barrage of tiny dioramas (Pozieres, Lone Pine), and a crushed Australian bugle picked up on Gallipoli lies dully with the torn shoulder straps and badges, a broken, rusted bayonet, some boxes of spent ammunition. Soon, it seems certain as they file down the corridors, they will find something of themselves. Only look long enough amid the half-known names, Passchendaele, Fleurbaix, and there will be their own. Somewhere beneath the tattered shoulder badges, the broken bayonet, a birth. . . .

Anzac, however, may not be enough to sustain Australia's national identity in a shrinking, complex world in which post-Hiroshima youth is trying to bail out of the Atomic Age. The Australian people are in the midst of change, for better and for worse, as the nation swings awkwardly from Whitehall to Washington, like a giant

88) Young Australians
89) Military parade, Sydney

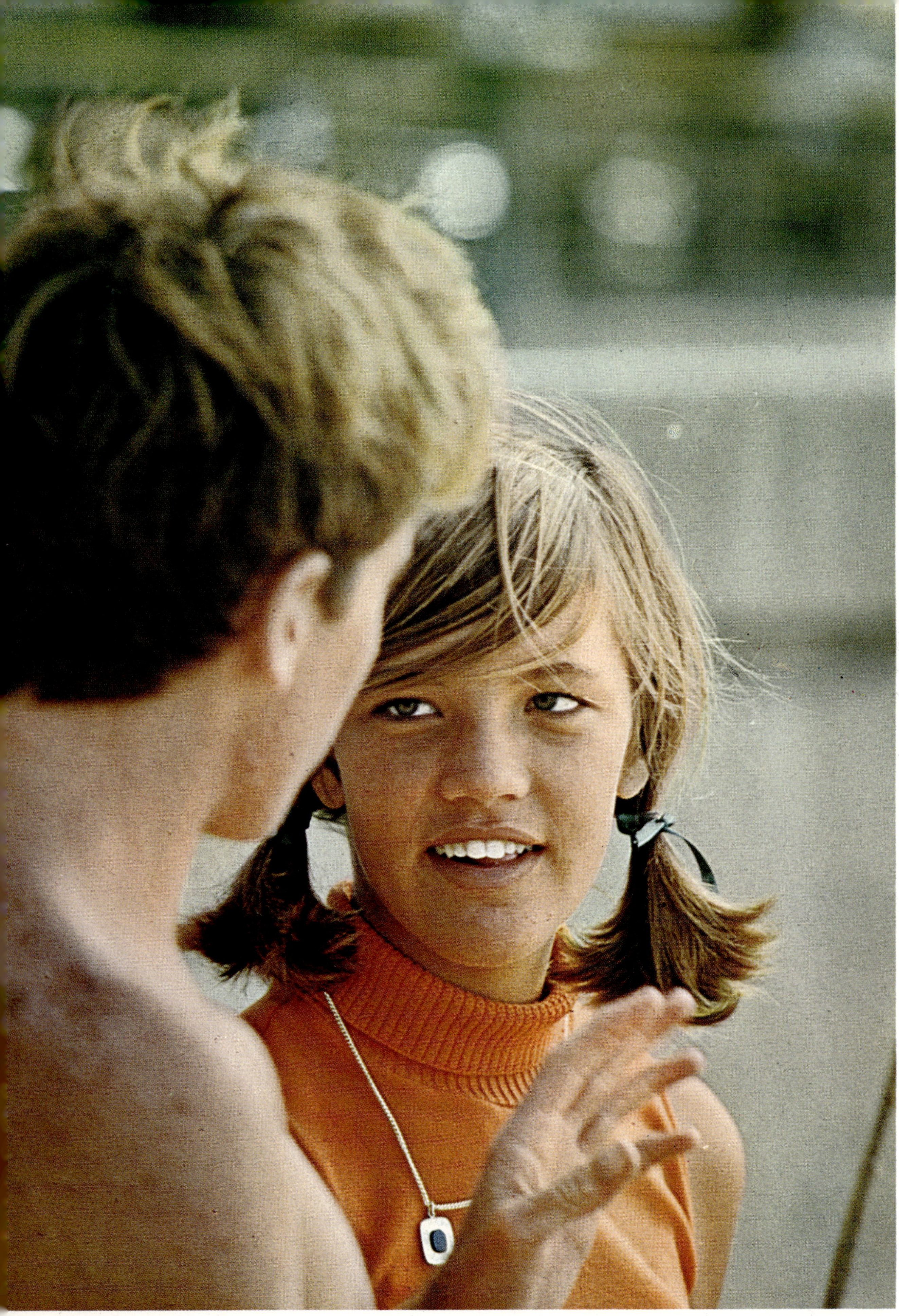

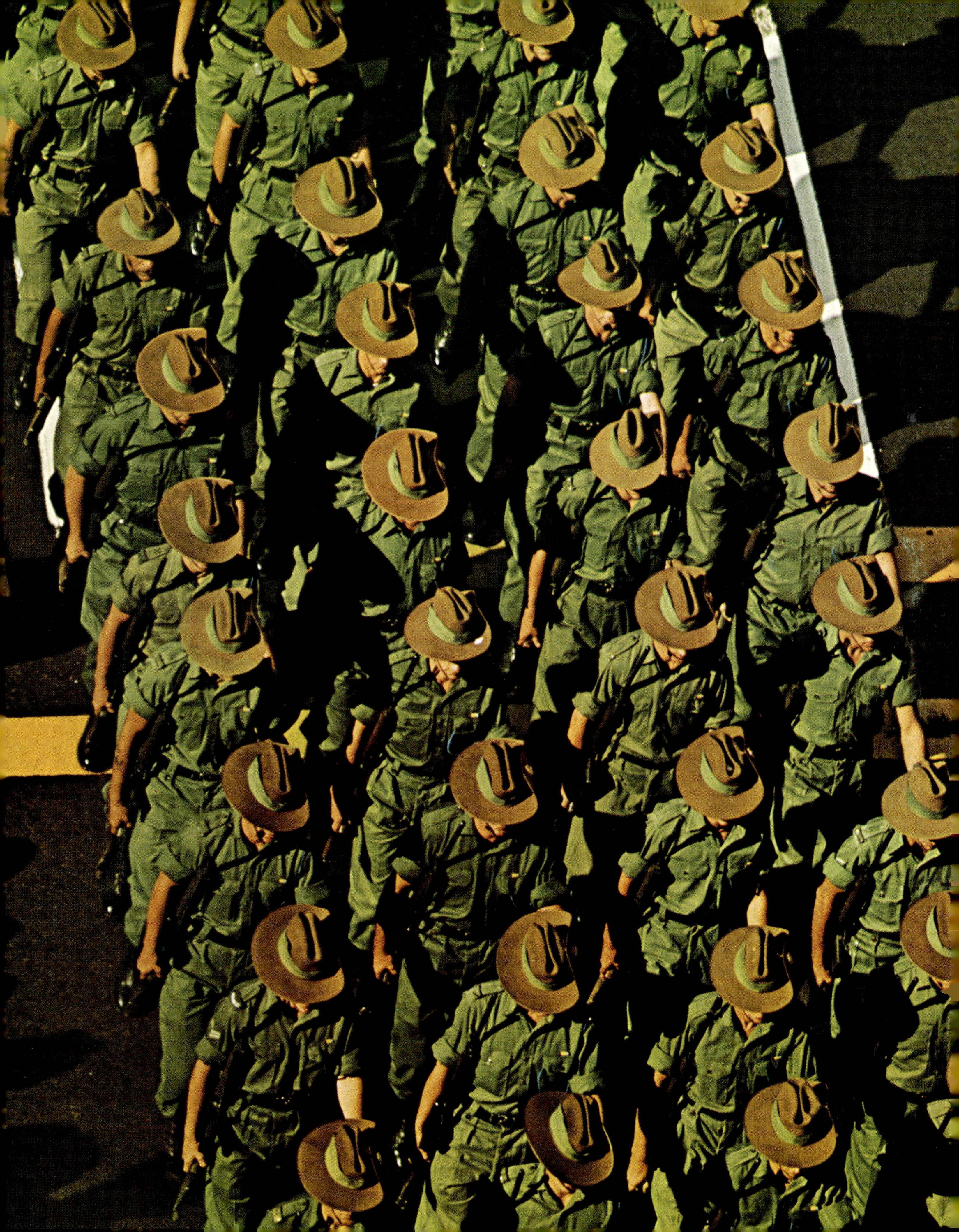

aircraft carrier caught in the tides of history. Australians once shouted from behind Mother England's skirts, but now she is receding and Japan looming forward in the ironic, molecular linking and disengaging of nations. Britannia, like one photograph superimposed on another, now has a Japanese face. Vietnam marks the entry of Australians into a troubled adolescence—the knife is under the stone now, tilting once-immovable attitudes. They approached the problems of Asia with the naivete of Far West children on their first visit to the Pacific, and they cannot extricate themselves now from the undertow. The Middle East volunteers fought "for Right and Manhood;" today's conscripts are not so sure.

A bloody invasion of Australia might cement the people in suffering and give them their dream, but nobody wishes that. Life may be grim in South-East Asia, but it is becoming more comfortable in Australia—whatever intangibles may disappear in the process. "Mate" is becoming a meaningless greeting which clerks mutter absent-mindedly in corridors when they cannot remember a name; "battler" one day no longer will be a compliment, for it will imply that a man lacks possessions and status in an affluent society. The chooks-and-chokos attitude to life will submerge beneath rockeries and landscaped gardens, the old staghorn finally disappear before indoor rubber plants straight from motor showrooms. Australians will succumb more quickly than most to "American" influences; a people diluted by distance, they will still dream of the bush, with mixed pride and dread (for it represents Death, too, in its way), but continue to die amid folds of fat in the suburbs. "My kids worry me," said a drinker in a bar. "They're growing up in a land of plenty. Australia was built on hard work and grog, not all these poofter influences coming in. . . ."

But life is certainly becoming more interesting these days, whether it lasts or not. The Church is slowly awakening to a realisation that it should be the conscience, not the servant, of the State, and bigger issues have overshadowed the old Protestant-Roman Catholic bigotry. The arts are flourishing as the philistines go on the defensive, the individual is still valued (though Wall Street may fix *that*), and the mental and physical isolation is passing. The Vietnam issue is a growing yeast within the old apathy—driving people who cannot stomach it to open protest. The nation still cannot afford equal pay for women, but tastes are improving (from plastic to dried flowers!), and Australians—once so dogmatic—are beginning to articulate their anxieties. And a proportion of New Australians have introduced a welcome gentleness into the national life (the southern Europeans for example, who cluster like gnarled little olive trees to watch their children play the strange game of Rugby League). An Old Australian rock fisherman said of the New Australians: "Once they looked like the rats under the house—an evil-lookin' mob, they looked. You wouldn't talk to them down fishin'. But now they're not only accepted—they're fishin' with Australians, and good mates with 'em. . . ." And a Dutch-born photographer said of Old Australians: "They are a lonely people, I think, as if they are still guests here

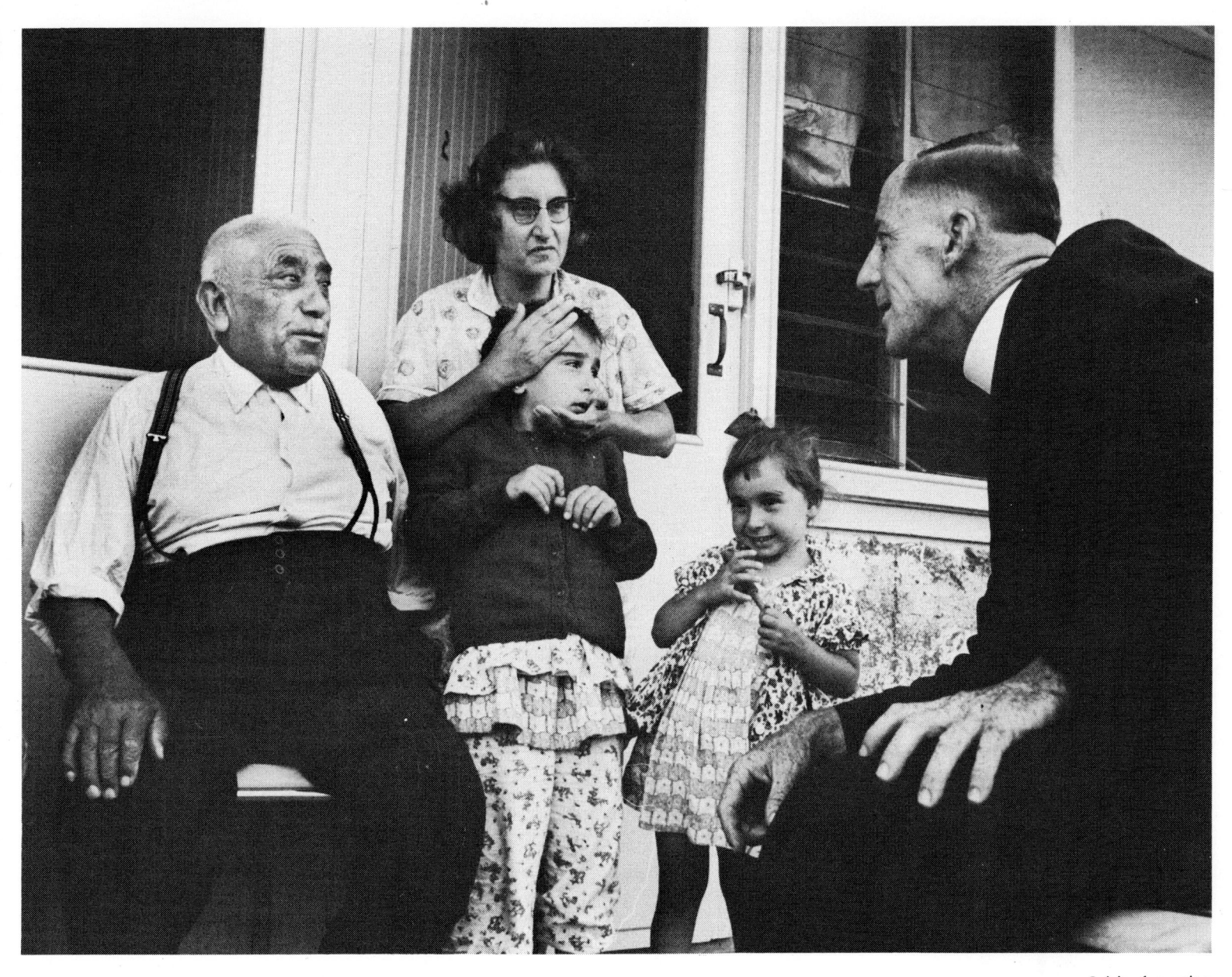

Spiritual meeting

in a hard country—I should like to photograph them through the bars of the shark net as they play on the beaches. But they have shown me an aggressive sort of sympathy when I needed it which is not very warm, but very practical. People have cared more about my feelings here than at home. . . ."

This is a pivotal period; Australians who care about this country's future should no longer luxuriate in the national virtues. Barring World War III, however, nothing dramatic will shatter Australians' lives for some time. Australians will probably grow more contented, and even more materialistic, as their hard old image recedes. And no more bushmen will break the circle of living to go down to Botany Bay. . . .

Artist, Hahndorf, South Australia

Members' stand, Melbourne Cup

Show time, Sydney

Faces at races

Fire crew, Sydney

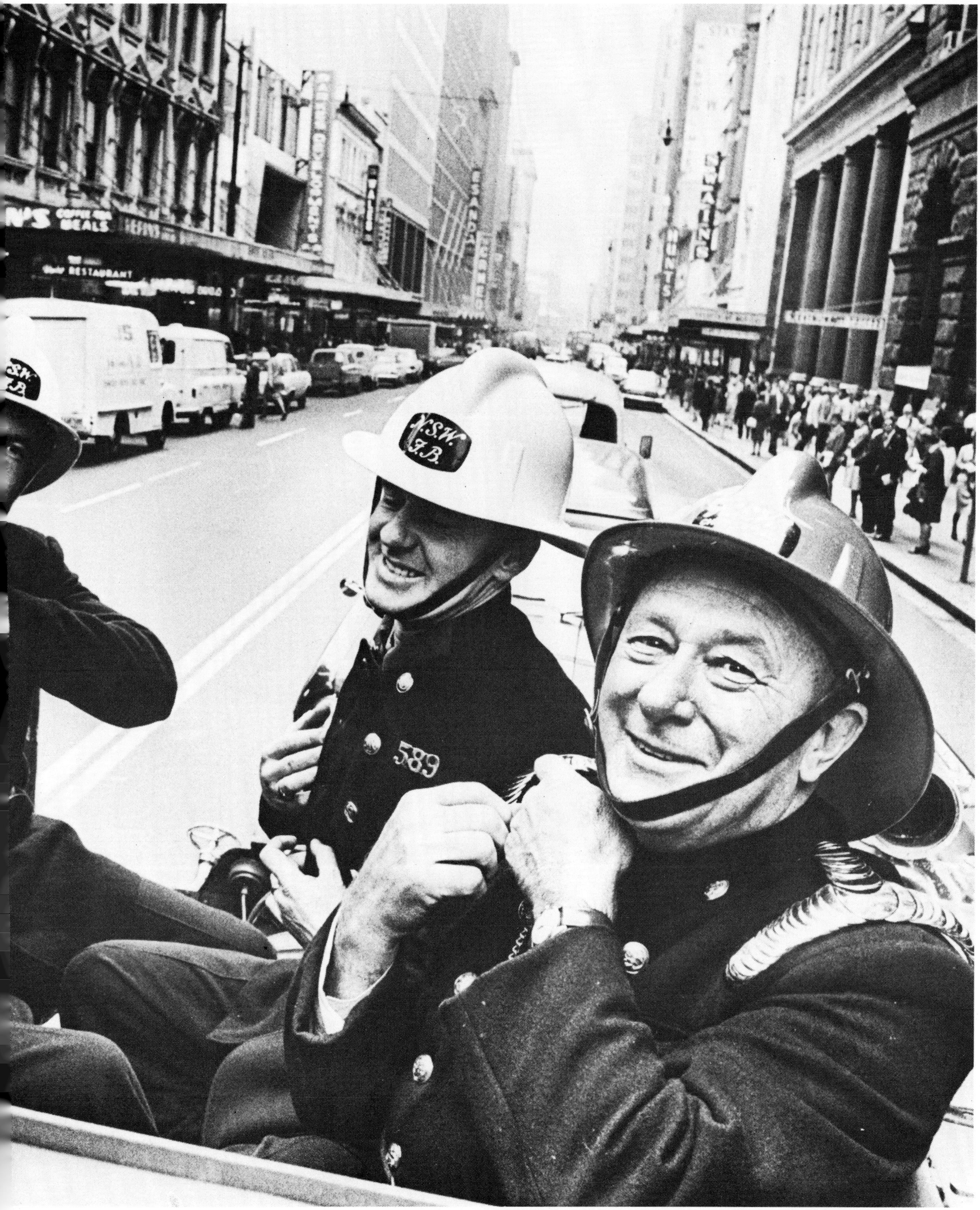
589

Health studio, Surfers Paradise

Sunbaker, Gold Coast, Queensland

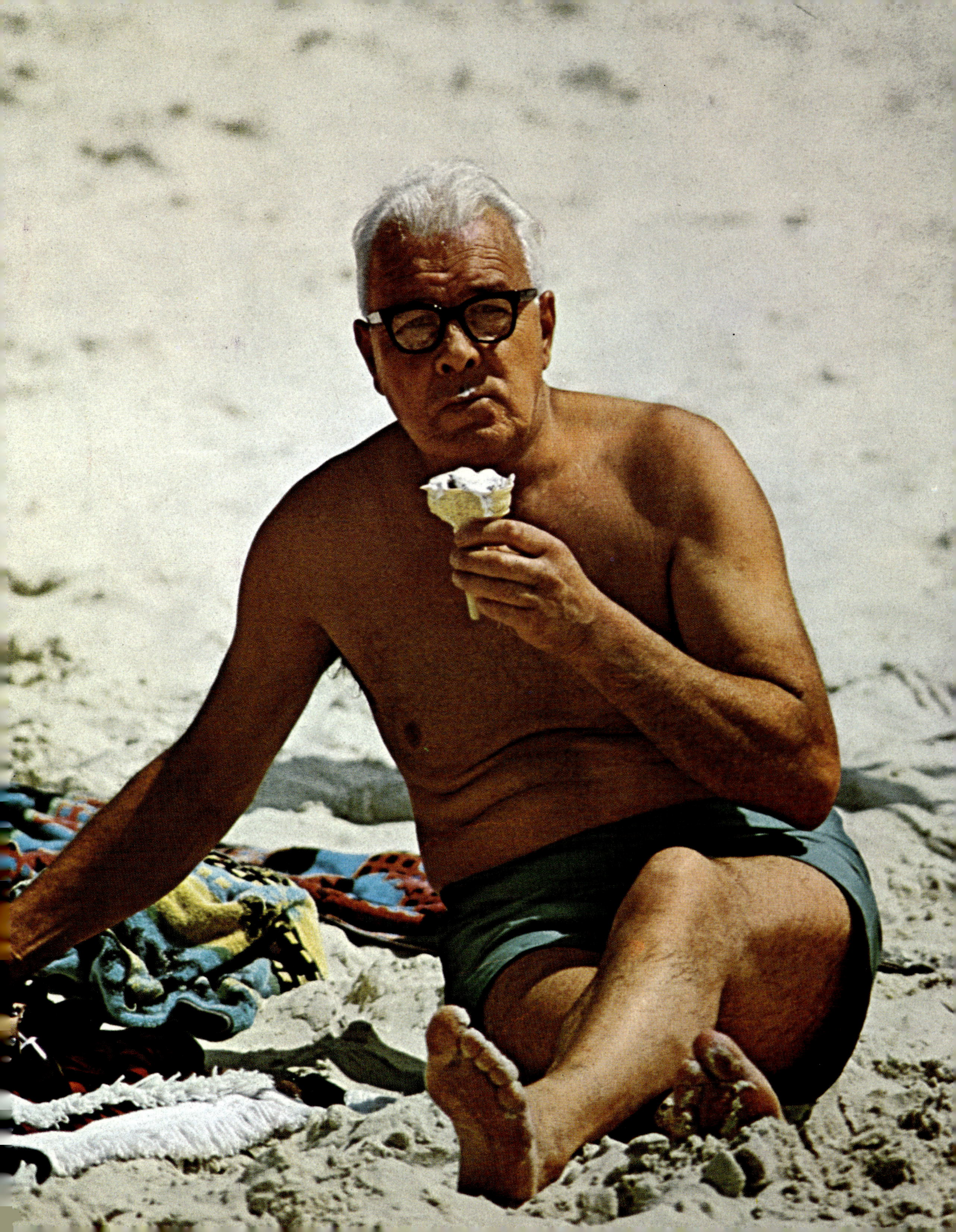

Gentleman, Melbourne Cup

Evening drink

The ring

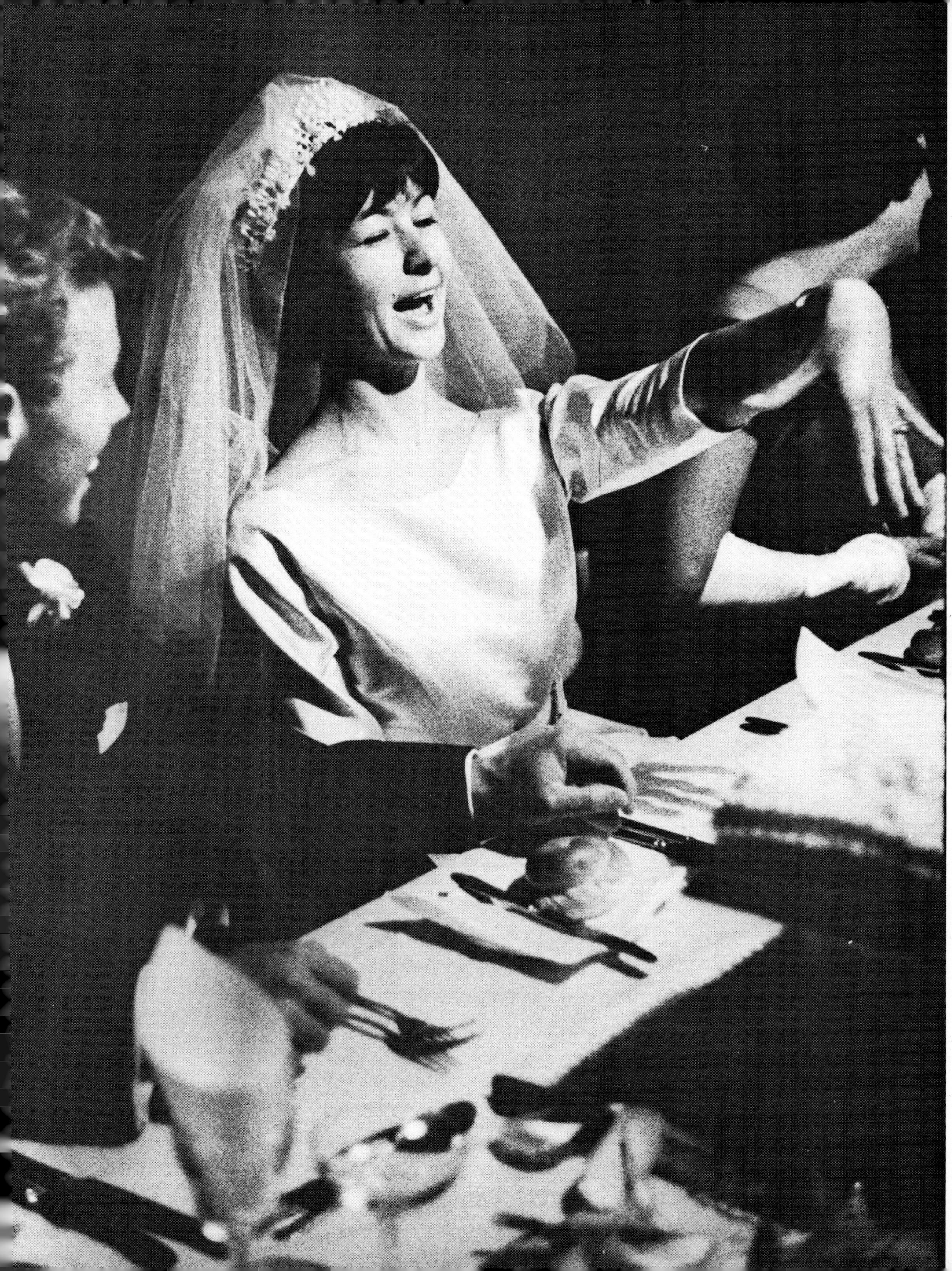

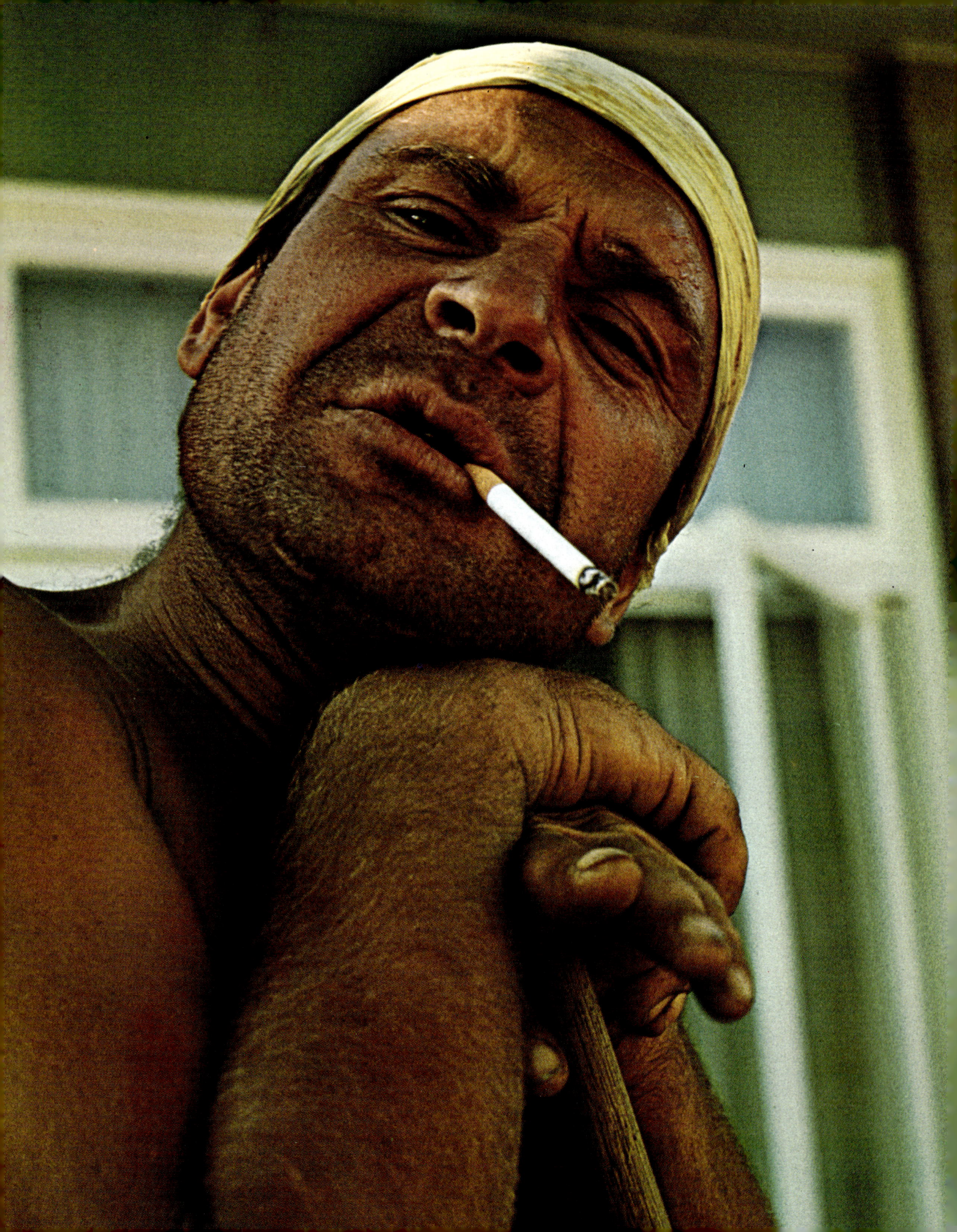

Punter, Adelaide
Mario

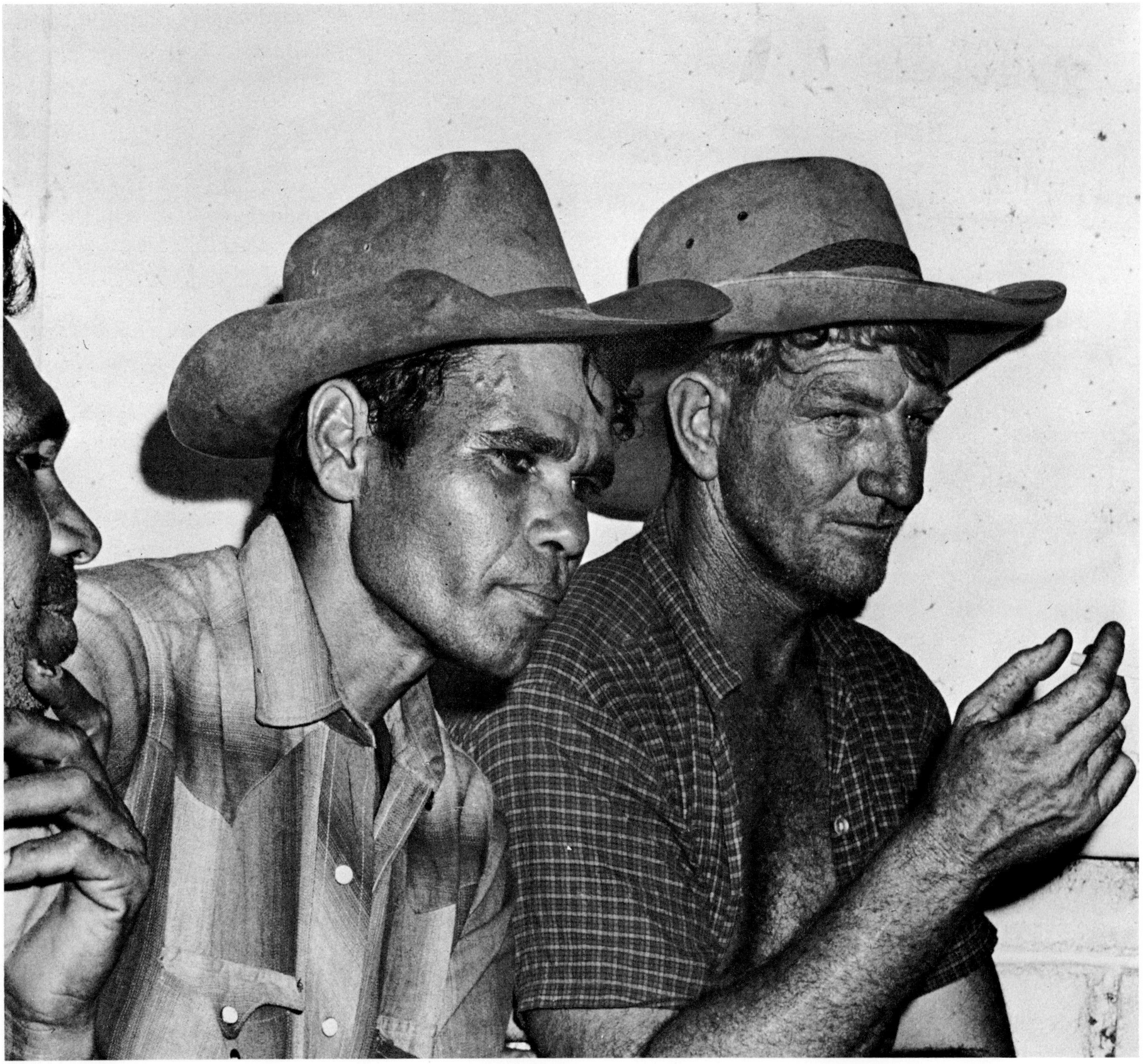

Australians all

Making damper, Ross River, Northern Territory

Wine casks, Hunter Valley, N.S.W.

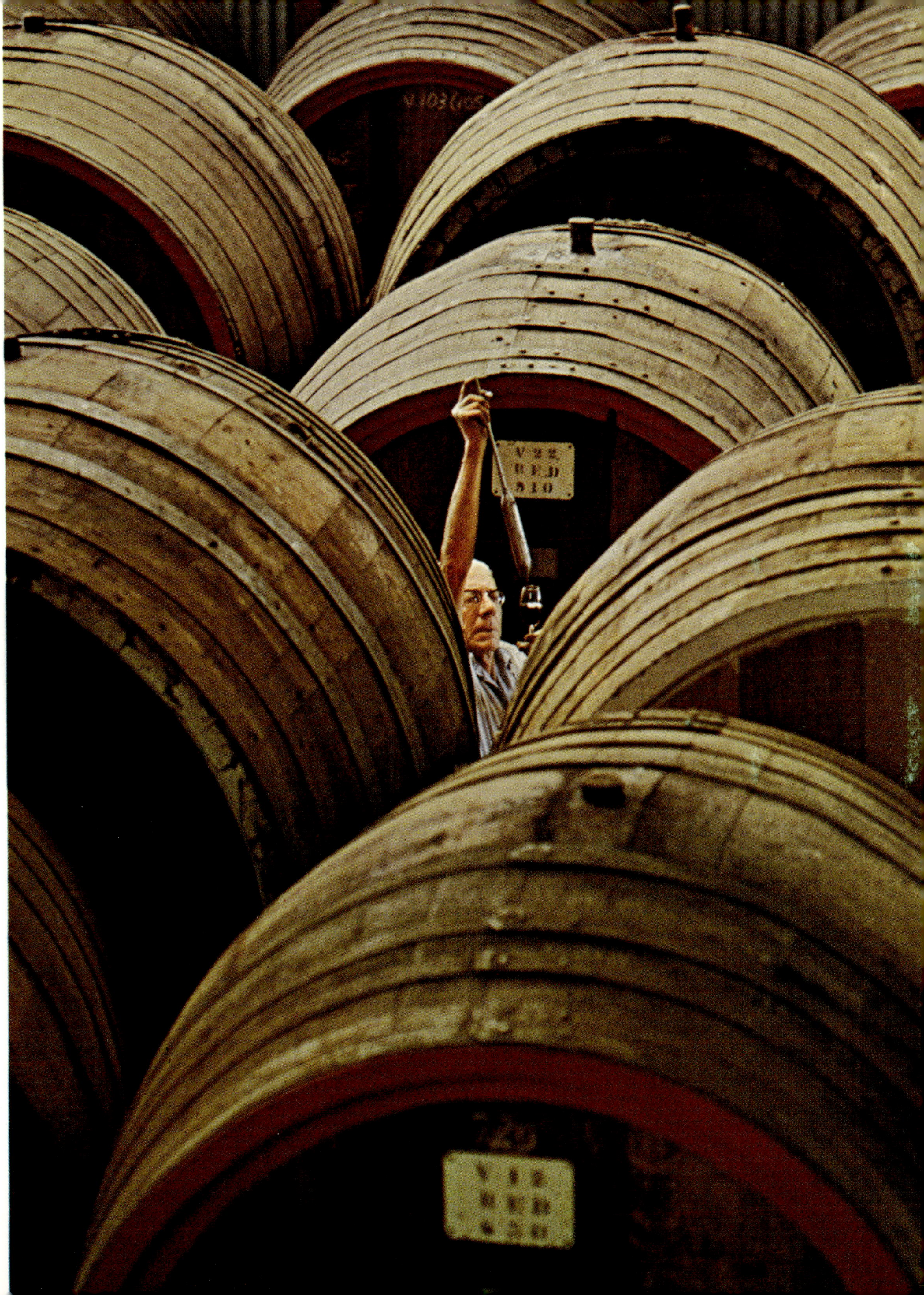
V 22
RED

Top) The Domain, Sunday   Bottom) Lunch break, Monday

Anzac Day

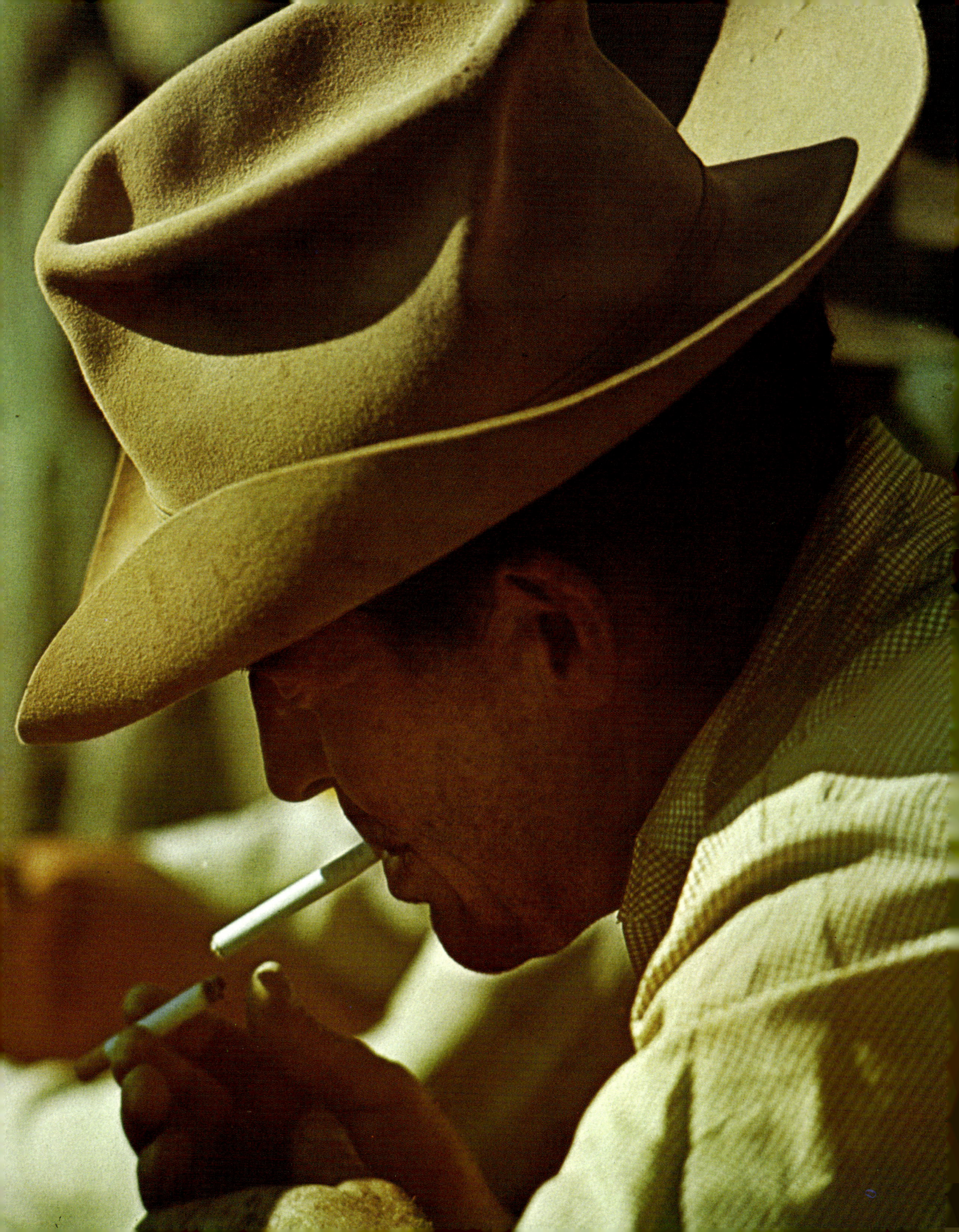

Maltese festival, Adelaide

Rodeo cowboy, Queensland

PLEASURE

HAPPINESS WITHOUT GUILT

Craig McGregor

Deep in the heart of the Surfers Paradise, that neon-lit, hamburger-and-hysteria jungle which is the capital of the Gold-Parking-Meter-Coast, is a holiday villa called PLEASURELAND. It's as good a symbol as any for that particular strip of Austerica, with its endless miles of Copocobanas and Miamis and Floridas and Surfriders and gaudy 15-storey motels and gaudier 25-storey hotels and multi-coloured petrol stations and Bar-B-Qs and Steak Houses and drive-in banks, cinemas and beer bars and barely a single square inch of public parkland (because the real estate is too valuable—one of these days they'll build the beach out too and then Surfers Paradise will have achieved its ironic apotheosis). Indeed I sometimes think that the Great Australian Dream is to turn this entire continent into a sort of super-colossal king-size PLEASURELAND with milk bars, fun parlours and plastic pennants lining the Birdsville Track and gold parking meters marching up and down the streets of Bourke and Cooktown and millions of jerry-built, three-roomed, fibro-and-fluorescent holiday villas dotted over every inch of the Australian countryside. Because Australians, whatever else one can say about them, have got their priorities right: they know that life is not meant for toil but pleasure, and even if pleasure's pursuit sometimes takes contorted forms (Surfers Paradise has zest, pace and an absolutely splendid vulgarity, but even I cannot stomach those aching miles of fake and tawdry glamour which stretch from Coolangatta to Surfers Paradise proper), at least they're after the right thing. Happiness without guilt, as Professor Manning Clark puts it. Or even happiness with gilt, if it's a SPECIAL and catches the sun.

The sun?

The sun is the private, ever-recurrent image which beckons the Australian towards pleasure. By now it has probably entered his sub-conscious, a sort of mandala with three spokes: a race memory bequeathed by those early settlers who threw up cool, solid-stone homesteads and cellar-dark verandahs to keep the Southern Hemisphere sunfire from their pale skin; a present experience of what the sun means, thrust deeper and deeper into the libido of dark-suited clerks in insurance skyscrapers watching bermuda shorts jiggle along the hotmix pavements and sports cars rasping up King William Street; and a wish-projected collage of tourist ads, Suncoast specials, Hayman Island holidays and Australian National Travel Association brochures which conjure up a vision splendid of a sunkissed, bikini-clad Australia Felix of the future, Tahiti on the Yarra. It is the sun which beckons the Australian towards the beach, where he has created a unique pop culture of surf lifesavers, board riders, summer barbecues and Christmas on the sand. It is the sun which beckons the Australian towards the bush, towards Sunday drives with the kids, picnics in the Dandenongs, bushwalking, caravan parks, and those tent towns which bestrew the 12,000 miles of coastline in the holiday season (19 p.c. of Australians go camping on their holidays).

It is the sun which beckons Alf to the backyard, pruning the hydrangeas with a rusty pair of Woolworths secateurs and allowing the Victa to tow him around the lawn on a Sunday morning; and Edna to the ladies' bowling club where, clad in a regulation white uniform with the hemline a regulation distance above the ground (which in very short and very tall women produces some bizzare sporting fashions!), she can pretend she's equal to the male, forgetting that she is as thoroughly segregated from the men's bowling club as she is from men's bars; and young Johnny to the Sandown car meet, driving through the cool of the morning in his Mini with wide-rimmed radials thumping over the bitumen and trannie blaring the latest hits, watching the birds flip past in their feminine Sprites and envying the moustached and cloth-capped oldies in their E-types who flip after them, all conjoined by the prospect of a day spent watching those machine age heroes, the racing car drivers, wrench pleasure from the threat of a carburettor death. It is the sun which, day after day, ricocheting off pavements, bouncing into sunglassed eyes, glinting on carpark windshields, sizzling on Skol-oiled backs and warming the baby slung in a Cozee-Seat beneath the rotary backyard hoist, promises to Australians, like the rainbow promised an earlier race, that in the end, despite everything, despite flood, war, Bomb, and disillusion, she'll be right, mate.

And yet the images of happiness, of pleasure, which most Australians pursue are probably far simpler and more basic than that. Like the family itself. It plays an important role in Australian life, perhaps more important than many other Western countries; two academic surveys, one of 10,000 Sydney adolescents and another of a small dairying community, found that there was a high level of unity in most of the families studied and, somewhat surprisingly, comparatively little friction between parents and their children. The average family has two or three children who often stay at home until they get married, the men at 27 and the women at 24; indeed it's the home, whether it be a triple-fronted brick veneer bung in Fremantle or a split-level architect-designed machine for living at Belmont or a narrow-fronted ironwork and frangipani terrace in Redfern, that is the focal point for the Australian's intrinsically suburban way of life. It's there that Barry Humphries' archetypal suburbanite, Sandy Stone, carries out his precious rituals of contentment: Sunday night down at the R.S.L. club, Monday night watching colour slides with friends, Tuesday off to the pictures, Wednesday cards with the family, Thursday a lodge meeting for Sandy and a visit to the dressmaker for Beryl, Friday a quiet night in the home, Saturday morning at the supermarket, Saturday afternoon at the footy and Saturday night watching the telly. . . . It's there that Australians get on with the gardening (TURN GRASS INTO LAWN! shout the motor mower ads in the Sunday papers, sure of a warm response from overfat Dads who are more likely to die of arteriosclerosis than almost any other bunch of Dads in the world) and the handyman work which has made them, frustrated pioneers all, an extraordinarily lucrative market for do-it-yourself books. When English migrants first arrive here they are always surprised to find that in the Aussie lingo there are no "houses," only "homes," and that the colour supplements are labelled IN THE HOME and BEAUTIFYING YOUR HOME.

Signs of progress, Surfers Paradise

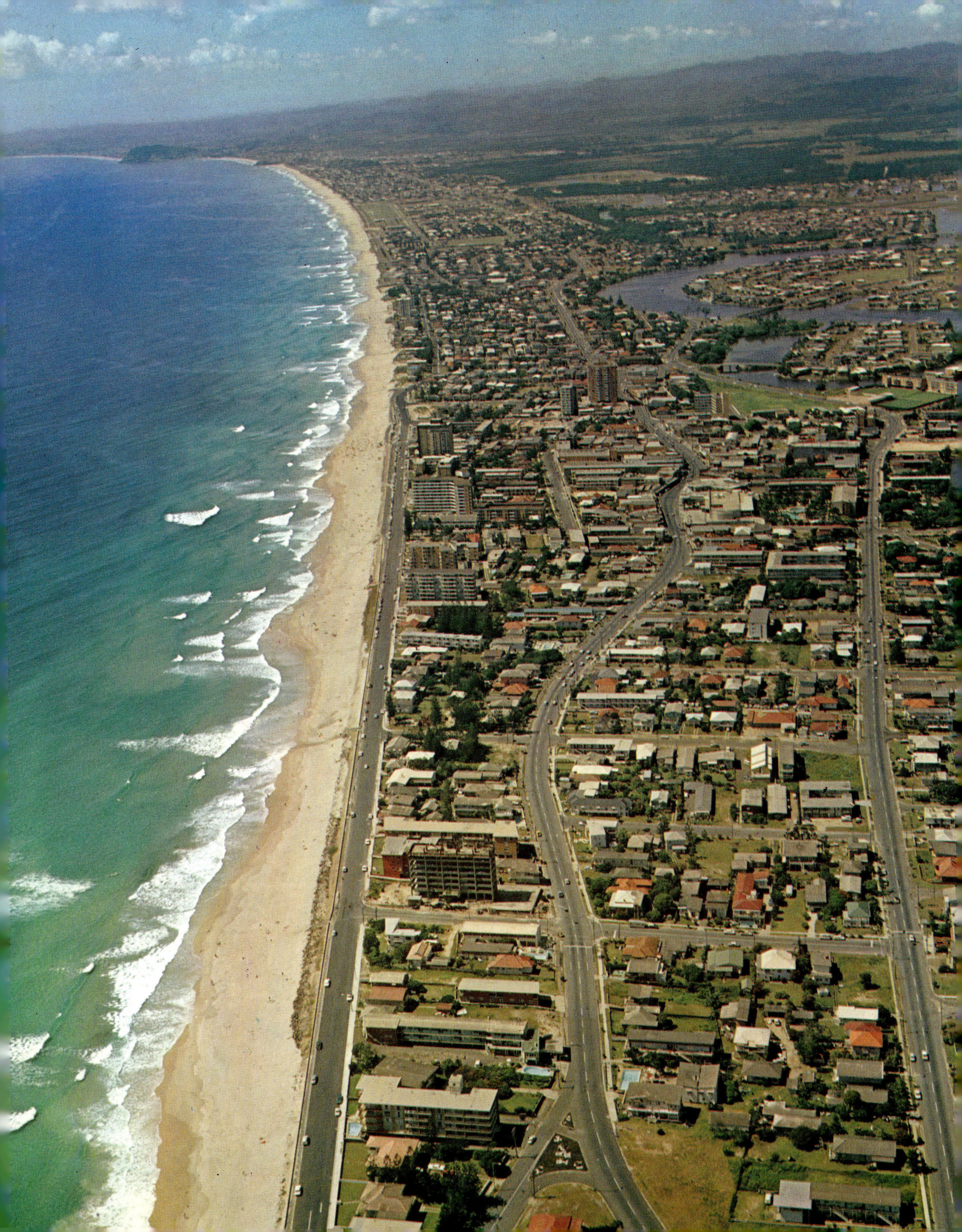

That's how Australians think of it: not just a place to live, but the centre of the world. A Melbourne housing estate study found that most men spent their weekends simply pottering around the home and making improvements to it; when they were asked what they would do with a windfall ten thousand dollars 70 p.c. replied "spend it on the home," and when their wives were asked what they'd do if they had more household help only 17 p.c. said they would go out more often—the others wanted to stay right where they were. That's what the good life means to most Australians: *stay at home.*

There are more adventurous souls, however, who seek headier pleasures than a cup of tea, a Bex and a good lie down. Like sex. A couple of years ago Dr. H. M. Carey, Professor of Obstetrics and Gynaecology at the Royal Hospital for Women, declaimed to me in suitably startled tones: "We're in the middle of a morals revolution. Today one in every three first children in Australia is conceived out of wedlock. It's absolutely staggering. Where will it all end?"

Well, like most revolutions, it doesn't seem to have torn society apart in the way churchmen and politicians have feared so televisually, but there certainly has been a dramatic change since the war years; Australians at last seem to be able to pursue sex with the same sort of open, purposeful hedonism they display in just about everything else. The VD rate has doubled in the last decade, the illegitimacy rate has almost doubled; medical authorities estimate that there are 90,000 illegal abortions a year in Australia, and that one bride in every five is pregnant when she gets married. Adultery is much less heavily censured than before, and the divorce rate has climbed to the point where one in nine marriages end that way. But there are even more obvious indicators of what's happened: bikinis at St. Kilda, strippers at the Cross, sex films in the city, exhaustive articles on the Pill in the *Women's Weekly,* soft-core pornography in the TV commercials, hard-core pornography at the stag dinners, *Portnoy's Complaint* in the bookshops, *Pix* gone nude, drag queens in all-male revues, skirts so mini that a dropped haircomb means indecent exposure—and that cornucopia of contemporary desire, the average Australian news-stand. The black, wowser-imposed puritanism which once held Australian life in a rigid mould of sexual conservatism has been broken at last, shattered by affluence, internationalism and a beach generation eager for kicks; a freer, more permissive morality has broken through. These days Australian women are heavier users of the Pill than any other women in the world. The Necessary Link between sex and childpain has been broken, once and for all; Australians have learnt that sex is not for procreation but for pleasure.

After sex, which nearly everyone indulges in, comes drinking, which three-quarters of the population enjoys. Australians are among the heaviest beer drinkers in the world: the average bloke gargles his way through about 22 gallons a year, but up in Darwin, where the temperature gets up to the hundreds, beer consumption gets up to the sixties. Toss in an extra gallon of plonk (wine) per head, plus nearly half a gallon of Scotch and other spirits, and you can see why a rich vocabulary has grown up about one of the after-effects: the chunder, liquid laugh or technicolour yawn.

Australians take their pleasures seriously, and perhaps none more so than grog. Their bars are usually spartan, lavatory-tile, chairless and cheerless affairs where the men can get on with the serious business of drinking without too many distractions (including women, who are banned from most bars). The beer gardens and cavernous lounges of those "new era" hotels which have followed the loosening of hotel trading hours are more civilised, but many have introduced self-service to speed up the turnover of middies, schooners and shorts. The clubs, which have begun to rival the pubs as drinking centres (they are open on Sundays, for a start) are perhaps the most sophisticated of all; the R.S.L. and Leagues clubhouses are often the most opulent and luxurious buildings in any town or suburb, and a peculiar style of mod-gloss architecture makes them as uniquely and recognisably Australian today as surf club buildings were in the "thirties." The wealthier clubs fly in entertainers from overseas, own yachts, farm out holiday cottages and excavate heated swimming pools for their members; the not-so-wealthy concentrate on the rows and rows of one-armed bandits which have made all this possible. Australians are inveterate gamblers: 90 p.c. buy lottery tickets, 60 p.c. bet on the horses, and as one form of gambling, such as two-up, dies away a new one springs up to take its place. One of these days bingo will be legalised, and then Australian women will have a chance to show that they enjoy gambling away the old man's pay packet just as much as, today, the old man does himself.

And yet—and I may be wrong about this—I get the feeling that gambling and the mass spectator sports upon which bookies depend, such as horseracing, are becoming less important to Australians. There has been a drift away from the mass rituals (horseracing, football, cricket) which the British brought with them from the Old Country to pastimes like bowling where the ordinary bloke can be a doer as well as a watcher. The move has been from land sports to water sports, from a seat at the Melbourne Cricket Ground to a seat in the family car, from mass culture to private leisure; for every person who goes to watch the cricket there's probably a thousand who go to the beach. Australians no longer have to huddle in gigantic sports stadiums for togetherness, or seek an elusive national identity in being part of a crowd; those sepia photographs of phenomenally crowded racetracks reek incurably of the past, and it's not just the thousands and thousands of grey hats which make them seem old-fashioned. These days Australians take their leisure elsewhere.

In the car, for instance. Affluence has made the ordinary family man as mobile as the toffs were a quarter of a century ago; the Sunday drive has become a national institution, the "Sunday driver" a national swearword. There's been a phenomenal growth of motels, and neon signs reading PACIFIC SANDS and LAKEVIEW and CAR-O-TEL and PASADENA LODGE have taken the place of the

116) Dinner for two, Sydney
117) Chair for one, Camp Cove
118, 119) Beach for all

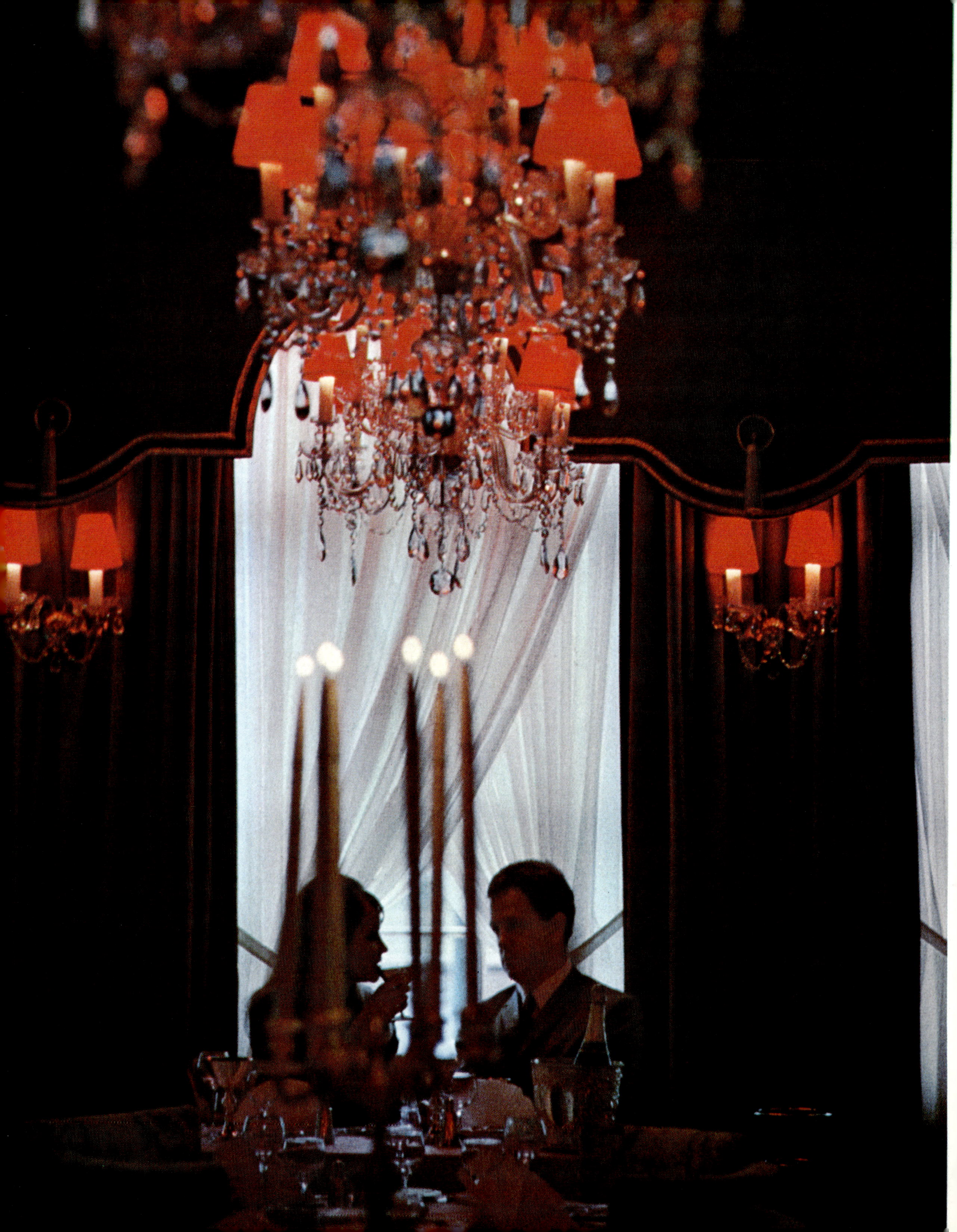

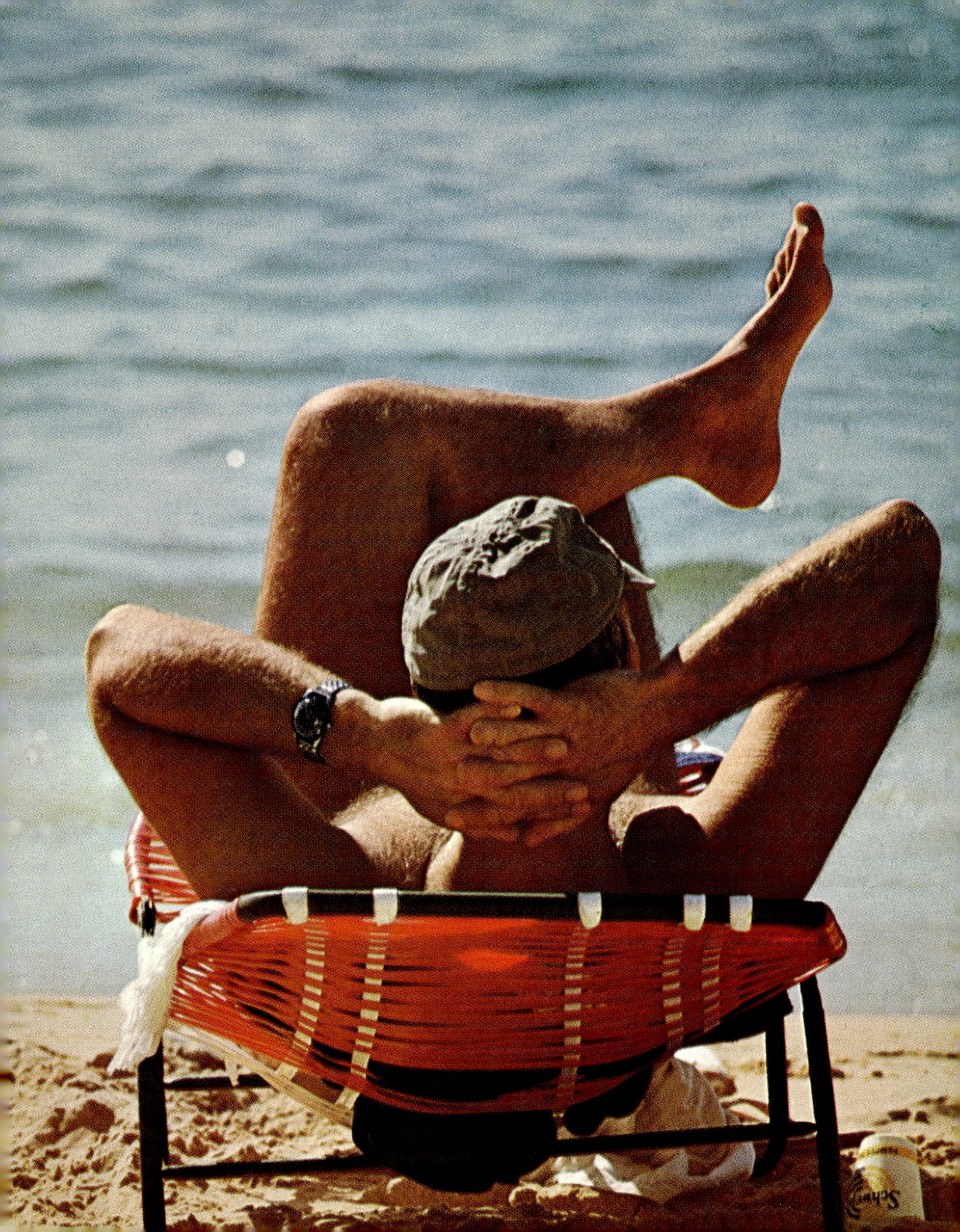

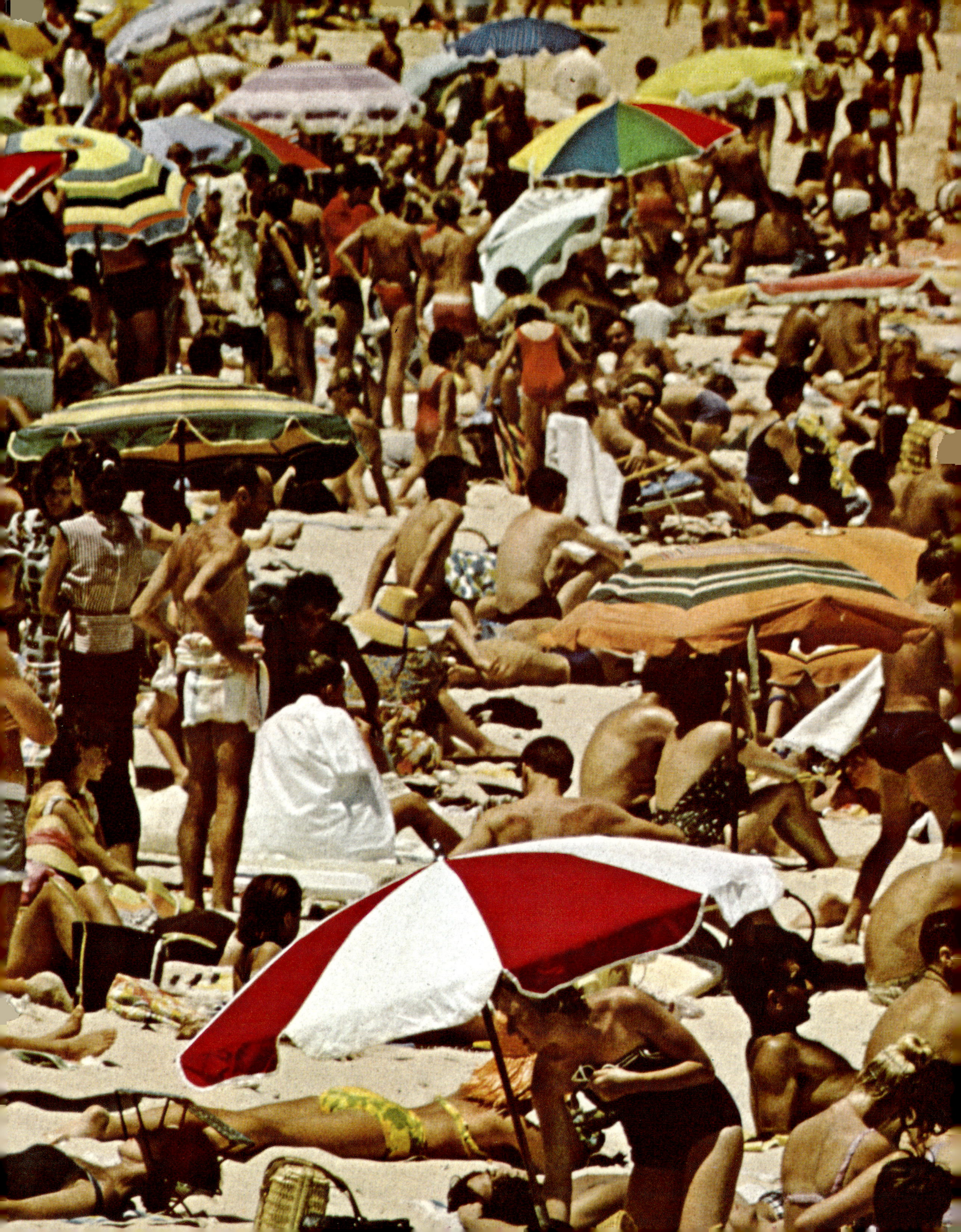

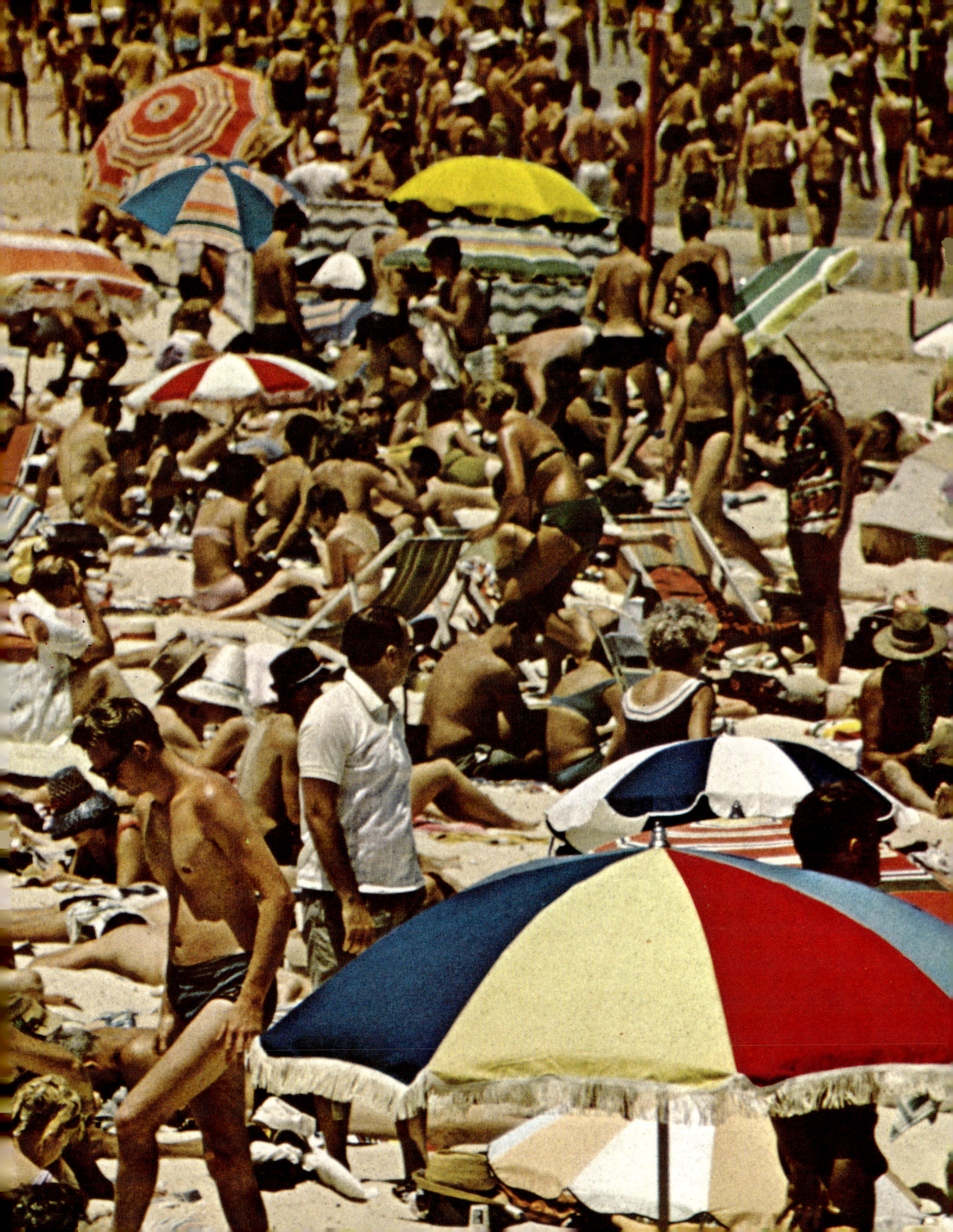

old guest houses and hotels to which steam trains brought hordes of dutiful holidaymakers. A few relics of the old breed linger on: the Victorian Department of Railways chalet at Mount Buffalo, a gloomy, cavernous, rabbit-warren of rooms and drawing suites which seems to have changed not one iota since the turn of the century, and the Hydro Majestic at Medlow Bath, wrapped in Blue Mountains mist and dreaming of grandiose yesterdays when watering spas, echo points, glorious views and the Bridal Falls meant "holiday" for most people. But they are anachronisms; nowadays three-quarters of all holidaymakers travel by cars, staying briefly at motels while they look around the countryside and enjoy the freedom which last year's hire purchase Holdy has given them. Almost a third of all cars sold in Australia are station waggons; it gives Alf room to put the kids to sleep on the trip from Adelaide to Surfers.

That's the other big change in Australian leisure: the swing to the beach. Australians have begun to come to terms with their environment; whereas half a century ago they fled to the mountains like well-bred Englishmen to enjoy the cool air and escape the sun, now they fan out along the coastline and pursue the sun. The new boom sports are nearly all waterborne: waterskiing, skindiving, boating, surf riding. Sydney Harbour has so many yachts it's had to introduce a registration system; even those untrammelled free spirits, the boardriders, have had to succumb to numberbrands on their fins. The glossy new holiday resorts are all on the coast, resplendent with hotels, motels, golf clubs, bowling greens and beachside boutiques, and often slapped down uncomfortably cheek-by-jowl with older fishing resorts where family outings, sandals, Dad in Army shorts, FRESH BAIT, oysters and mucking about in boats are still the order of the day. Almost the entire eastern seaboard is slowly being parcelled up into development lots so that harried city dwellers can escape once in a while to a seaside weekender. The lack of planning is appalling, but a rescue operation has been mounted and some resorts, such as Noosa in Queensland, and Merimbula near the Victorian border, have already achieved a striking man-made beauty. Australia will never create its own Riviera, as Surfers Paradise proved, but at least the beaches will be free.

Of course, the spectrum of pleasure is infinitely broad. Every day in Australia thousands of people go tap-dancing, collect stamps, learn ice-skating, sing scales, arrange flowers, read books, attend concerts, play darts, fly kites, practise yoga, raise pigeons, walk dogs, go fishing, build model aeroplanes, sew, knit, embroider and involve themselves in innumerable other pastimes, fashionable and unfashionable. It's easy to delineate the mass activities and spectator sports which Australians indulge in together, impressive through sheer crowd size, forgetting that for many pleasure means quieter and more secretive things: a letter to a friend, a stroll in the sun, or just sitting and thinking. The pleasure is never undiluted. Ants climb into the holiday sugar, the kids get sunburnt, a broken beer bottle slices your foot open, the car won't start. And it is limited: not for the Australian the subtle poetry of infinitely slow twilights, chianti and cypresses in Tuscany, one's first Michelangelo, West Indians and dollybirds in the tube. But it has its own rough balladry: a beer at the Lakes and Ocean, sixpenny rides on the merry-go-round, pelicans and cabbage tree palms at Forster, frosty mornings in the back of the ute, an axe bites into timber at Deep Creek camping ground, the reeds quiver and wild ducks break for the sky. Australians have always poured most of their imagination and creativity into transforming the commonplace, seeking happiness in the rituals of leisure—family life, mateship, holidays, sport—which give their lives meaning. They are looking in the right place, because in the 20th century it's pleasure, not work, which fulfils the man. I wish them well.

Rock fishing, N.S.W.

122, 123) Horseman, Trephina Gorge, Northern Territory

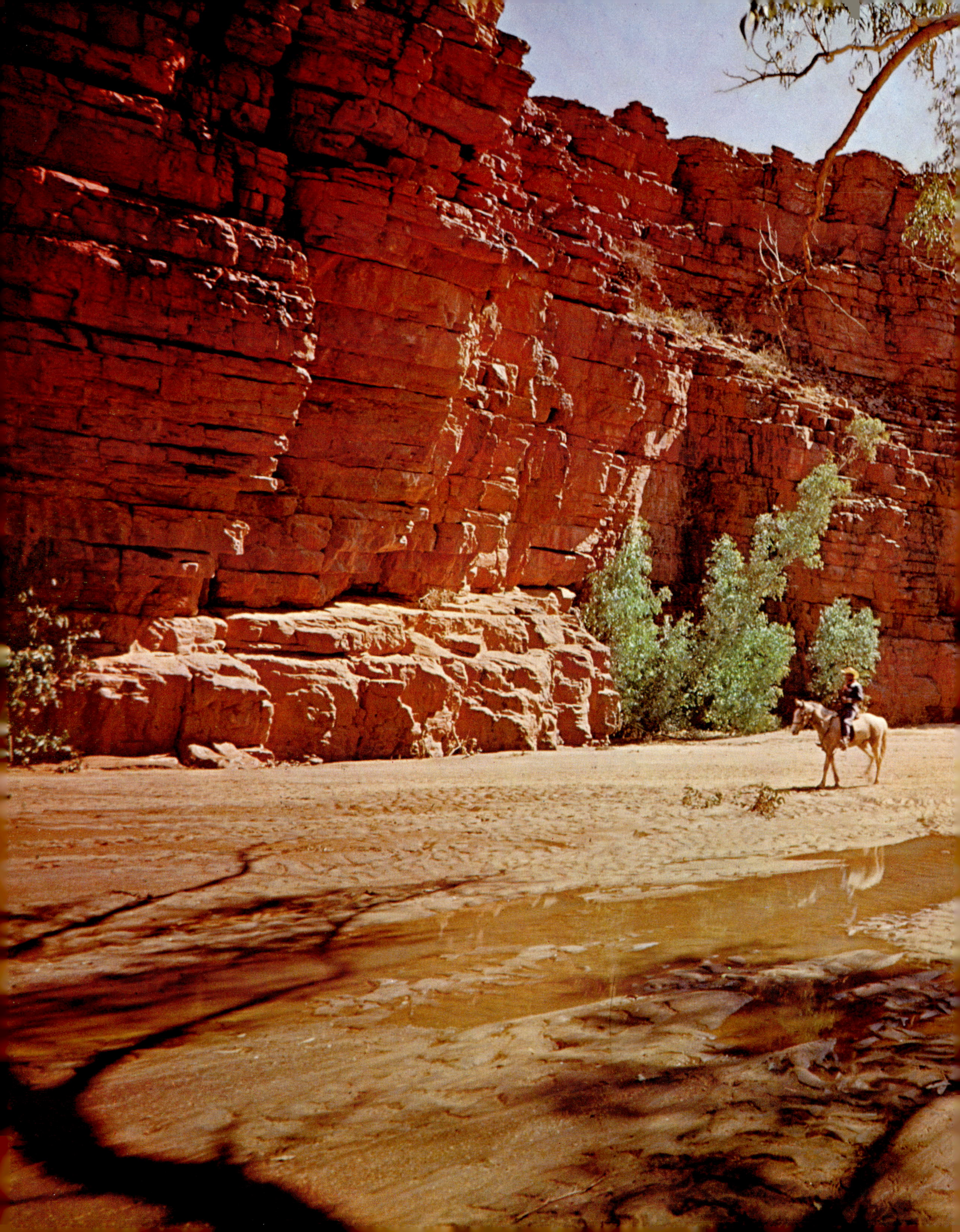

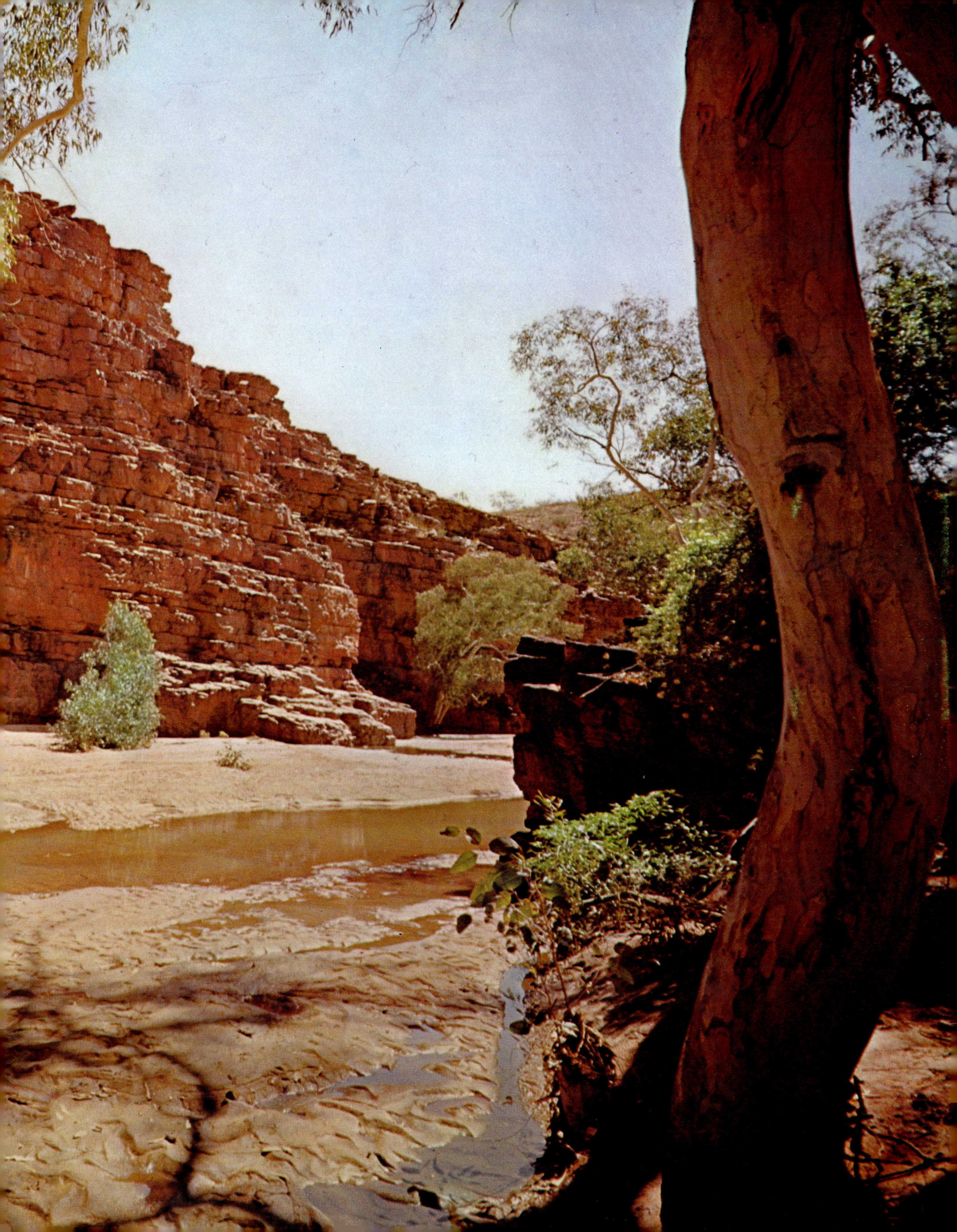

126, 127) Above the snowline

King's Cross entertainment

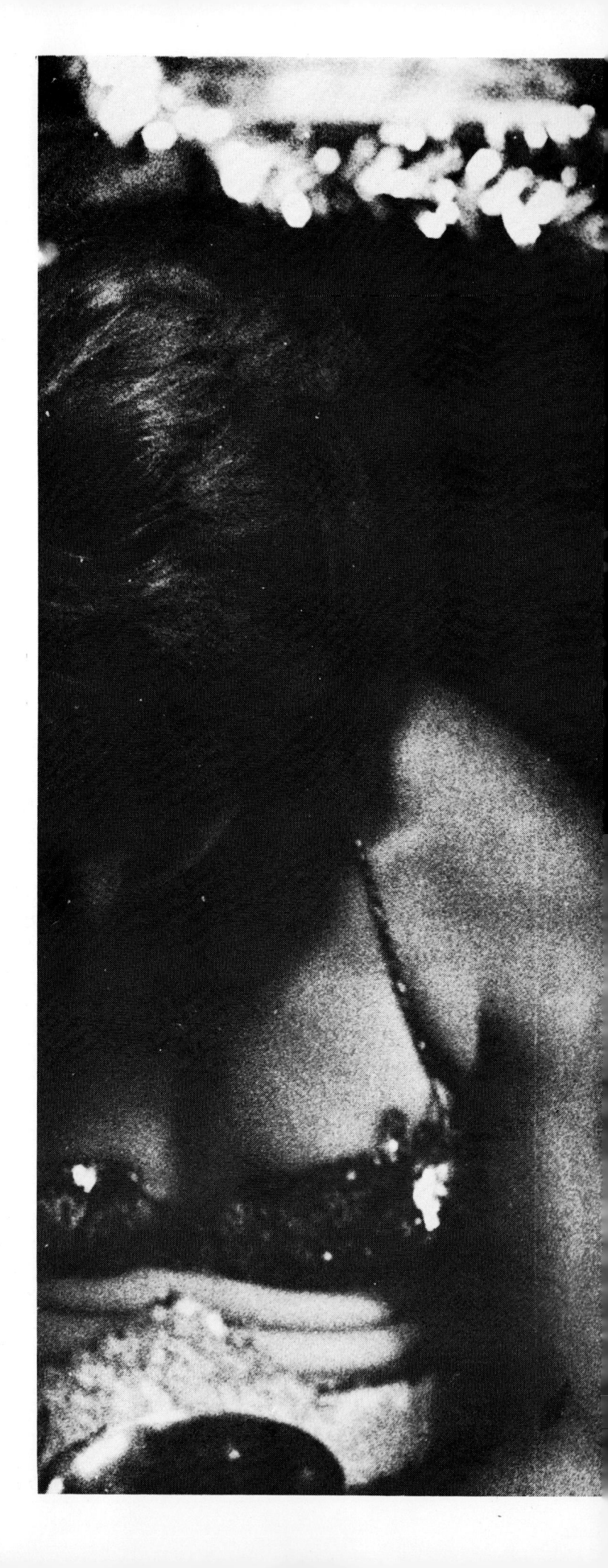

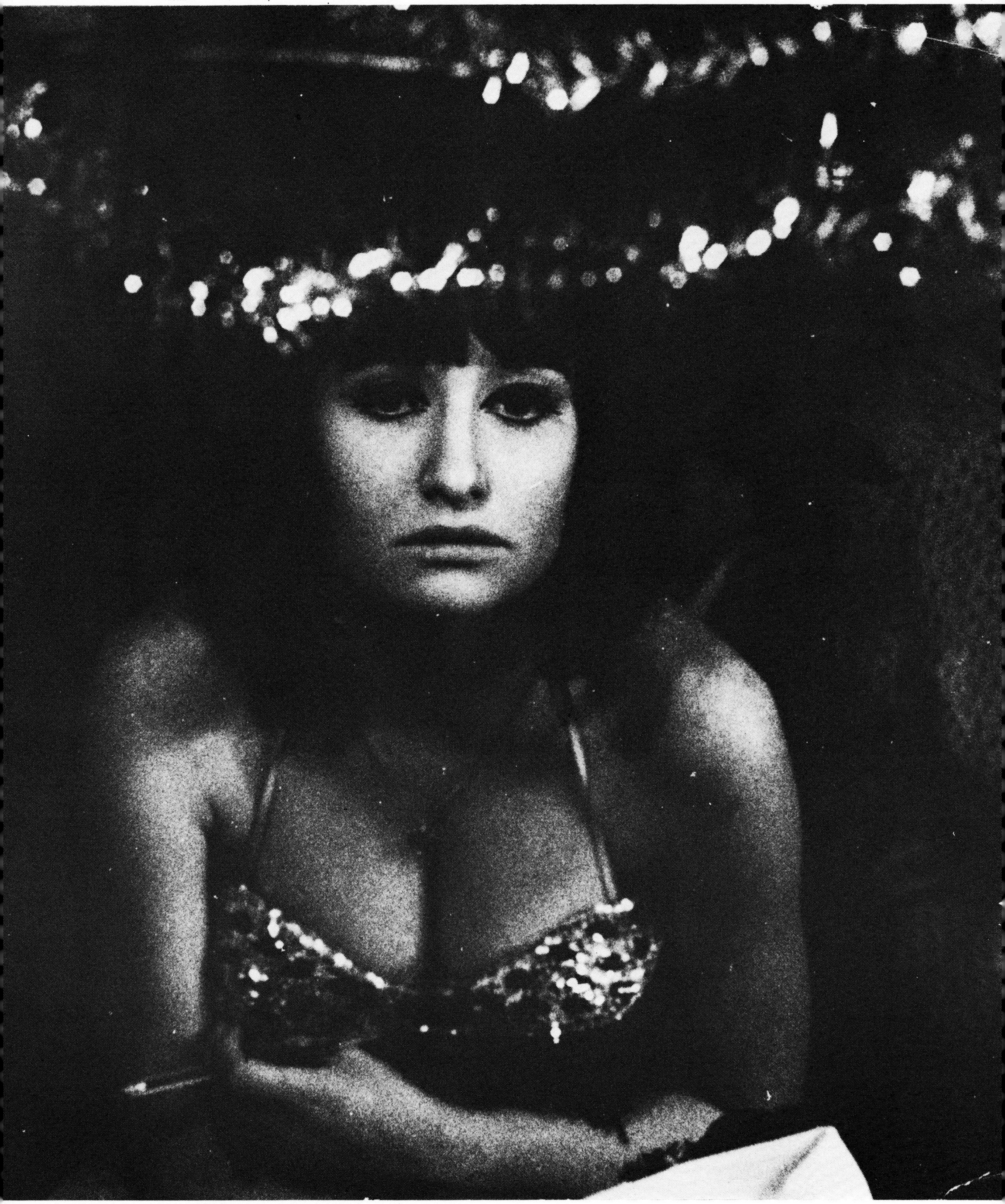

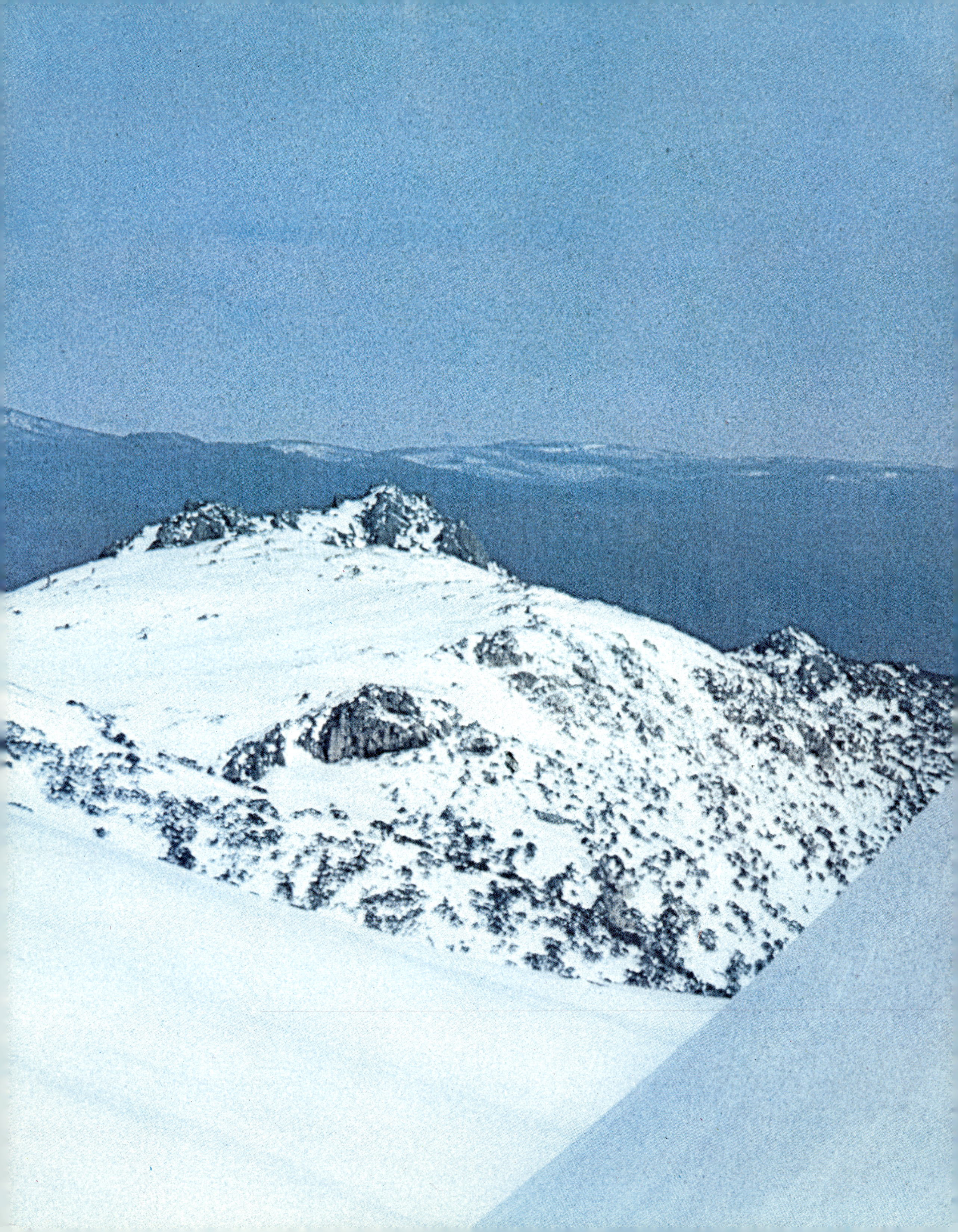

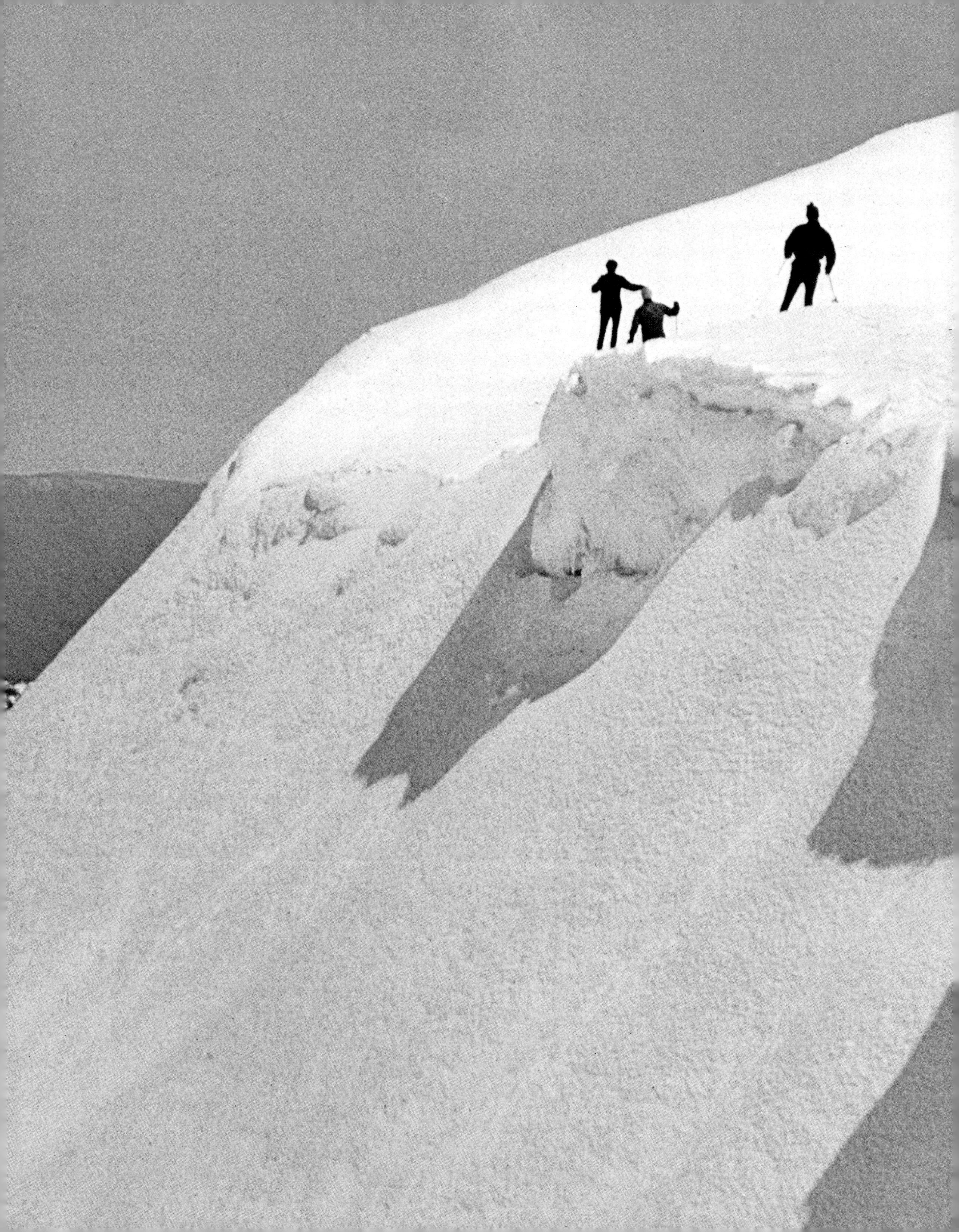

COLLINGWOOD
Founded
1893
JSP·837

GINGER
15TH AV
TOMATO
20c LB
BANANA
3 LB 20c
SWEET
PINEAPPLE
3 FOR 20c

Rodeo, Northern Territory

Above left) Football adoration, Melbourne
Left) Fruit stall, Queensland

Helmsman, 'New Endeavour', off the Queensland coast

Windsor Castle Hotel, Paddington

Board transport

Learner slopes, Thredbo Valley, N.S.W.
134, 135) Topless A Go Go, Sydney -

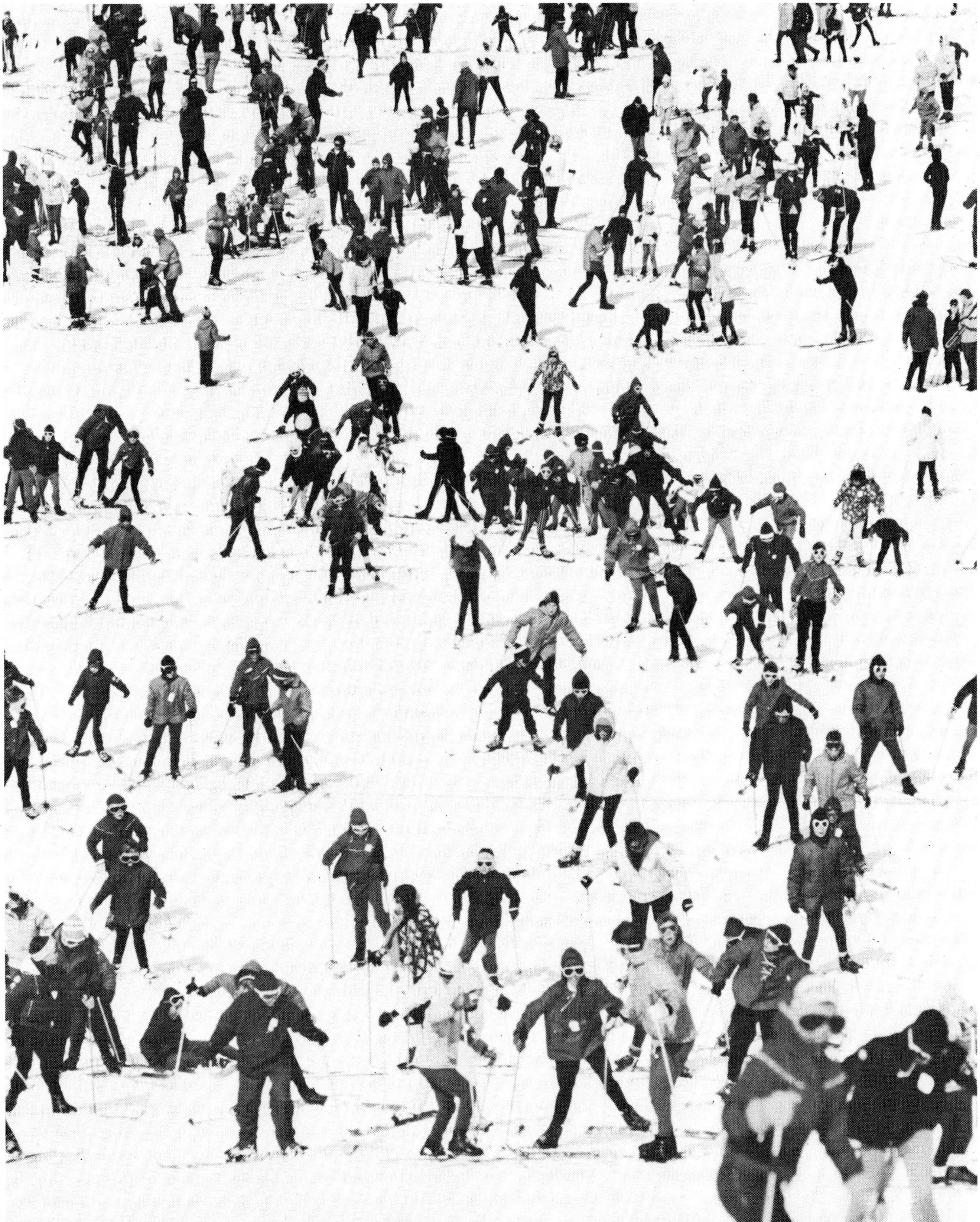

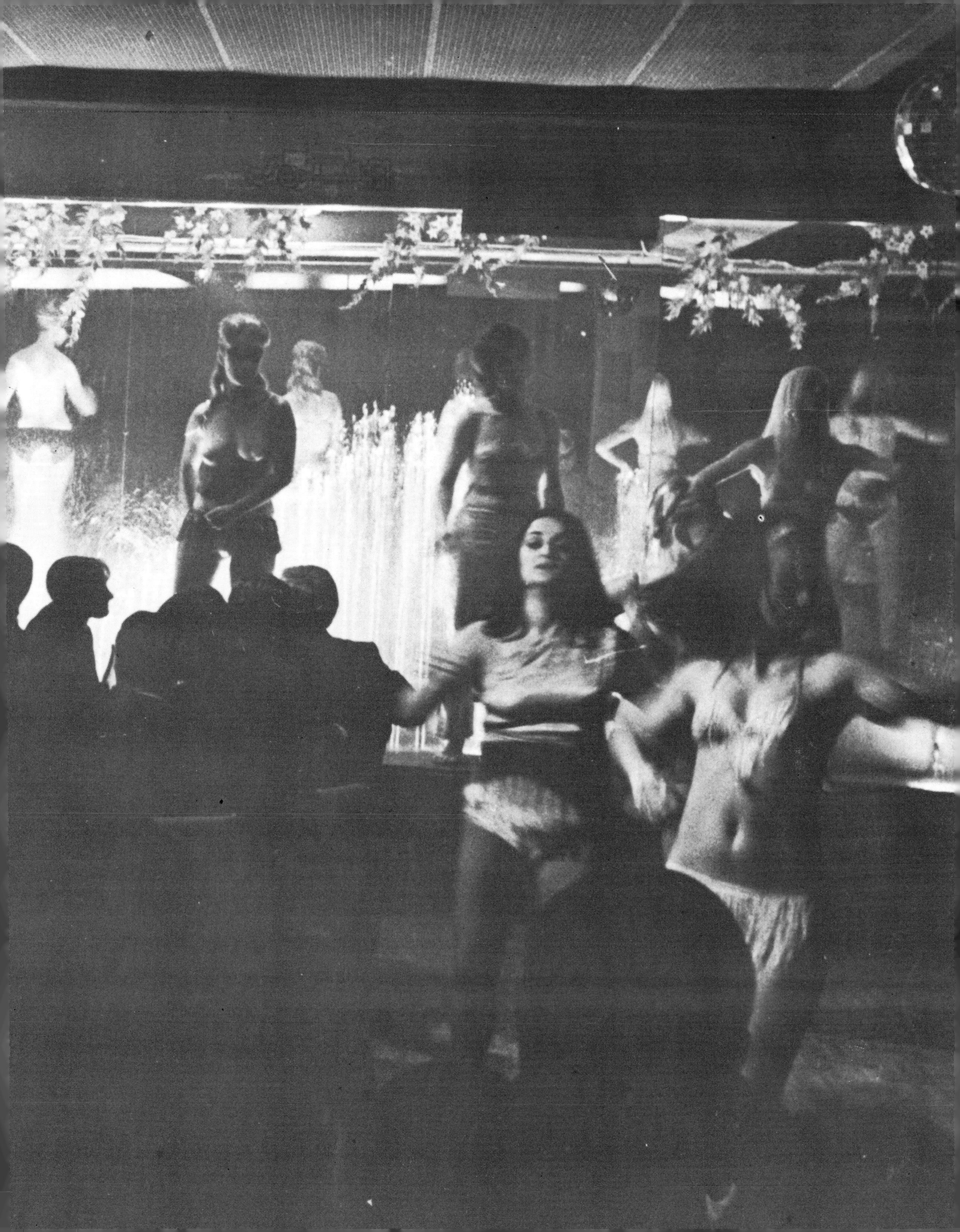

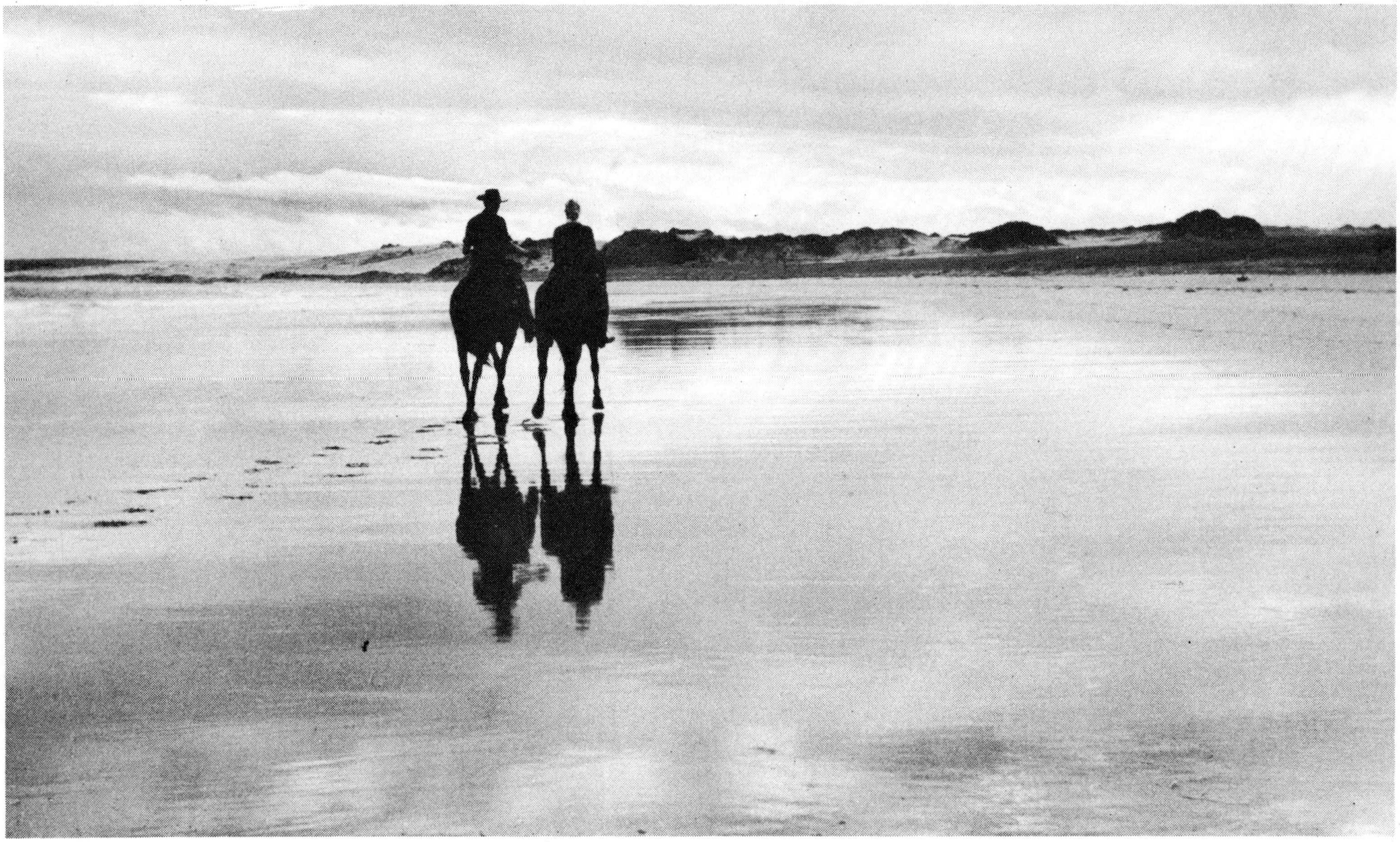

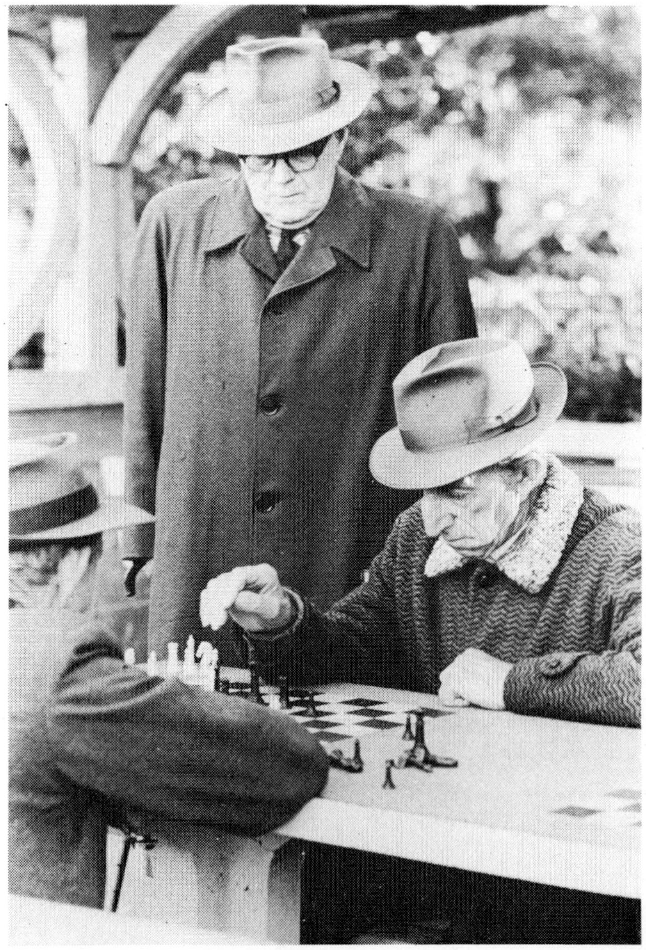

A day is passed . . .

SPORT

THE GREAT AUSTRALIAN TALENT

Harry Gordon

Not all Australians are expert swimmers; some rely on a splashy, uneven sidestroke, combined with a ragged putt-putt kick, and there are others who have never mastered the dead man's float. In Australia there are swarms of earnest five-minute milers, and duffers who spray golf balls around fairways with drunken imprecision, and tennis players who can't even jump the net. There are horsemen who fall off, surfboard riders who have trouble standing up, cricketers who can't bowl a leg-break, and divers who do belly flops. There are, to be frank, a lot of also-rans in Australia.

In some overseas minds this would be regarded as violently improbable. To these minds, Australia is a country which produces winners . . . Sedgmans and Hoads, Elliotts and Landys, Konrads and Frasers. They do not realise that beneath all that thick athletic cream, a great deal of very plain milk exists. The sad truth is that the losers of Australia have been deprived of their identity.

Suppose we ask the question: which Australians have achieved international eminence in their fields? And suppose we ask it, not in Australia (where our lists might be loaded a little selfconsciously with sopranos, scientists, writers, artists, politicians, soldiers and a flier), but in Stockholm, or Tokyo or San Francisco. A group of knowledgeable Swedes or Japanese or Americans might be able to come up with the names of a few non-sportsmen like Nellie Melba, Joan Sutherland, Judith Anderson, Errol Flynn, Patrick White, Morris West, Sidney Nolan, Alan Moorehead, Sir Robert Menzies and maybe The Seekers. But they could probably name, without much trouble, at least twice as many people who have made their reputations in sport.

Now what does all this prove? Simply that the tennis player and the swimmer, along with those veteran performers the kangaroo and the koala, have become part of the brand-image of Australia. Simply that sport is considered by many people around the world to be the great Australian talent. Whether this is a desirable state of affairs, or whether it is fair to opera singers and also-rans, is beside the point; the fact is that the image does exist, and it is totally justified. Australians have had an impact on world sport that is quite out of proportion to the size of the country's population; and as a result, Australia is often identified mistily as an isolated, faraway hot-house which catapults into the outside world an endless succession of champion tennis players, swimmers, surfers, runners, golfers and jockeys.

Consider, briefly, just a small selection of the athletes from Australia who have invaded the highest levels of international sport in the years since the end of the Second World War. A freckled, jagged-nosed man called Rod Laver became the second person ever to perform the Grand Slam—which means that he won the world's four major tennis titles in one year. But there are many who doubt that this made him the greatest of the Australian tennis players; Frank Sedgman, Lew Hoad, Ken Rosewall, Ashley Cooper, Neale

Fraser and Roy Emerson were some who dominated the world field for a time. Shoals of Australian swimmers broke every world freestyle record during the 1950s and 1960s, and at the 1956 Olympic Games they took 14 gold medals; they included John and Ilsa Konrads, John Devitt, Jon Henricks, Lorraine Crapp, Kevin Berry, Terry Gathercole and the late John Marshall, but the two finest of them all were the husky rebel Dawn Fraser and the blond seaweed addict, Murray Rose. John Landy and Herb Elliott ran the mile faster than any rivals, Jack Brabham won three world driving championships. Midget Farrelly and Nat Young slid down the face of precipitous waves as they steered their surfboards to world titles. A succession of lithe and graceful girls, from Marjorie Jackson and Shirley Strickland to Betty Cuthbert and Marlene Mathews, challenged and beat the great Russian, Dutch and English girl sprinters, and a quite dissimilar group—little men with lined, drawn faces and slender frames and powerful wrists—came to dominate the English racing scene. These were the professional jockeys, headed by Arthur "Scobie" Breasley and George Moore. Peter Thomson made it almost a habit to win the British Open Golf Championship, and Bruce Devlin plundered some of the richest purses on the American circuit. Heather Blundell won the major squash titles with some monotony, Stuart Mackenzie kept on winning the Henley Diamond Sculls, Sid Patterson and Russell Mockridge pedalled like machines, and Ron Clarke ran vast distances faster than Nurmi or Zatopek or Kuts.

These champions, and some scores of others, represent the summits of sporting endeavour in Australia; but it is important to note that all of their sports are played in great depth . . . right through the belts of not-quites, on-the-way-ups, middling-fairs and duffers down to kids like the Maroubra Tadpoles, a bunch of earnest 11- and 12-year-olds who march up and down their beach behind a lightweight surf reel, learning to become lifesavers. All of these people—some consciously, most sub-consciously—extract from sport a deeply-grained sense of satisfaction, the kind of pure, sometimes exultant satisfaction that other people might gain from singing or folk-dancing or growing roses. The truth is that sport is an elemental part of the Australian way of life, deeply rooted in the consciousness of the people. Not only do Australians play sport with zest and watch sport with interest . . . they also talk sport constantly. Not long ago a distinguished American journalist confessed, after a visit to Australia, that he was hard put to recall any conversations in which sport did not intrude in some fashion. "If the other party is at all vulnerable," he wrote, "Australians will talk sport as if they existed for nothing else."

This preoccupation with sport, which some critics might call an obsession, is the result of a complex of geographical, historical and sociological factors. Geographically, the most striking characteristics about Australia are the largeness, the isolation and the comparative emptiness of the place. With some four people to the square mile (against 327 in Europe), it is essentially a country for vigorous, space-devouring endeavour . . . for vast parklands and fields and arenas. There is no sense of constriction, and it is consistent with the mood of space-freedom that the native brand of football is played on a large elliptical field, roughly 200 yards long—or about twice the size of an American football gridiron. The isolation (which might ordinarily have been counted a disadvantage, because it does discourage competition from overseas teams) has somehow spawned a chip-on-the-shoulder desire to excel in fields which command international attention and respect. And the size of the population has had the effect of sharpening enthusiasm. Peter Thomson, the golfer, once put it this way: "Nothing helps you climb like a bit of success, and in Australia you can distinguish yourself without too much ability. You don't have to make your way past so many others. To get to the top in a country like the United States, with a couple of hundred million people, why, it must look insuperable to a young boy—way beyond him." Add to the other facts of the atlas a softly temperate climate, thousands of miles of coastline where wide sands collide with an uncompromising surf, and fertile pastures which provide an abundance of high-protein diet—and it comes as no great surprise that this is a continent which abounds in restless, virile energy.

In its earliest era, during the nineteenth century, sport in Australia was primitive, lusty and boisterous. It came first, in disorderly fashion, to the goldfields—and it offered scope for betting and an alternative to brawling. "Kick when you see a head," was the laconic instruction to the frontiersmen who gambolled around the goldfields, playing a referee-less mixture of Gaelic football, soccer and rugger. Games like cricket and the English and Irish variants of football were exported to Australia in the 1840s and 1850s—at a time when the playing of organised ball games was mainly the privilege of the English upper classes. In the new land, there was no highly stratified society, and there were no fancy ideas about which people should play which games. This staunchly egalitarian approach has always been a feature of Australian sport, and there can be no doubt that it has contributed immensely to the high standard of prowess.

Professional foot-running boomed around the goldfields, mainly because running was a pure form of contest which required no equipment other than a couple of feet. The centres of this sport were the old gold towns of Stawell and Bendigo, where, long after the first strikes were exhausted, the inhabitants were still inclined to plunge heavily on their favourite runners. Even now, the Stawell Gift and the Bendigo Thousand survive as the two richest professional foot-races in the world.

Other, less fundamental, sports than goldfields football, fighting and running arrived during the nineteenth century. The first visiting English cricket team arrived in 1851, and a few years later a team of full-blooded aborigines (the owners of unlikely names like Mosquito, King Cole and The Twopenny Tiger) visited England; in the year of the first English cricket visit, the national horse-racing classic, the Melbourne Cup, was born. Some enthusiastic amateur devotees of track and field were competing before the turn of the century; an Australian, E. H. Flack, won the 800- and 1500-metre events at the first modern Olympics in 1896, but it is significant that he lived and trained in London. Tennis came to Australia soon after the turn of the century, and the first national sports hero in the modern sense was Norman Brookes—who in 1907 won the Wimbledon championship and led the Australasia team (the other half was the New Zealander, Tony Wilding) to a Davis Cup victory. All of these sports were uncluttered by the undertones of class which pervaded British games during the same period; they all offered diversion in a country where diversions were few, and they all caught the vigorous, almost cheeky mood of the new country. It was natural enough that as the nation began to grow with some purpose, sport was already a closely integrated part of the life of the people.

Sociologically, there are several explanations why sport has made such a deep impression on the soul of the Australian people—and not all of them are necessarily flattering. As a long procession of critics from D. H. Lawrence to Miss Googie Withers have often pointed out, Australian society is emphatically male-dominated. Conversation counts less than performance, and performance on the sporting arena can be a means to success—both financial and social. The tennis promoter Jack Kramer, who says he is often recognised in Australian streets but never in American streets, admits candidly, "When you're a champion sportsman in Australia, you're important in a way you like to be."

Culturally, the nation had little to offer until recent years; there was not much theatre production, only a smudge of classical and jazz music, and a shortage of lively periodicals. It was scarcely surprising that so many talented artists, musicians, singers, actors and writers had to go overseas to find recognition. All of this, of course, meant that there were few fields of interest to compete with sport.

Australia's comfortable living standards (without extremes of poverty or great wealth) and the comparative classlessness of Australian society have both had the effect of enabling any youngster to play almost any game. The exceptions are a few sports which do impose financial barriers, like yachting, polo, skindiving and skiing. It is interesting, but usually fruitless to search for occupational denominators in the teams Australia sends to Olympic Games. The track and field team which competed in the Eighth Commonwealth Games at Kingston, Jamaica, in 1966, included a grazier, a physicist, a shipwright, a theological student, a machinist, a couple of typists and several schoolteachers. The swimmers included a dental surgeon, a television journalist, a bank clerk and a student lawyer. The world champion breaststroke swimmer Terry Gathercole was a plumber, and his team-mate, the Olympic backstroke champion John Monckton, was a carpenter. It may be pertinent to note that *every* member of the American swimming team which competed in the Rome Olympic Games, both men and women, was attached to a university, a college or a high school. With two exceptions—one was a teacher at Indiana

University and the other a university student who had been drafted into the army—all listed their occupation as "student."

Forbes Carlisle, who was a lecturer in physiology at Sydney University before he made a lucrative if rather unlikely switch to swimming coach, is convinced that the Australian attitude to sport owes a lot to migrant breeding. "It takes initiative, drive and a considerable amount of courage to pack up and migrate to a distant country," he says. "These qualities are passed on from generation to generation, and they make an ideal basis for sport."

These diverse splinters from our background help to explain the Australian attitude to sport; they also suggest reasons why, during the first half of this century, Australia produced a large number of champions in many fields . . . men and women like the swimmers Fanny Durack, Frank Beaurepaire, Alex Wickham and Boy Charlton, the cyclist Hubert Opperman, the sculler Bobby Pearce, the tennis players Norman Brookes, Jack Crawford and John Bromwich, the sprinter Jack Donaldson, the cricketers Don Bradman and Bill Woodfull, the boxer Les Darcy and the billiards player Walter Lindrum. But they do *not* fully explain the emergence, since around 1950, of battalions of super-atheletes—people who are able to dominate, singly or in groups, entire sports.

The sports at which the super-atheletes have performed best are tennis, swimming and running. It is sometimes overlooked that before the present golden age began, Australia was not a major world force in these sports. She was producing some good tennis players, but until Frank Sedgman won the Wimbledon singles championship in 1952, no Australian had held the title for 20 years. At the 1936 Berlin Olympic Games, Australia could only produce one swimming finalist, and at the 1948 London Games no Australian swimmer won a gold medal. Between 1896, when Flack won his two middle-distance titles, and 1952, when Marjorie Jackson and Shirley Strickland won gold medals, no male or female runner had scored an Olympic win. Suddenly, around 1950, the losing began to stop. Since that year, Australian tennis players have played off in 17 Challenge Rounds for the Davis Cup (and have been beaten only three times), and they have won Wimbledon with a regularity that has become almost tedious. The swimmers had their most glorious patch at the 1956 Olympics, but have been breaking world records and winning medals with some consistency since then; and so have the runners, led by Landy, Elliott and Clarke.

What made the dramatic difference? Mostly, it was just a matter of plain hard work. No single factor has had more to do with the success of Australian athletes since the mid-century than the coaching of Harry Hopman (tennis), Percy Cerutty and Fran Stampfl (athletics) and Forbes Carlisle, Harry Gallagher, Sam Hereford, Don Talbot and Frank Guthrie (swimming). All of these men believe basically in conditioning, and they set their charges huge amounts of build-up preparation. Hopman, who is possibly the most successful sporting coach in the world (the 1966 Challenge Round was his 19th as Australia's non-playing captain, and his teams have won all but four of these) confesses a little disarmingly that he doesn't try to teach his boys how to hit the ball. "If they are Davis Cup players, they know how to play their strokes," he says. "What I try to do is bring them, at exactly the right moment, to exactly the right pitch of physical and mental conditioning." He does this by imposing massive doses of running, skipping and gymnasium work, and by simply talking to them . . . relaxing them, inspiring them. Hopman tries to tailor each player's physical program to his individual needs, building up some bulges and whittling others down, rather like a sculptor working on someone else's statue.

Some of the other coaches tinkered with ideas that are slightly off-beat; Forbes Carlisle has used ergometers (to measure the capacity for work), hypnosis and pre-race hot baths, and wiry old Percy Cerutty has mixed Plato, rolled oats and dried fruits with his running schedules. But all have built their reputations basically around the simple proposition that the performance of a swimmer or a runner improves in direct ratio to the amount of physical preparation he has done.

Apart from the growing influence of the coaches, other trends have been apparent in Australian sport during recent years. The success of Australian tennis players and swimmers has caused a discernable falling-off of interest in the traditional summertime game of cricket. There was a time, not so long ago, when a boy's first and most cherished ambition was to become a Test cricketer . . . when he sat up at night to hear the Test broadcasts from England, and played cricket across a curved bitumen road against a telegraph pole in the balmy early evening, with haloes of buzzing insects lurching through drunken figure-eights around the light-bulb above him. These days, his heroes are more often the tennis champions who sometimes manage to travel the world for ten years without catching one grey glimpse of winter; these days he might be swimming twelve miles a day at the age of twelve.

Another sport which has faded, for quite different reasons, is boxing. It has been a casualty of affluence, and there is sad significance in the fact that most of its local recruits these days are drawn from the aboriginal population. Australia's first great boxer was Young Griffo, whose favourite bar-room feat was to stand on a pocket handkerchief and take bets that he could dodge any punch thrown at him without raising his hands or moving his feet from the handkerchief. He always won. He came from The Rocks in Sydney, never trained, got drunk often, and had no punch—but he fought draws with Joe Gans, Little Chocolate and "Kid" Lavigne, and came to be known as the greatest featherweight in the world. There were other great Australian fighters, like Les Darcy (who achieved folk-hero status, in company with Ned Kelly, Smithy and Phar Lap), Dave Sands, Ron Richards, Vic Patrick and Jimmy Carruthers. But the old ring adage about a hungry fighter being a good fighter is an accurate one; nowadays, it seems, only aboriginal youths can be relied upon to be hungry.

The same affluence which hurt boxing has boosted a number of other Australian sports. It provided extra swimming pools, plus equipment for water-skiing, snow-skiing, skin-diving, golf, tennis and sailing. "You want to know why negro boys don't take on tennis," the American Davis Cup player Arthur Ashe confided not long ago. "Because it costs them 40 dollars just to get a racket, and Negro boys can't afford that. Here in Australia, though, any kid has a tennis racket . . . just any kid."

Of them all, the sport which has expanded most during the past few years is boating; some 160,000 Australians now take to the water every weekend, and the craft they use range from some 2,000 Herons (which are small, cheap and easy to handle) to a couple of 12-metre yachts which fought in 1967 for the right to make a 500,000-dollar challenge for the America's Cup. Between the humblest Heron and the mighty 12-metres are dozens of classes . . . dinghies, skiffs, catamarans, Flying Dutchmen, 505s, big ocean-going sloops and yawls and ketches, and squadrons of 18-footers which scud around Sydney Harbour, carrying up to 1500 square feet of sail apiece, followed throughout by ferryboats and launches on which bookmakers shout the odds. Australian yachts' successes in the 1964 Olympic 5.5 metre class (with Barrenjoey, skippered by 60-year-old Bill Northam), the Admiral's Cup, the world Flying Dutchmen, 505 and catamaran titles, and her three gallant, expensive assaults on the America's Cup have caused her to become rated one of the three major yachting nations in the world. (The other two: the United States and Britain). Boating has long been a popular sport on Sydney's Harbour and Melbourne's Port Phillip Bay—but the factors which have caused it to boom are bigger incomes, extra leisure and the growing congestion on Australian roads. This crowding has made the enjoyment of leisure time driving, which not so long ago represented a means of escape at the weekends, almost an impossibility; now people are heading instead for the sea—and pessimists are predicting that if the boom continues, the nation's waterways will soon become almost as crowded as the roads.

The huge influx of migrants since the last war has brought not only a softening of prejudice, an appreciation of minestrone, and a raffish continental colour to some old suburbs; it has had a large effect on Australian sport. Soccer, which for many years tagged behind Australian Rules football, Rugby League and Rugby Union, has become so popular that officials of the other codes are worried. Teams with names like Juventus, Wilhelmina, Slavia, Polonia, Croatia and Budapest play in the main cities; the sport has taken on a new explosive quality, with fights breaking out and referees being chased—but the crowds are bigger than they ever were. And in the Victorian Football League, stronghold of Australian Rules football, names like Jesaulenko, Ditterich, Silvagni and Barassi are among the popular heroes. It is a little ironic that Europe should have invaded the native

Australian Rules Football, Melbourne

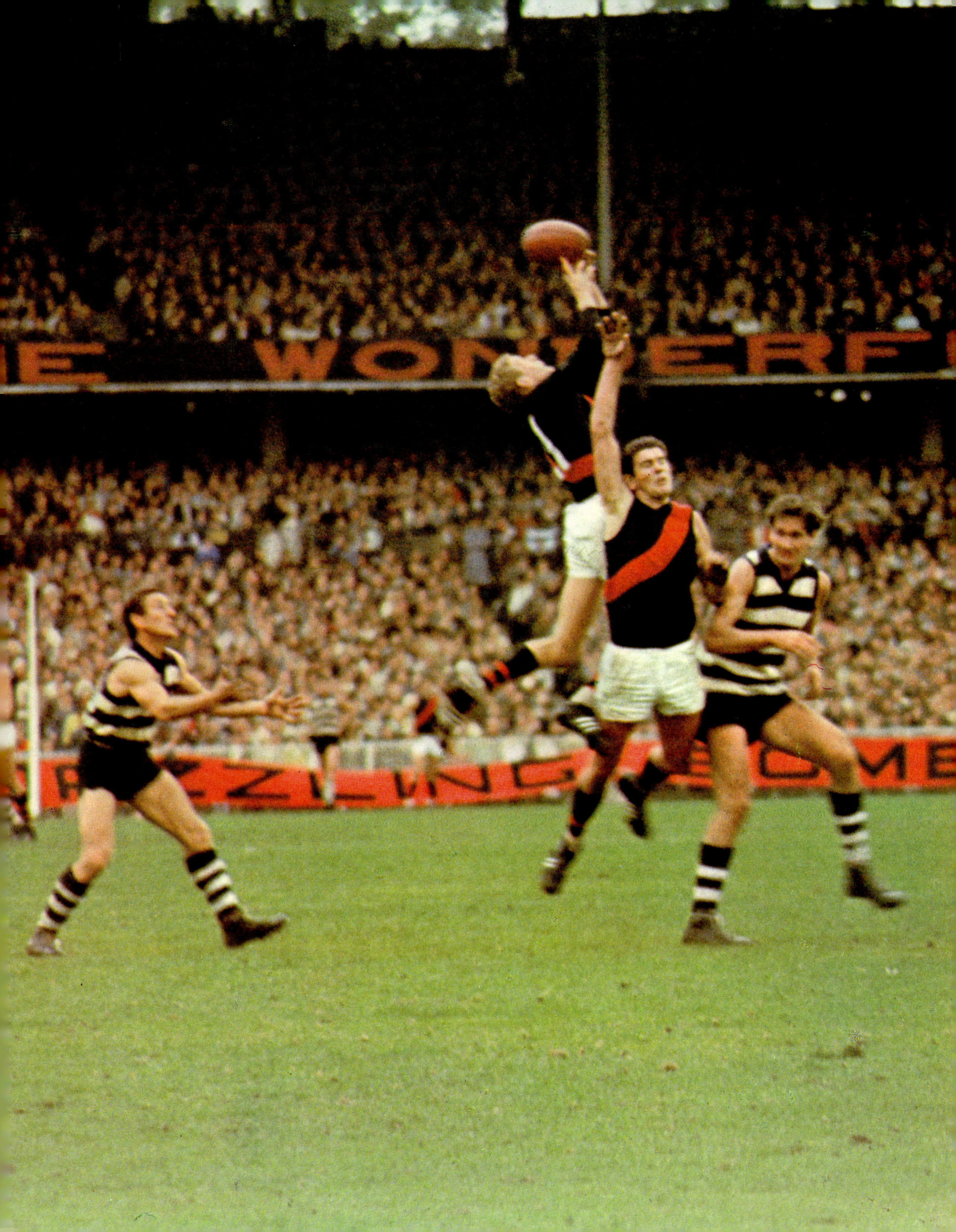

Australian football game, which has never invaded any region north of the Murray River. Australian Rules football is a remarkable sport; it contains more rules and less mayhem now than it did as a half-breed code on the goldfields, and it attracts far greater crowds than any of the other football codes. It is spectacular and tough, it communicates to spectators a sense of personal involvement, and its greatest stars, like Peter Hudson and Ted Whitten, achieve a god-like status that is denied to cricketers and Olympic champions. But its following is confined to the southern States of Australia.

Another sport which might be considered native, but not national, is surf lifesaving. The contestants, splendidly tanned and fit young men, are members of the remarkable Surf Life Saving Association—which during 60 years of existence has rescued 150,000 surfers on Australian beaches. Its carnivals are ritualistic, distinctively Australian affairs which involve high-stepping marches behind colourful banners, rescue-and-resuscitation contests and surf swimming races. They produce the kind of spectacle which looks fine on travel posters advertising Australia; but the sport is mainly confined to a belt of coastline in New South Wales and southern Queensland, plus a couple of small stretches in Victoria and Western Australia. In recent years, particularly since the success of Midget Farrelly and Nat Young in surfboard championships, the association has had some trouble in attracting members; many youngsters have preferred to buy a board and search for the rapture that sometimes comes with board-riding, rather than join a club and put in hours of rostered, unpaid beach patrol work.

Australians have a passion for gambling on almost anything—but the event they bet on most is a horse race, the Melbourne Cup. On Cup Day, the first Tuesday in November, two things happen; dainty stenographers and doughty matrons and maiden aunts invest in office sweeps (it is the only money they ever spend on gambling), and just about all work stops for three and a half minutes. Trams grind to a halt so that transistor radios may be heard, and cities take on an On The Beach stillness as the whole nation waits and listens. An indication of the reverence accorded to this event, and to turf champions generally, is the presence of the great Phar Lap's stuffed carcass in a glass case in the Melbourne Museum.

But perhaps the strangest aspect of sport in Australia—particularly in view of the general propensity for gambling—concerns professionalism. Jockeys apart, it is just about impossible to discover one pure professional who makes his living from playing sport competitively in Australia. And this in a country which is considered far more sport-minded than England (which has full-time professional footballers), Canada (which has full-time ice-hockey players) and the Philippines (which has full-time jai-alai players). The Jack Brabhams, the Peter Thomsons and the Bruce Devlins, the Rod Lavers and the Ken Rosewalls have to go overseas to make their money—and the professionals who give coaching lessons or run shops attached to clubs don't really count as full-time sportsmen.

The Hill, Sydney Cricket ground

148, 149) Ski trail, Perisher Valley, N.S.W.

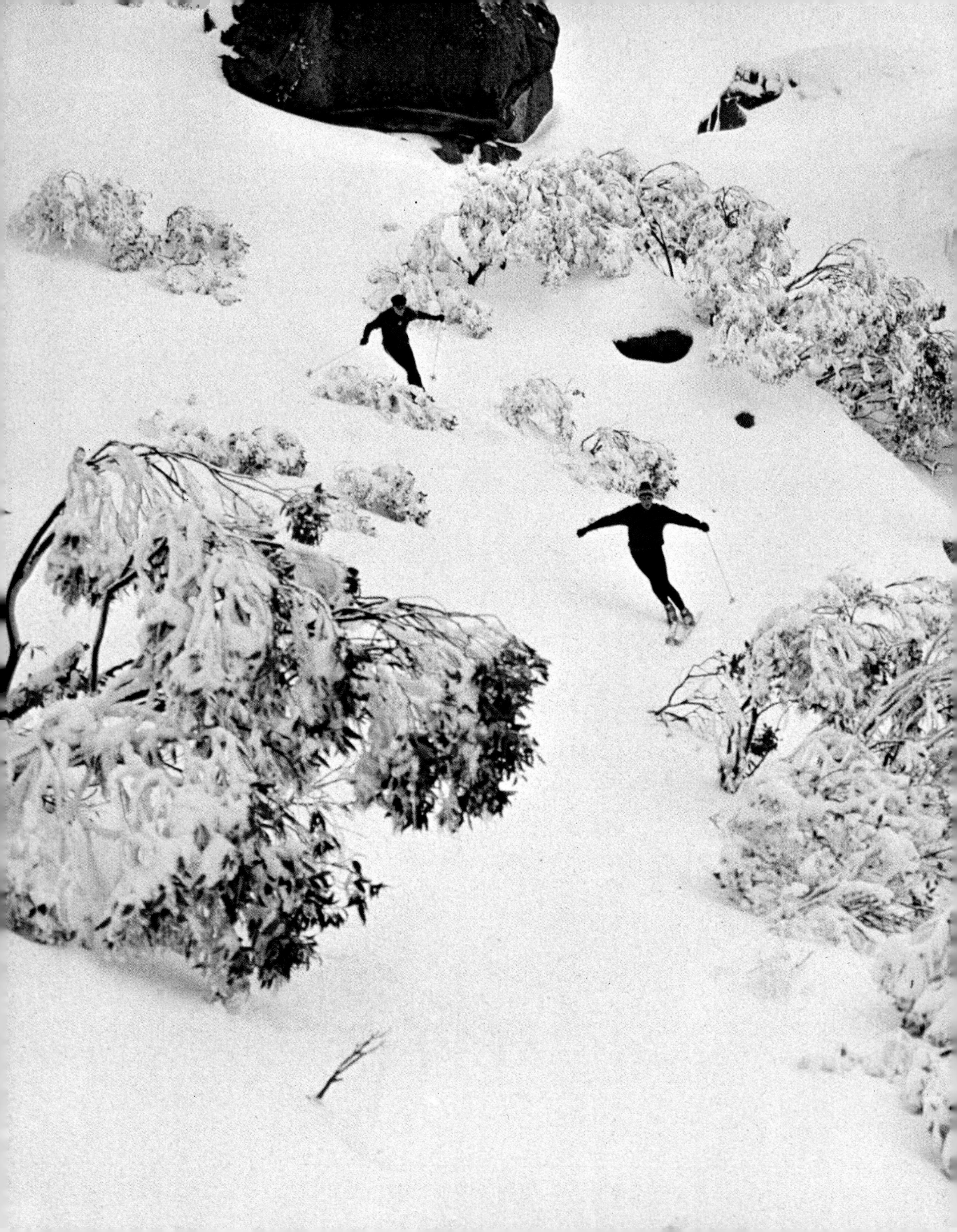

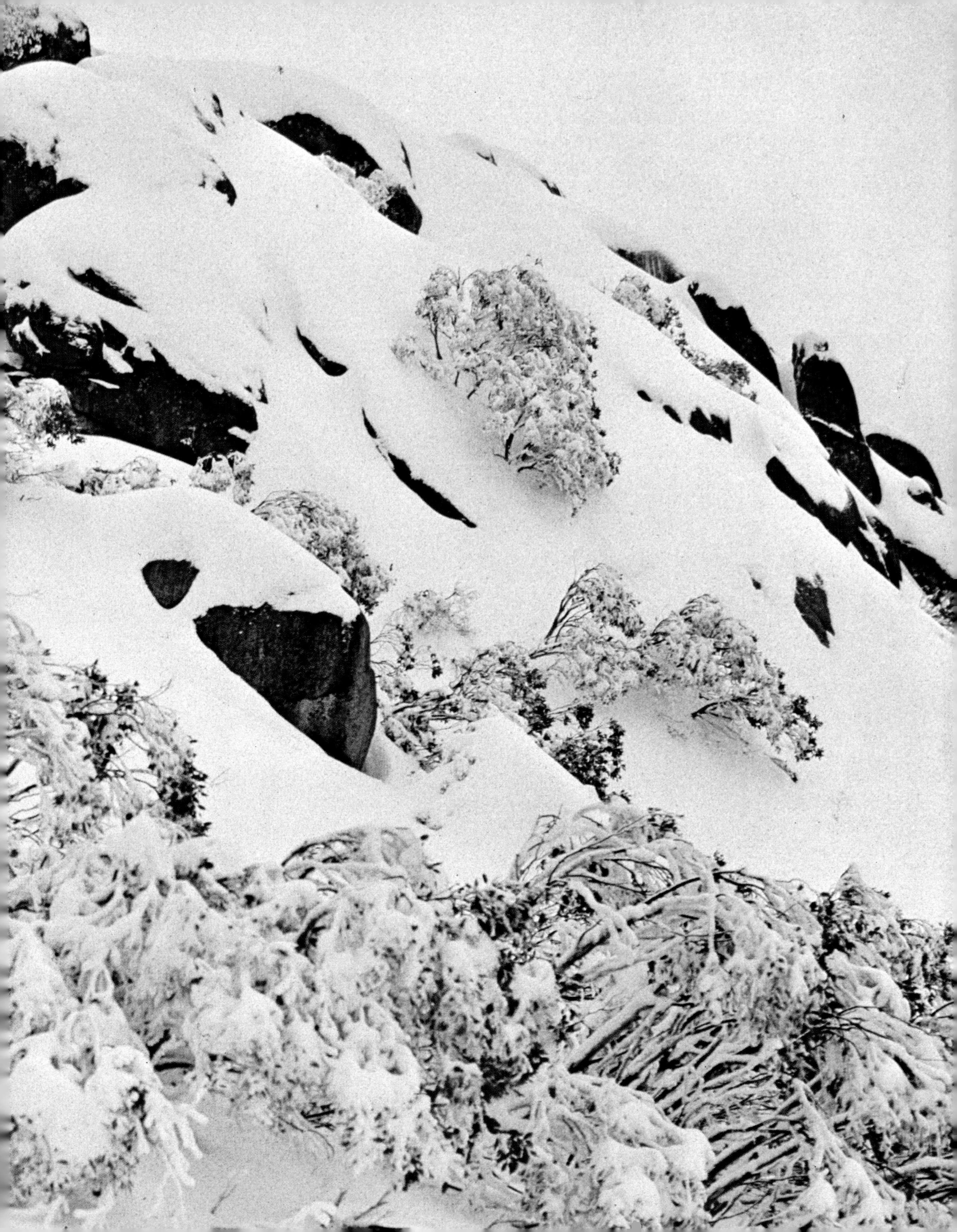

Boxing champions double up as fruiterers and electricians, Stawell Gift runners work as encyclopaedia salesmen and plumbers. The Melbourne footballers who attract crowds of nearly 100,000 at one match never get beyond semi-professional status; the great Barassi spends his days selling office furniture. Even the young men who make a full-time profession out of the sport which masquerades as amateur tennis have to go overseas to find the good "expenses."

It could be that the only pure, made-in-Australia professionals outside of horse-racing are the aboriginal boys who stand grinning on the sideshow boards in their cheap, bright and shiny dressing gowns while a spruiker prods a bass-drum and yells, "Who'll take on the black boy?" Whether this is a comforting thought depends, I suppose, on your point of view.

Sporting devotees

152, 153) Dragon class yachts, Sydney Harbour
154, 155) Surfboat race in heavy seas

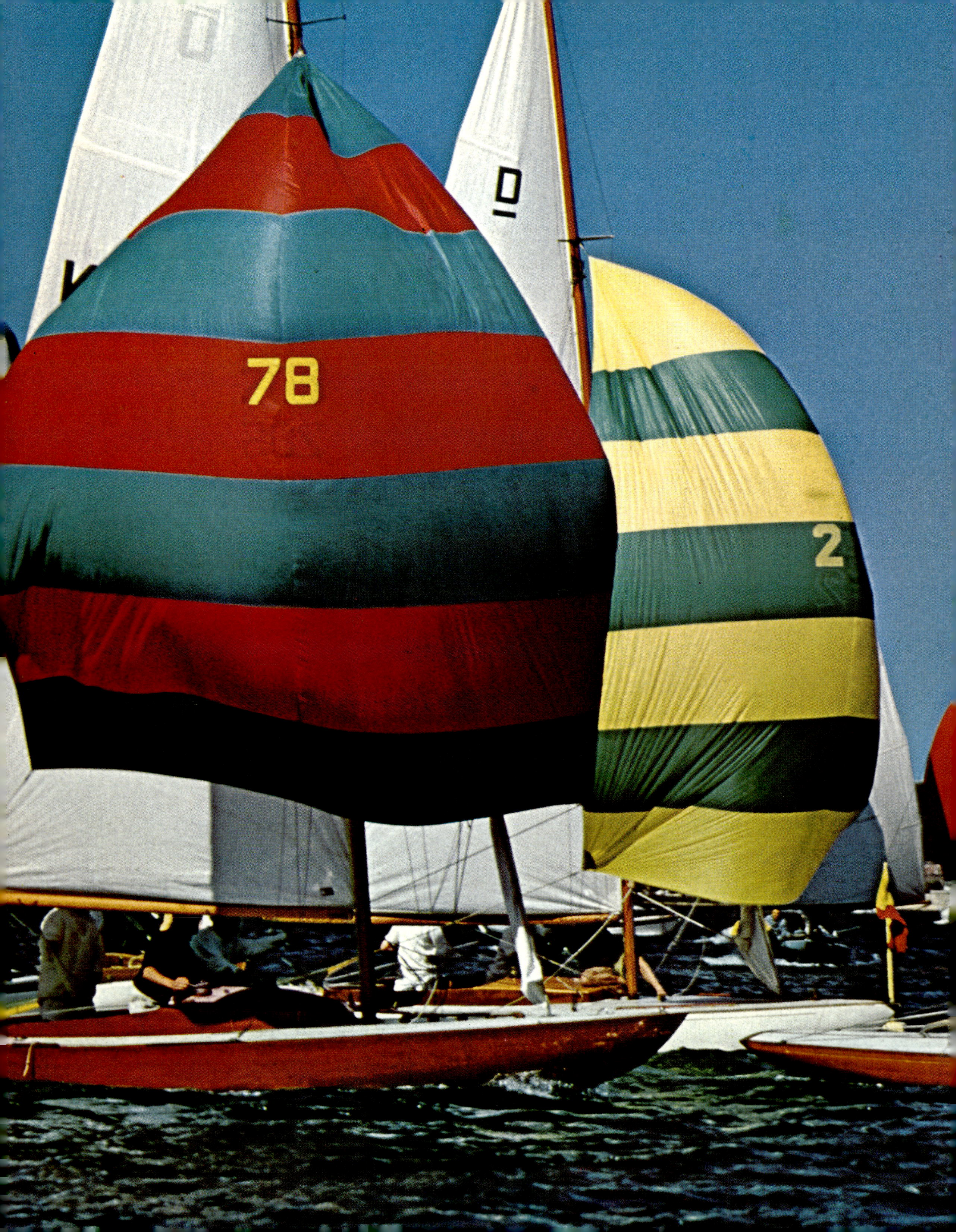
78
2

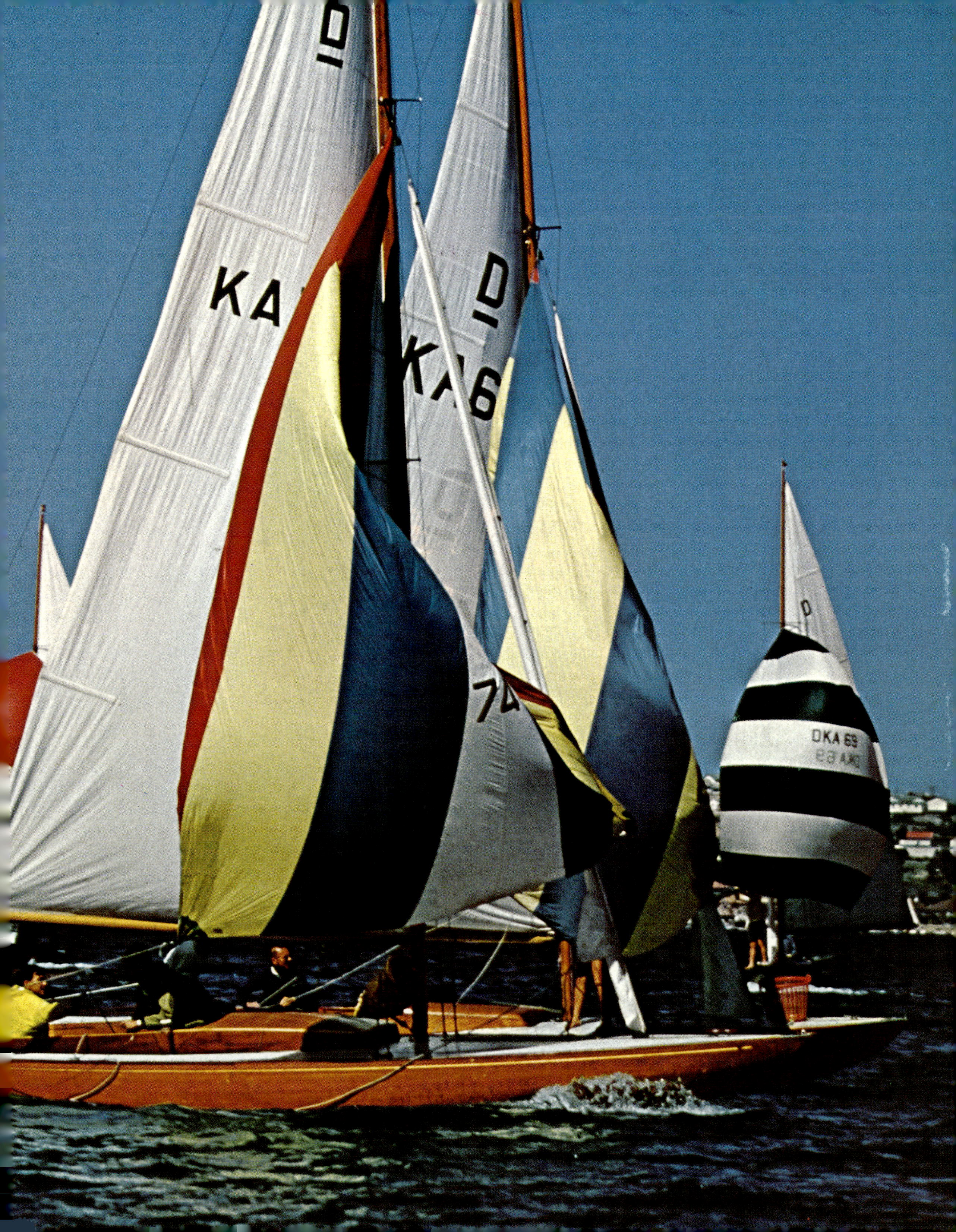
D
KA
D
KA6
74
D
DKA 69

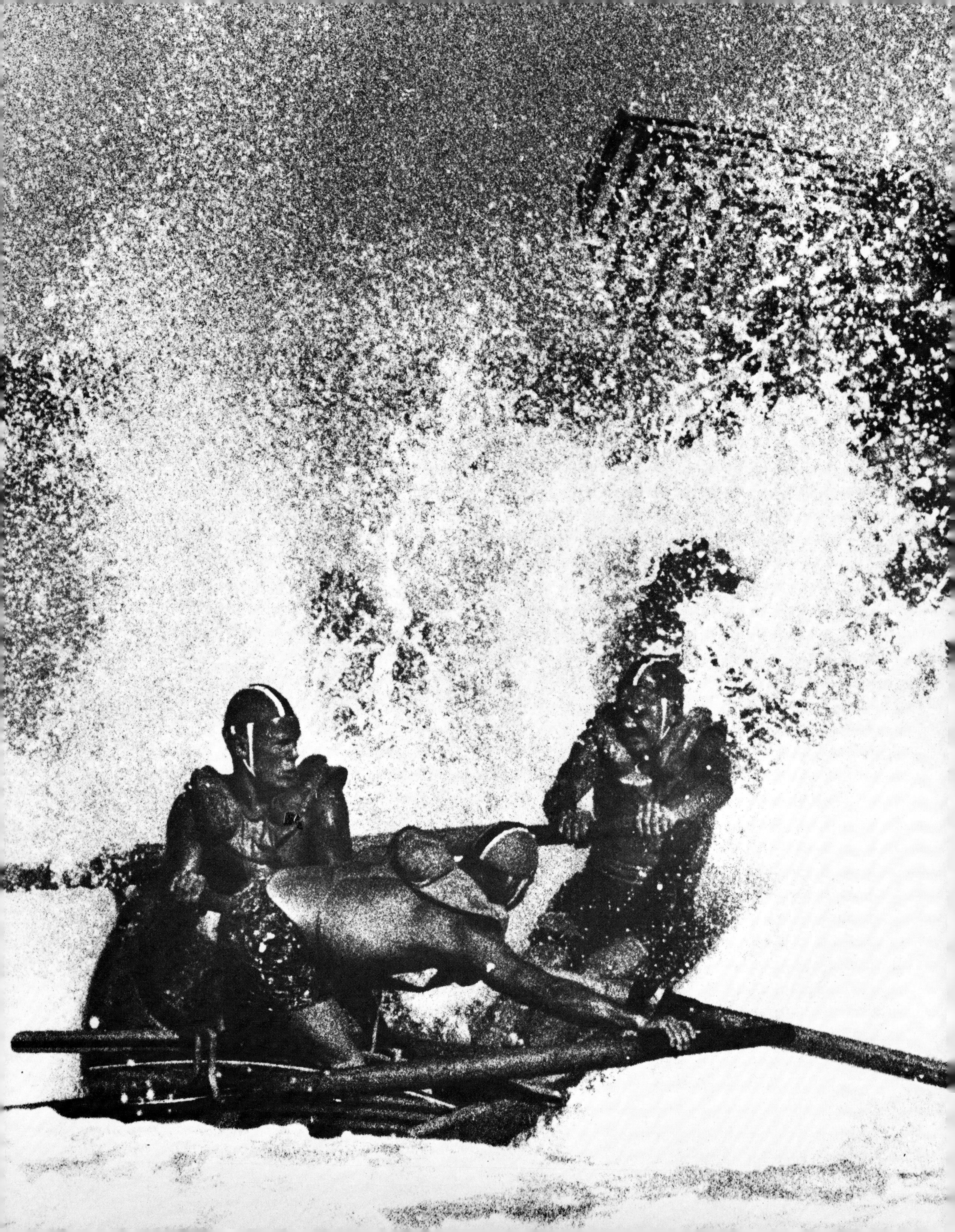

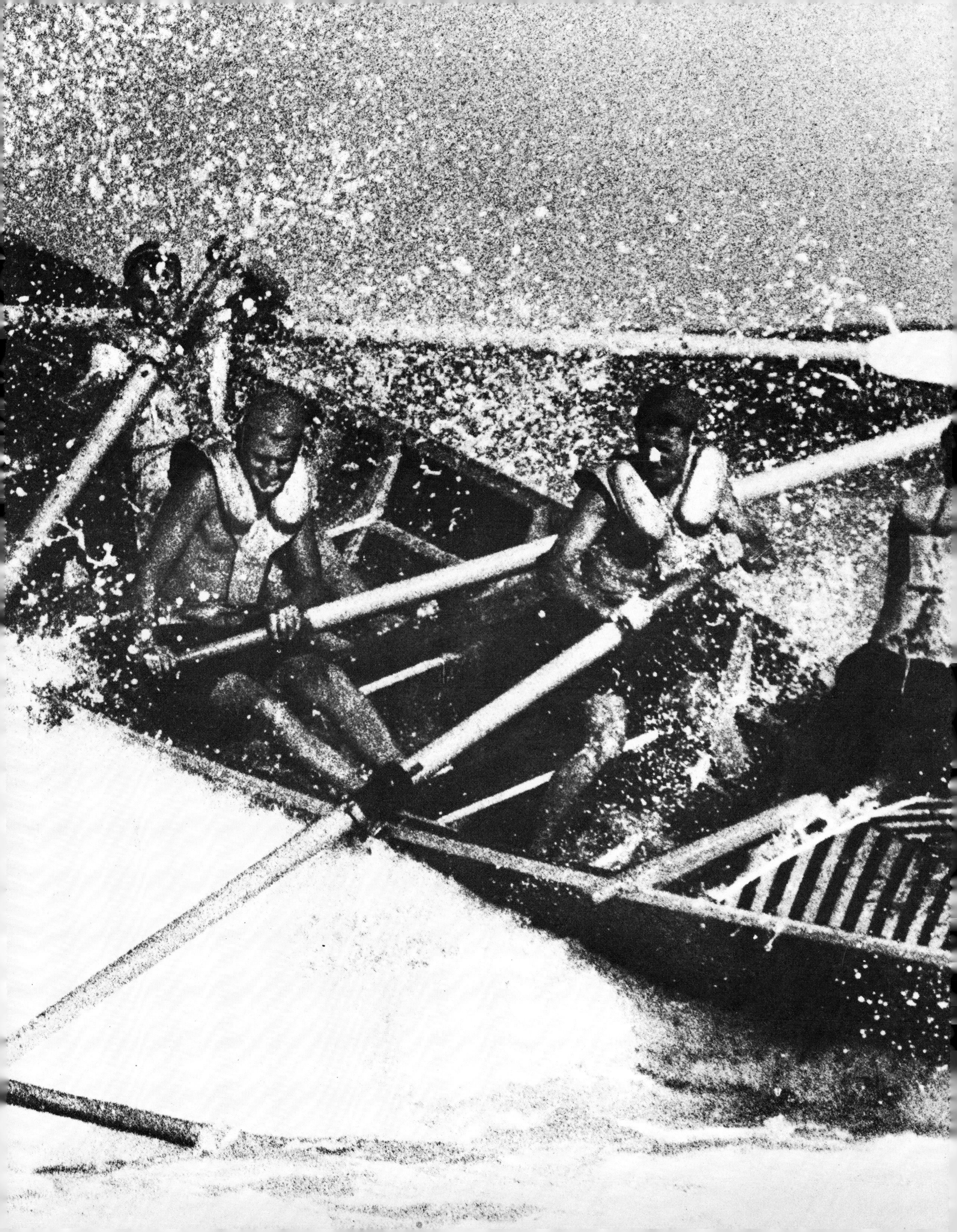

Sprint finish, Melbourne

Bradley Head, Sydney Harbour

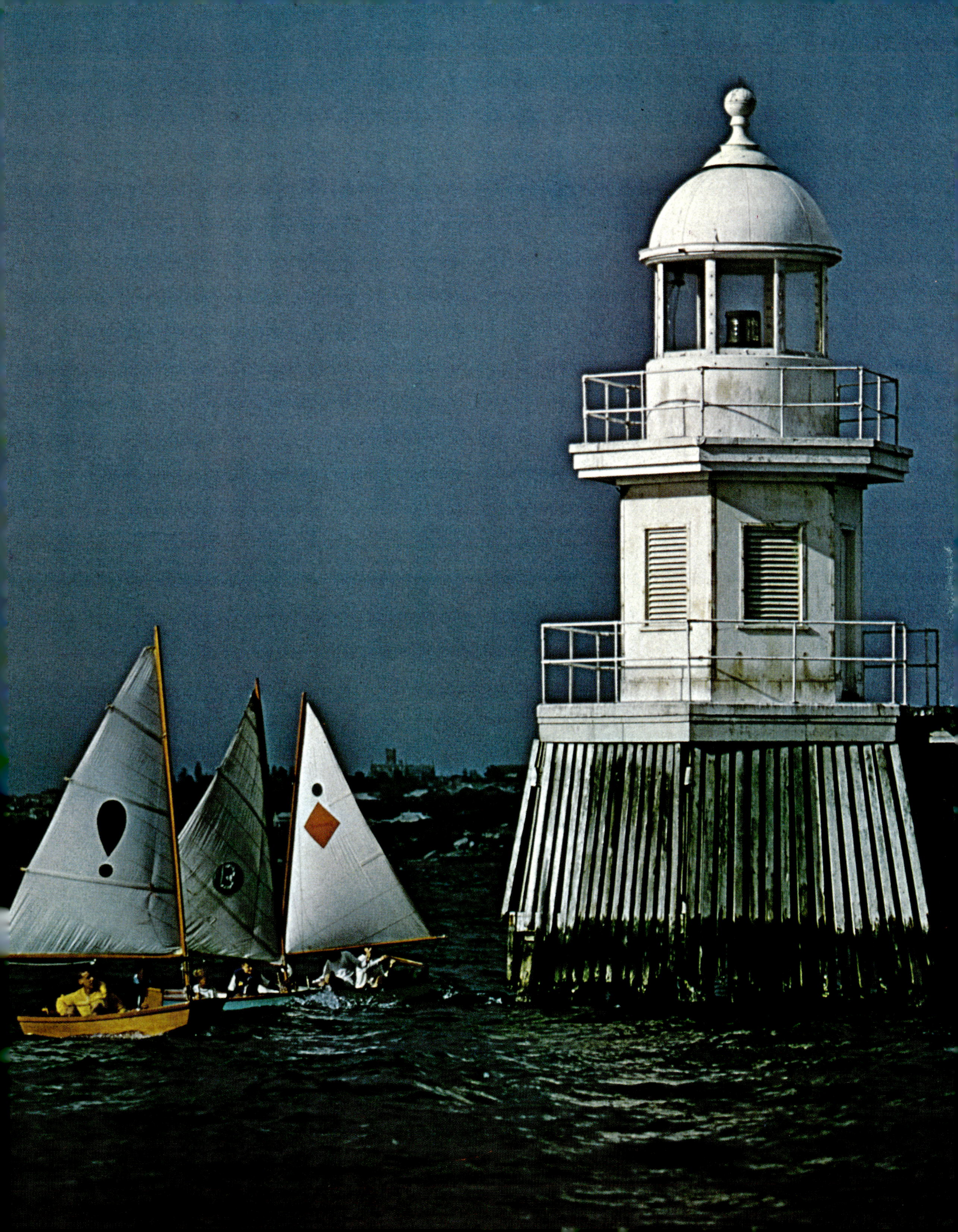

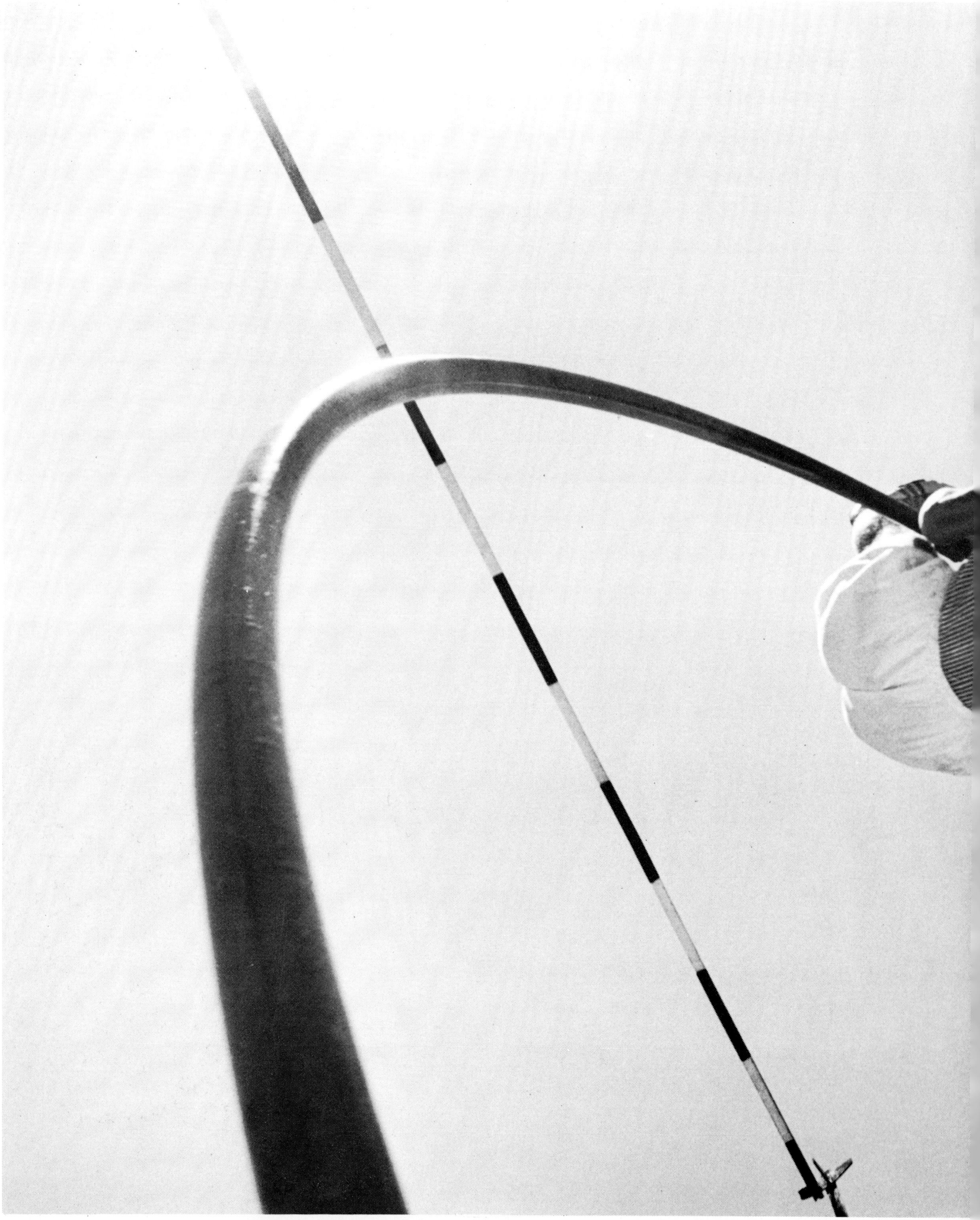

Pole vaulter, Perth

Miler, Olympic Park, Melbourne

Junior and Senior League Football

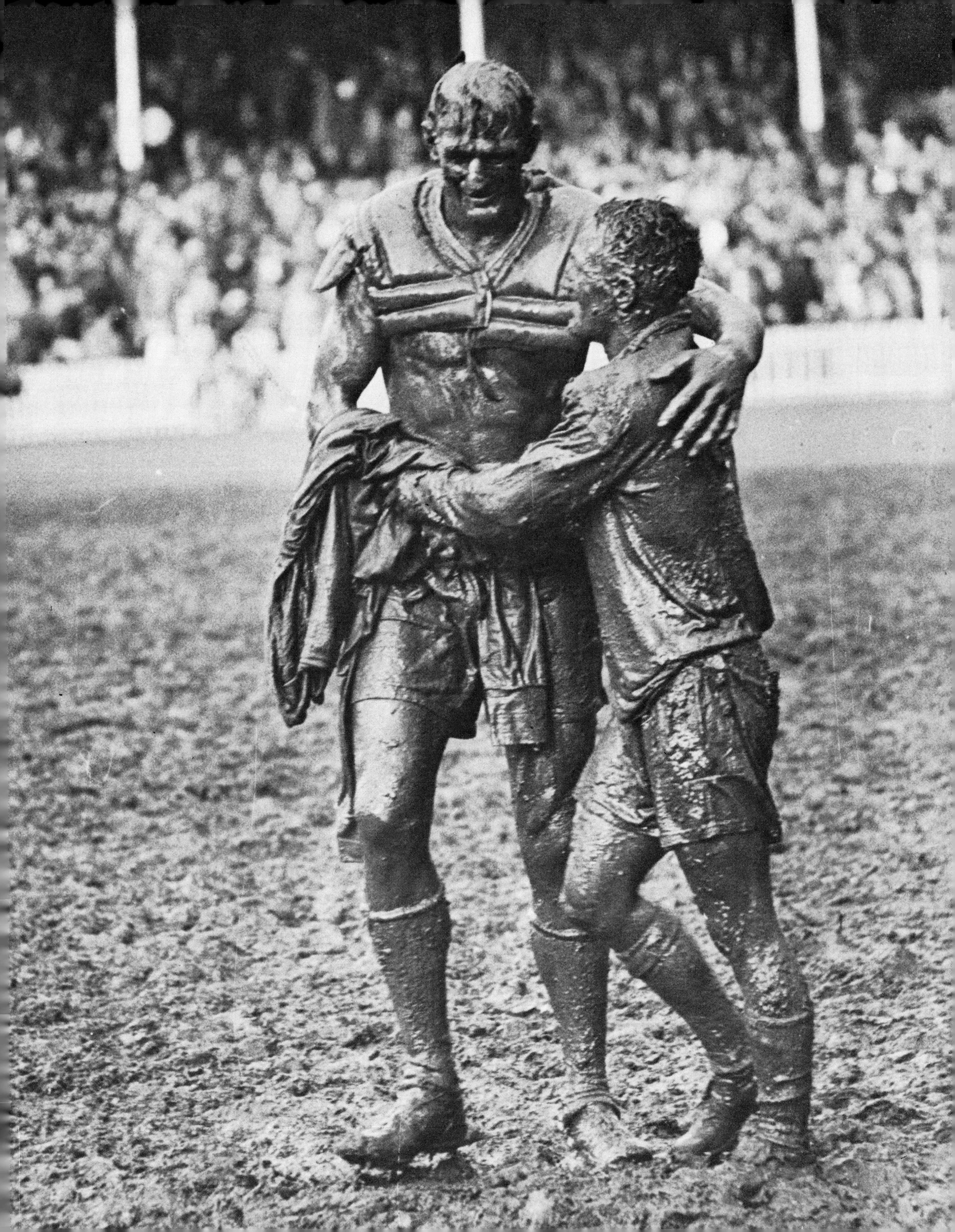

CULTURE

ARTISTS AND FLATLANDERS

Geoffrey Dutton

Australia is a country of terrifying contrasts. These are not simply the geographical clichés of the vast, bare outback and the crowded cities, or the sweep from apple orchard to avocado plantation. There are far more shattering contrasts between the Australian's easy-going confidence and his almost total ignorance of the rest of the world; between his she's-right-sport acceptance of the good, sunny life and his indifference to the starving or murdering of millions of his neighbours; between his support of war after war and his living in the only country in the world that has never known a war on its soil; between his intense, genuine egalitarianism and his unfailing support of every type of white imperialism.

A perpetual child, either under the mother-figure of Britannia or the Uncle Sam-figure of America, the Australian has always prided himself on his manly independence. When he was a pioneer he sent his magnificent horsemen to shoot down his fellow-pioneers, the Boers. Since then, whether the war was a senseless holocaust, a culmination of blunders, or a mad escalation, he blithely sends his soldiers to it and cheers them for heroes when the poor devils come home. The first, biggest and ugliest sculptures, and the most inert pieces of masonry his children see, are war memorials. Over the years he has killed, cheated or scorned aborigines and Italians, Frenchmen and Japs. To his credit, however, though probably thanks to luck and isolation, he has never been particularly anti-Semite. Far away in the bottom of the world, he has been bewildered by the cultures of other peoples, or simply ignored them.

The function of the arts is not merely to be a mirror to nature, but to be a link between man, his environment and his intimations of eternity. Where the contrasts between man and his environment are too violent, art either scarcely exists at all, as in the first struggles of pioneer settlers, or else is forced to concentrate on eternity, as in the meditations of prisoners or saints. But if the contrasts are not too violent the artist welcomes them, as out of these he draws the equilibrium of art. "Without Contraries is no progression." The essence of the average Australian is that he is oblivious to the contrasts under which he lives. He therefore wants a flat culture, a culture like a stage on which dancers perform or a canvas which artists decorate. "He's got his feet on the ground" is the highest compliment an Australian can pay an artist, or any man. Yet heaven is above, and the grave is below the ground. There is almost no tragedy in Australian art or literature, and almost nothing of what W. B. Yeats called "the vision of evil." The country itself, so vast and unaccommodating, has in many cases filled in for the human complexities or spiritual dilemmas that are the basis of art in most countries. Hence the extraordinary emphasis in Australia on landscape painting and pastoral poetry.

A nation's culture is more than an amalgam of its several arts; it involves the surroundings in which people live as well as their attitudes. An aesthetic consideration of the man-made environment of Australians might easily lead one to the conclusion that Australia is visually the ugliest country in the world. This would be unfair. The black industrial cities of England, Europe and the USA are more hideous than anything in Australia, and there are no slums comparable with those of Calcutta or New York. Yet in terms of visual environment, Australians probably have less aesthetic feeling than any other people in the world. It is only very recently that the formation of National Trusts has made people aware of the few beautiful historical buildings that do exist. Australians are supposed to be nature-lovers, yet they will rush to the beach to desecrate a paradisal bay with a rash of squalid shacks. A group of surfies will drive far and fast to an idyllic coast where they will camp and rise early in the morning to catch the big waves in marvellous sweeps of white on blue, the beauty of pure form and controlled grace; but in the sandhills where these gods camped there is a fly-swarming heap of opened cans and broken bottles. Farmers and graziers attack flora and fauna as if they were enemies. From Esperance in Western Australia to Rockhampton in Queensland one sees the native bush cleared, flattened and burnt, to the very edge of the roads; not only are its subtle and unique beauties lost, but it is not even left as a windbreak. There are many country towns in Australia full of characteristic and attractive buildings, rich in historical associations, whose councils are happy to see the main street a wilderness of petrol pumps and tatty flags where fine old buildings had been. Hungry for money, the councillors should all be sent on a trip to the USA to see what can be done not only in preserving local history but also in making it a good source of tourist revenue for the town. At the moment it looks as if the paintings of Russell Drysdale will be the only remaining record of what Australian country towns once looked like.

Artists are the weeds in the concrete of progress. They push up something living, they break up sterile conformity. They have never been daunted by the philistinism of Australian attitudes, and the amazing fact is that in 1971 Australian indigenous culture is more healthy than it has ever been. Perhaps the greatest of all Australia's bewildering variety of contrasts is that Australians, and not only young Australians, have a remarkably open mind towards modifications to their culture that come from within. If their mates say it's all right, they are prepared to give almost anything a go. They are in this the heirs to the serious traditions of self-improvement of the 19th century Mechanics Institutes and the bourgeois who insisted on paintings on his wall and books on his shelves, however dreary some of them may seem now. Australians have never been hostile to poetry, even if what they liked best was not aesthetically always the best: Banjo Paterson and C. J. Dennis sold in vast quantities. (It is interesting that in 1966 an Australian edition of translations of the visiting Russian poet Yevtushenko sold more copies than any other book of poetry since C. J. Dennis.) Music has always flourished in Australia, and Melba and Joan Sutherland have achieved as great a fame as any athlete. Recently, however, music has graduated from the performing to the creative level with the emergence of a number of brilliant young composers. It seems hard to remember that only fifteen years ago an A.B.C. announcer could quite unselfconsciously say "We will now have half an hour of Australian music. We will begin with 'A Suite of Old English Dances' by Sir Arthur Benjamin." Australian books are now published and read in numbers undreamed of twenty years ago. Public architecture is noticed as never before; apart from the Sydney Opera House, poor embattled giant, the work of Roy Grounds (his Melbourne Arts Centre is already a masterpiece), Robin Boyd (also Australia's most intelligent writer about what man has done to the face of Australia), Peter Muller, Harry Seidler and many others has provided an excitement in architecture long denied to Australians.

The greatest success story of all is modern Australian painting, and, more recently, sculpture. It has all been so quick that Dobell, Drysdale, Nolan and Arthur Boyd are already Old Masters, though the last three are still alive and painting. The crafts, pottery, jewellery, enamelling, and also industrial design, are healthier and more noticed by the public than they have ever been. And behind it all, the anti-culture of the wowser, though still strong in some quarters (especially Melbourne), has begun to crumble with the realisation that virtue is not safeguarded by banning books and films; Australians, always authority-nervous, still allow an absurd and inconsistent censorship, but there are continual protests and the situation is better than it was ten years ago.

It all sounds remarkably cheerful. Yet, true to Australian traditions of violent illogical contrasts, Australians welcome what artists produce but would not be too happy to have an artist in the home. They are not curious how he lives, whether on the basic wage or not; they do not even care whether he lives in Australia or somewhere else. In fact, most of them live in cities and a few still hold out in London, while Russell Drysdale, Clifton Pugh and Albert Tucker live in the country. Drysdale lives in beautiful unspoiled country north of Sydney, but with his countryman's love of simplicity and solitude (and yarning over a beer), he would be just as happy under the cold stars on the red sand of the far outback. Sidney Nolan, the St. Kilda tram-driver's son whose gentle, rather donnish, manner goes with an omnivorous intellectual curiosity, once told me has never been tempted to paint an English picture in his life. The light is totally alien to him. Yet he lives in London where he sees his Australian visions most clearly, and comes home fairly frequently for long spells to refresh not only his eye but his very pores. Arthur Boyd, as Leonard French remarked recently, is probably the safest of all the Australian artists in London, as he has erected the most skilful walls around himself. I have seen a tweedy Boyd disguised perfectly as an English country gentleman, and half an hour later back in his studio neither less nor more himself, amongst his peaceful remembered landscapes and the tortured imagined world of the sexual crises of his lovers, who, like their creator, have their subtle jokes as well. His brother-in-law, John Perceval, recently artist-in-residence at the Australian National University, Canberra, is often surly to the world but always lyrical to nature, whether in a Highgate garden or the bush. Lawrence Daws, who is apologetic about the Canaletto-precision of his surveyor-trained panoramas of Canberra

Len French, Melbourne

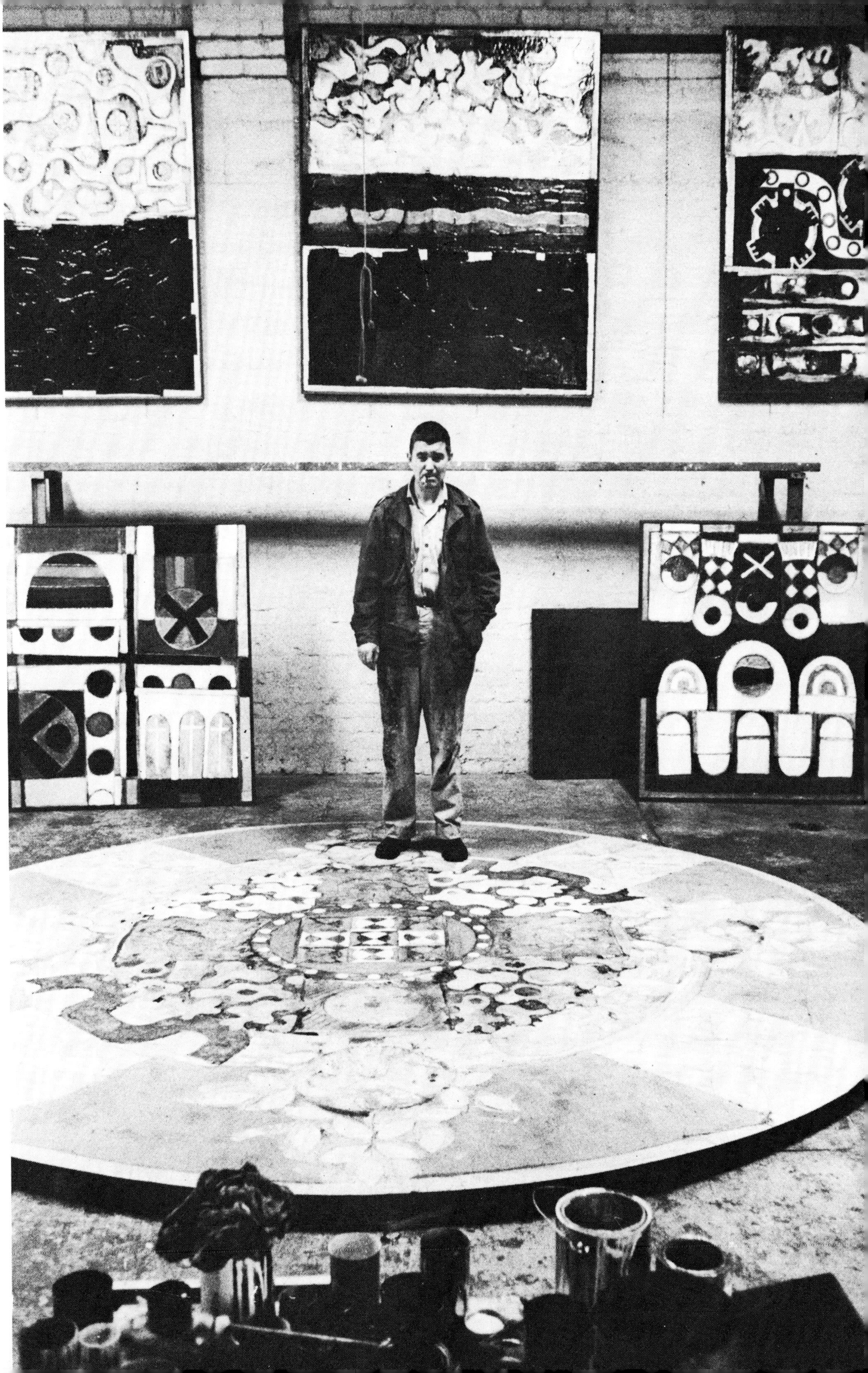

in the look-out above the city, is fighting back towards a figurative style from the splendour of his abstracted symbolism, and is equally at home in London or Adelaide, dividing his time between the two. The brightest young expatriate, Brett Whiteley, came back to Australia not so long ago, seeking the good life after painting the sex-murderer Christie in London.

Len French's hieratic immobility, splendid in gold and cathedral-glass reds and blues, seems an unlikely product of flat, drab Australia, where, as D. H. Lawrence said forty years ago, "they clatter around like so many mechanical animals, always vaguely, meaninglessly on the go." On the grand scale, French's stained glass in Canberra and the Melbourne Arts Centre is masterly. Albert Tucker, who once had a harsher vision of evil than any other Australian painter, now lives and paints happily in the bush near Melbourne. Fred Williams, who has a more austere and abstracted view of the bush, has become the painter perhaps most universally admired by the critics. Charles Blackman, the most poignant of image-makers, has returned from London and is living in Sydney, which is undoubtedly the artistic capital of Australia. There are many other admirable and sought-after artists living there, such as Friend, Olsen, Rapotec, Hessing, James, and a very strong younger painter, Kevin Connor, to name only a few. But good artists and sculptors are scattered all over Australia, the elegant Robert Juniper in Perth, Robert Boynes in Adelaide, Robertson-Swann in Sydney, Clifton Pugh in the house he made himself in the bush near Melbourne, Norma Redpath in Melbourne when she is not seeing her bronzes cast in Italy. Other outstanding sculptors are Max Lyle and Robert Klippel.

There are private art galleries in every Australian city and some country towns, booked up with exhibitions for months ahead, and an art prize every week or even more often. Art is "in," and a number of artists are quite well-off, though not of course as reliably affluent as master plumbers or medical specialists. The artists would also be the first to make the sceptical reservation that painting can be a good investment, and you don't have to go to the bother of reading it or listening to it.

As for writers, they can take their chance. Two of the most successful writers in the English-speaking world are Australians, Alan Moorehead and Morris West, but Moorehead lives mostly in London or Italy and writes few books about Australia, while West lives in Sydney but never writes a word about Australia. Otherwise, only a handful of writers can live off their writing, and most make less than a moderately industrious baby-sitter. It is interesting, however, that with the shift in education towards Australian books, the hidden best-sellers (well over 100,000 copies in some cases) are books like Alan Marshall's *I Can Jump Puddles* or Colin Thiele's *Sun on the Stubble*.

Patrick White is Australia's one writer of acknowledged world stature. Several informed English and American critics have declared him to be the most significant novelist writing in English today. White is accepted in Australia now, especially amongst the young, but when *The Tree of Man* and *Voss* were published they were reviled by Australian critics, including authorities such as Stewart and A. D. Hope; White is now the idol of academic critics, which probably causes him more alarm than those early attacks. White's moral austerity in his novels and plays, and his fierce criticisms of the shallowness of Australian life, its unapprehended contrasts, led to ludicrous charges that he was somehow "un-Australian," as if being Australian was something that could be comfortably separated from the human condition. His tragic view of life, and his unafraid vision of evil, also discomfited people who depicted him as a sour, austere misanthrope, a label which amuses his friends who know him as a man as sensitive as he is witty; he is also a first-class cook, and has surrounded himself with one of the best private collections of Australian painting.

It is impossible to draw any lines of connection or influence between other worthwhile Australian novelists. Thomas Keneally, with six novels published, has varied in style from the gothic to the satirical, although related moral dilemmas unsettle all his books. Randolph Stow is a shy Western Australian haunted by his ancestors and succoured by childhood. Judah Waten is an older writer who keeps the clean simplicity and concern for ordinary people that characterised his first book, about Russian Jewish migrants, *Alien Son*. Perhaps the most talented of all the young novelists is Peter Mathers, whose first novel, *Trap*, about a part-aboriginal, is not always easy reading but is bursting with originality of material, ideas and technique. His second novel, some four years in the writing, is due to be published late in 1971. On a lesser scale, minor successes have been scored in the last year or so by Barry Oakley in Melbourne and William Marshall, originally from Sydney and now living in Europe.

The poets are easier to group, and more numerous. Australia has some of the best lyric poets in the English-speaking world, Judith Wright, David Campbell, Douglas Stewart, and, when they absent themselves from more didactic occasions, A. D. Hope and James McAuley. The Old Master of Australian modern verse is Kenneth Slessor, who stopped writing in the 1940s, at the peak of his powers (unlike Wordsworth). Together with R. D. FitzGerald, whose talent is more narrative than lyrical, these poets write about Australian history and exploration, about the wrongs of the convict past, and about the eternal subjects of man and woman and nature. Except for Campbell and FitzGerald, they do not write about Vietnam. Why should they? The greatest lyric poet of the 20th century, Rainer Maria Rilke, wrote his worst poems about the first World War. Judith Wright, much influenced by Rilke, is after the beyondness of things when she writes about a place, or a bird, and she goes as deep as only a poet can. The same non-temporal obsessions give permanence to A. D. Hope's sexual rage.

Yet although mere comment on the temporal scene is dangerous to poets, it is extraordinary how remote the older Australian poets have kept themselves from the major events of their time. There are a few exceptions, such as Vincent Buckley's excellent "Political Poems," which damn demagoguery and corruption rather than any particular political event, and, most notably, Bruce Dawe, who is brilliantly bitter over Australian moral hypocrisy and laziness about Vietnam and other public issues. The typical older Australian writer is not *engage*. Dawe is. Yet it is interesting that a number of fine young poets, virtually *engagees,* have swept Australian poetry into a new movement in the last two or three years. Outstanding are Les Murray, Michael Dugan, Michael Dransfield and Garrie Hutchinson.

There is now far less of a tendency, in Australian novelists, artists and poets, to withdraw from what might be termed 'world issues'. It was as if all the basic contradictions of the Australian way of life were simply too much to squeeze into artistic form, or else the images of eternity were more appealing than those of everyday life. There was too much work to do in building up a valid tradition from the past (e.g. Nolan's Kelly and Burke and Wills series, Douglas Stewart's play *Ned Kelly,* R. D. FitzGerald's *The Wind at your Door,* McAuley's unsuccessful epic *Captain Quiros*) to leave much energy for interpreting the present, whether national or international. The artist or writer as conscience of his people has been a conception remote from Australian reality. How much is missed may be gauged from a random sample of the great conscience-stirrers of the 20th century: Thomas Mann, Pasternak, Yeats, Auden, Silone, Sartre, Faulkner, Picasso, Grosz, the young Russian poets today. Only Patrick White can keep them company.

It is a paradox, then, that while many artists have turned back or looked inwards, contemporary journalists, commentators and cartoonists have been busy as never before. The guts and brains and backbone of the Australian body politic have never been so closely examined. This comes partly from the daily papers, especially *The Australian,* partly from the cartoons of Petty, Tanner, Molnar, Martin Sharp, Rigby and others, and partly, in broader scope, from books such as the seminal *The Lucky Country* of Donald Horne, Craig McGregor's *Profile of Australia,* and, easier on the national ego, George Johnston and Robert Goodman's *The Australians.* Australians are at last being thoroughly subjected to self-criticism, the first essential of a dynamic, as distinguished from a traditional, culture. Columnists such as the poet Max Harris and Julie Rigg; TV documentaries and news programmes such as *This Day Tonight,* the face-to-face interviews conducted by Bob Moore, and the ABC's somewhat restrained *Four Corners;* journals like *Nation, The Bulletin, Sunday Review,* literary quarterlies and *Australian Book Review*—all these have made Australians take stock of subjects and prejudices that were scarcely mentioned or even generally suspected twenty years ago. The variety of these analysts is also encouraging. For instance, Australia's three most powerful cartoonists have entirely different styles: Petty of *The Australian* has a fluid, wriggly line that chases a moral dilemma into every odd corner; Tanner of *The Age* makes strong, lairy, irreverent statements that are frequently very independent of the policies of his employers; Molnar of the *Sydney Morning Herald* has an architect's precision and a classical wit. The extremely high quality of Australian cartooning may be measured by the fact that Pat Oliphant, a pleasantly average Adelaide cartoonist, nowhere near approaching the quality of the three just mentioned, who now lives in Denver in the U.S.A. won a Pulitzer Prize for his work in the late 1960s.

The sick member of the Australian cultural community is the theatre and film industry. Since the foundation of the Australian Council for the Arts a lot more money has been available, but most of it has been poured into opera and ballet rather than into drama and film. The results have been quite impressive, particularly with the ballet; it has had ideas from Robert Helpmann and talent from its dancers which have put it into the international class. But the drama has wobbled and flopped, after a good start with Lawler's *The Summer of the Seventeenth Doll,* Alan Seymour's *The One Day of the Year,* and Patrick White's four plays. J. C. Williamson's, the only big commercial entrepreneur, has consistently underestimated Australian taste with dated comedies (wasting the talents of that fine actress Googie Withers), or potted extracts from Shakespeare, or else by playing it safe with U.S. musicals. It is characteristic of Australian theatre that Googie Withers goes to London to act in a new Ionesco and comes home to play a moth-eaten Maugham. It is left to the Old Tote in Sydney, or to John Sumner's Melbourne Theatre Company, or semi-professional or amateur groups of which there are so many of quality that it would be invidious to name only a few, to bring the public the plays that are filling the theatres of Europe, London and New York. Various Australian plays have been produced since Patrick White stopped writing for the stage, but none has had an outstanding success, except for Michael Boddy and Bob Ellis' *The Legend of King O'Malley,* which has shown how knockabout entertainment can have real political relevance and popular acceptance.

Up till now, Australian attitudes to war have been symbolic of her general intellectual and cultural involvement with the outside, international. world. She has operated on the volunteer system. Those who wanted to go, went; if they were lucky enough to come home again they were hailed as heroes. No one really asked what it was all about. So it was with culture. Australians were happy with paintings of gum trees, the latest Maugham, or Gladys Moncrieff warbling amongst the gladioli, and if a bunch of cultural volunteers wanted to go and fight on the artistic front in Paris or London, well it was all right, as long as they came home famous, although in some cases their fame was resented, somewhat paradoxically, as being in some way "un-Australian".

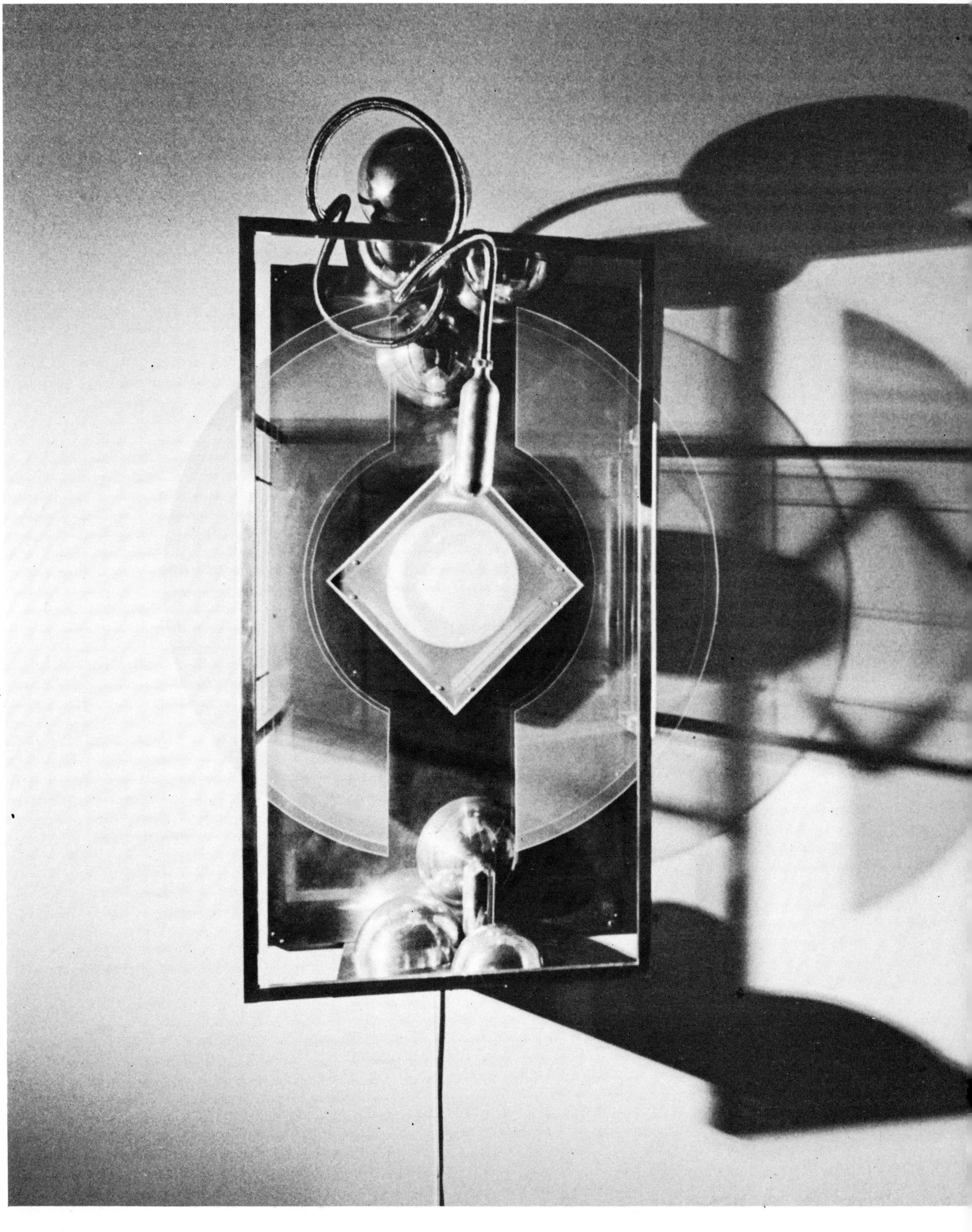

But suddenly conscription, which had split the nation asunder in two world wars, slipped quietly through in peacetime and as a result Australian conscripts are dying in Vietnam in an undeclared war. Australia has been catapulted into the international scene. With less disastrous results, this is exactly what artists, writers and musicians have done to largely unsuspecting Australians. While ordinary citizens still harbour illusions of insular safety, the country's intellectual and artistic leaders are citizens of the world. Every now and then one comes home and shows the people what they are really like. Barry Humphries, for example, fills theatres all round Australia (those same theatres that were empty for J. C. Williamson's threadbare offerings) with satires on sacred suburbia; he may then return to London, where amongst other things he is responsible in part for the brilliant comic strip "Barry Mackenzie" which mocks the Australian abroad.

No group is more international than the young musicians. Richard Meale made his name in 1963 with *Las Alboradas,* which is as spare and spiky as Australian wildflowers but Spanish in inspiration and European in its avant garde technique. Those who have heard his major work, *Nocturnes,* say it may be the finest Australian music yet written. Peter Sculthorpe's *Sun Music* reflects the composer's passion for his country, where a man on the red sand can be as solitary as the sun in the sky, but he has learned from Messiaen, electronic music or Japanese *Noh* music. Nigel Butterley, who in the late 1960s won the international Italia Prize, has developed works from the songs of Australian birds, but an important piece like *Laudes* is a song of praise prompted by European churches, and has some affinities with the paintings of Len French. Other very talented composers, such as Margaret Sutherland, Dorian Le Gallienne, George Dreyfus and Larry Sitsky, are just as international, not only in technique but in the source of their inspiration. However, it is also encouraging that Australian composers are setting Australian poems to music, as for instance Malcolm Williamson has done with the work of James McAuley.

The easy-going Australian public has, as it were, to wake up to the fact that its artists have run away and come back while it has been standing still. Of course this has been happening all the time with scientists and engineers, but somehow they are expected to be international while art in general is expected to be genuinely Australian. The result of the artists' defection is that, to keep up, Australians have to find out what the wide, wild world is all about, and not just cuddle a koala under the shade of a Union Jack, wearing American clothes, and watching the glorious, brainless Pacific Ocean. Australians are extraordinarily amiable people, and there are signs that they do not mind being awakened. People of all sorts, from taxi-drivers to businessmen, come to listen to poetry readings at the Adelaide Festival of Arts, or listen to chamber music at art galleries, or flock in thousands to retrospective exhibitions of Drysdale or Nolan, or support Musica Viva (a remarkable organisation which brings the world's finest chamber music players to Australia). Australian ballads

Mike Kitching, Sydney

John Bell, Sydney

174, 175)
John Olsen, Sydney

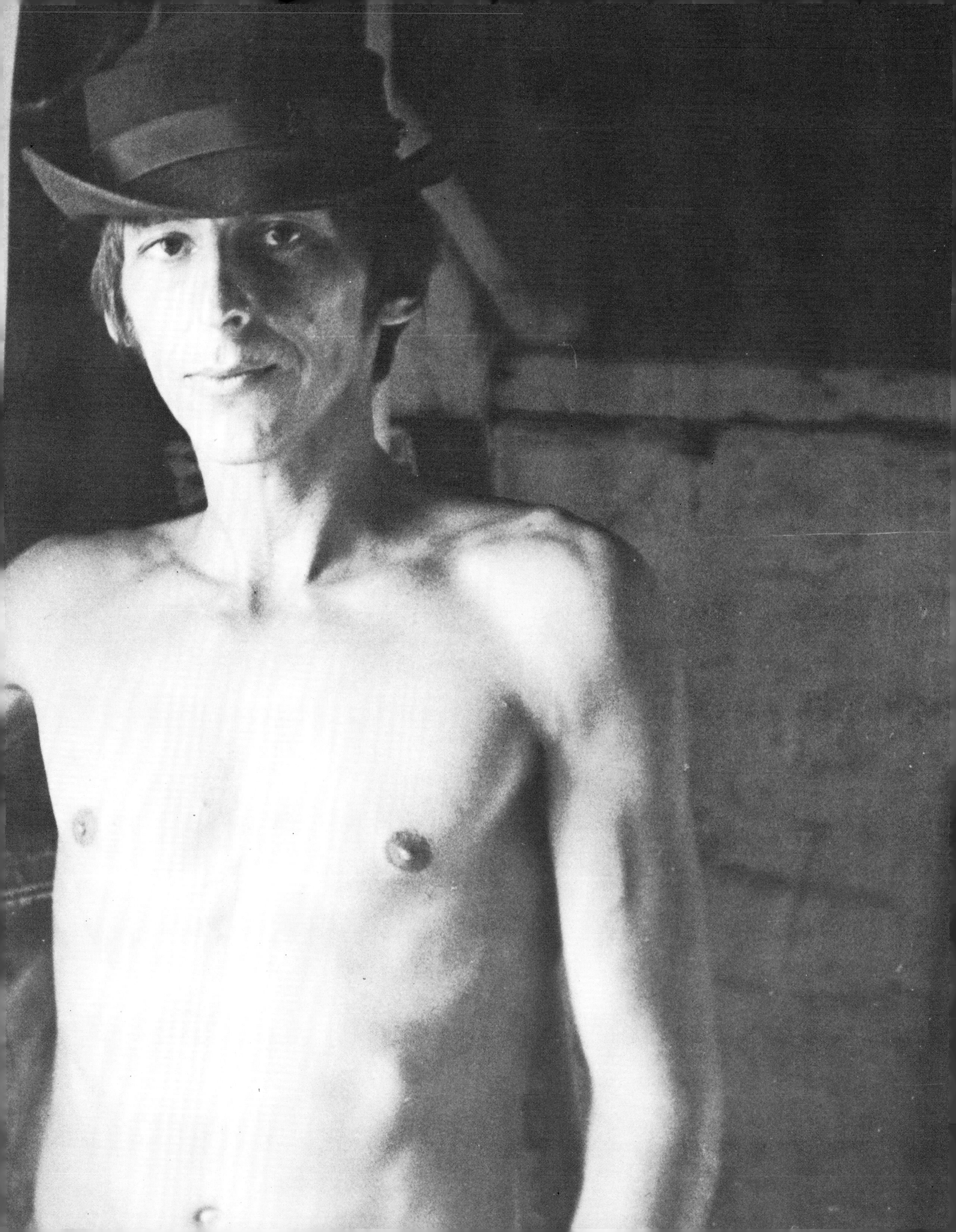

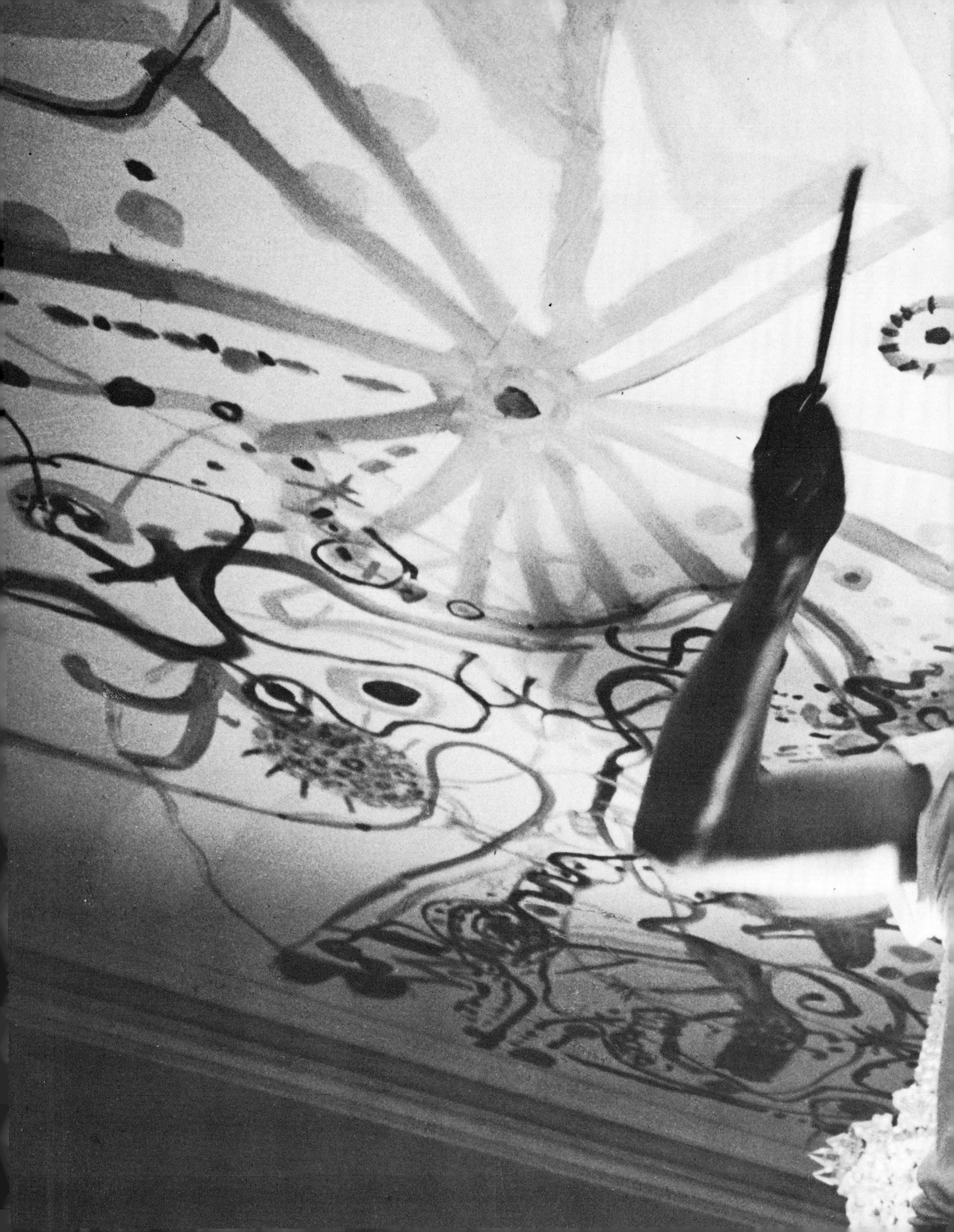

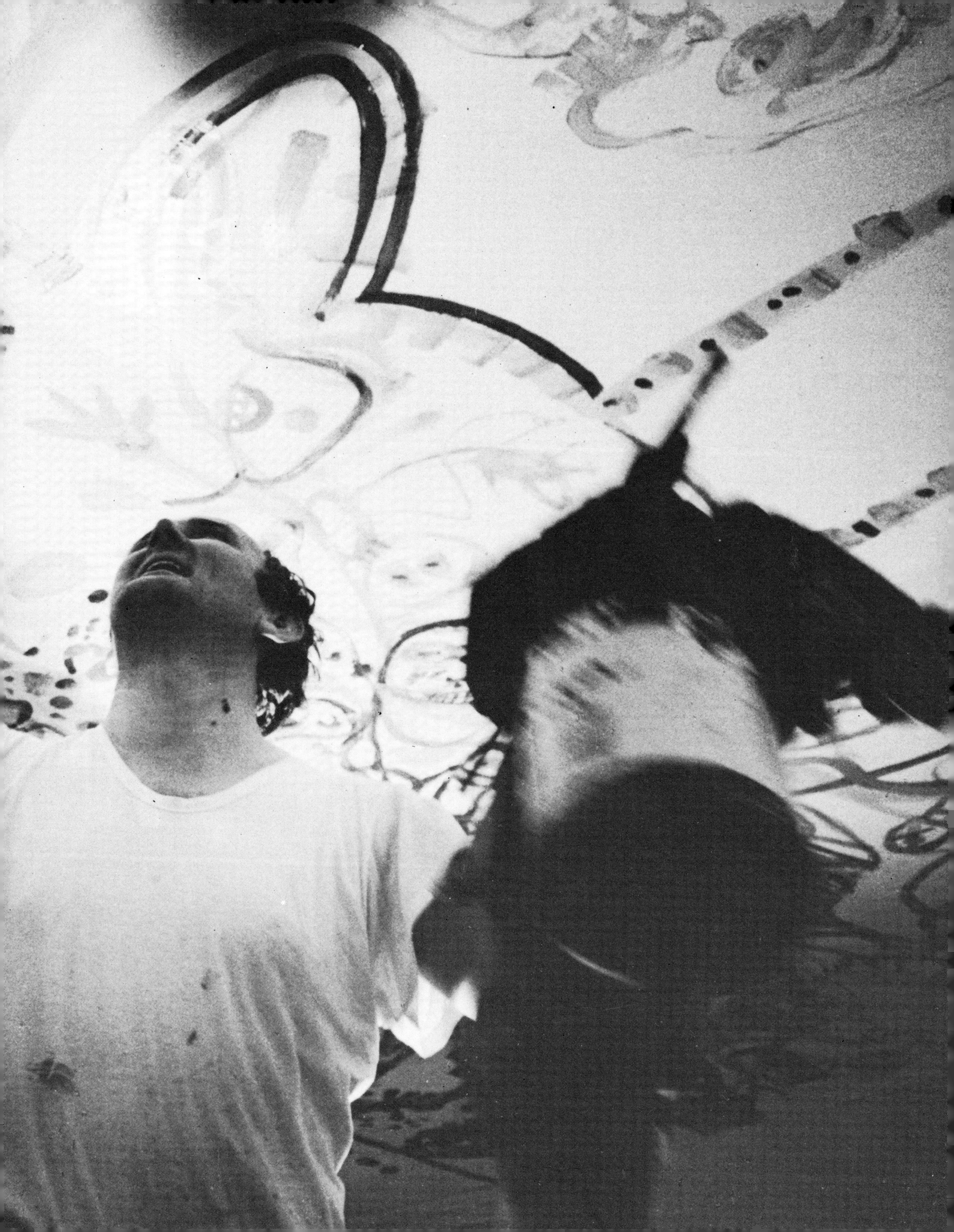

are sung in schools where thirty years ago the children were lucky to know "Waltzing Matilda." Modern ballads have been composed, and although the craze for ballad-singing is on the wane, people like Gary Shearston have made their impact.

Artists, writers and musicians are always prophets in that they reveal to ordinary people the shape and meaning and sound of what lies beyond the world of flat appearances. (Of course they, above all, know that no people are really ordinary.) Australians, inhabitants of a vast physical and intellectual flatness, have suddenly found themselves in possession of a culture which, wherever the bits have come from, has built new hills and excavated new valleys all around them. Walking home on a dark night, the good citizen may find himself flying through space. It is no longer safe to put one's feet where the ground used to be.

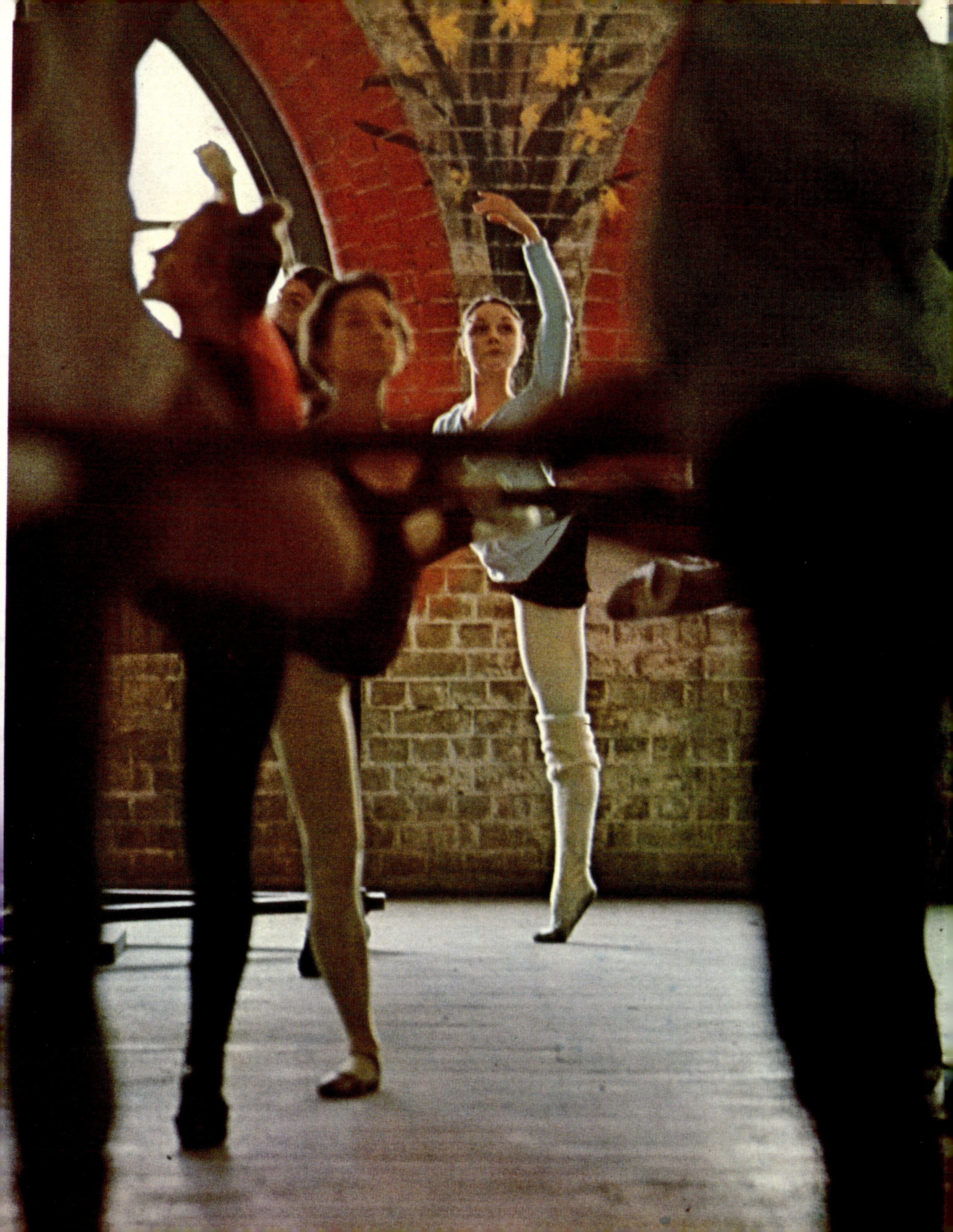

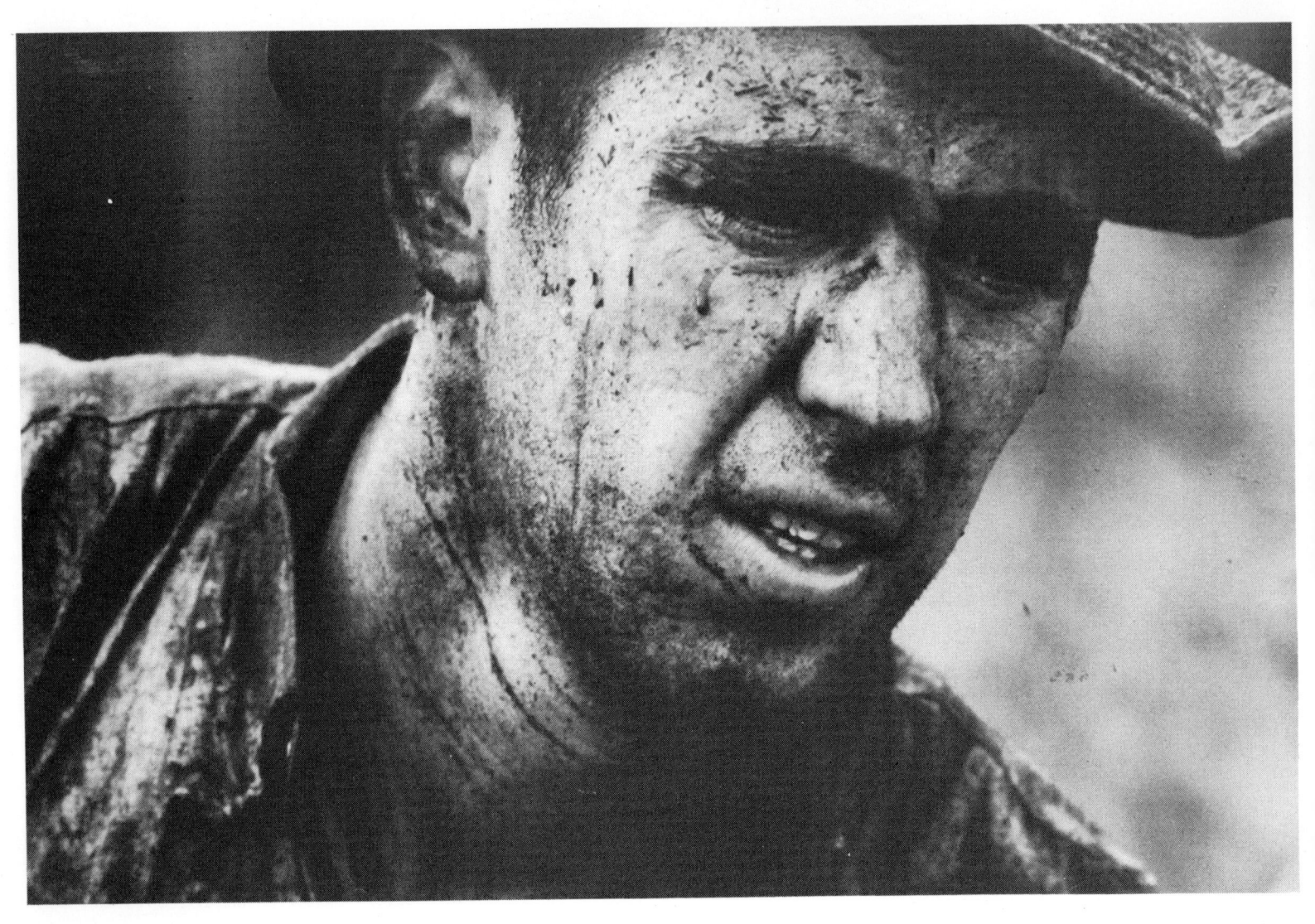

Cane cutter, Queensland

PROGRESS

CHIPPING AWAY AT A CONTINENT

Patrick Tennison

Apart from a scattering of ancient aboriginal carvings and bark paintings, anything man-made in Australia today is the result of human effort within only the last 180 years. It's an impressive achievement: twelve million people; huge capital cities covering up to 650 square miles each; a network of smaller settlements which extends from minor cities to one-horse towns of a post-office, a pub and a couple of shops; 26,000 miles of railway track to provide the nation's digestive system . . . and, in 1971, a gross national output which was worth $29,000 million a year.

These are the most obvious monuments to almost two centuries of striving, but there are others. The nation's 180 million sheep provides one-third of the world's wool and earns Australia almost $700 million a year. Wheat brings in another $543 million a year; we produce so much there is trouble over our surpluses, and political scufflings because the best market happens to be China, a country that is hungry for it — but Communist. Dairying yields almost $530 million a year. And then there are the minerals. "OIL—non-existent in payable quantities in Australia, as far as geological surveys and exploration have been able to establish." So wrote political commentator Don Whitington in his book *Ring the Bells* published in 1956. Less than a decade later this opinion was utterly out of date. By the mid-60s Australia was in its liveliest period of mineral discovery. Oil and natural gas had been discovered in Bass Strait off the Victorian coast, in the Roma area in Queensland, at Barrow Island, Gingin and Yardarino in Western Australia, at Moomba and Gidgealpa in South Australia. New nickel and copper discoveries had been made near Kalgoorlie in Western Australia, and iron ore exports soared (though early sales were made at what many consider an embarrassingly low price). Bauxite discoveries at Weipa in Queensland and Gove in the Northern Territory inaugurated new mineral industries and prospects for the whole country. A century ago, gold was the mineral that helped populate Australia. Today, oil, bauxite, nickel, copper and iron ore are the minerals that will bring new wealth.

All these things are part of the chipping away Australians have been doing in their vast continent these last 180 years. That 1788 beginning was a reluctant one. To the scant standing monument of those aboriginal carvings and cave paintings came groups of shackled convicts and their soldier warders. There was little of the American dream about that early Australian settlement. It was scarcely more than a matter of grubbing an existence out of a strange and often bitter pasture. And Australia remained colonial long after the U.S. won a youthful independence. The colonial is never the ambitious adventurer that the independent national is. The U.S. splurged into opulent mass development while Australia stumbled and shuffled under an often disinterested colonial policy dictated from the other side of the world.

That early Australian development period called more for muscles than brains—so it got more muscles than brains. Land had to be

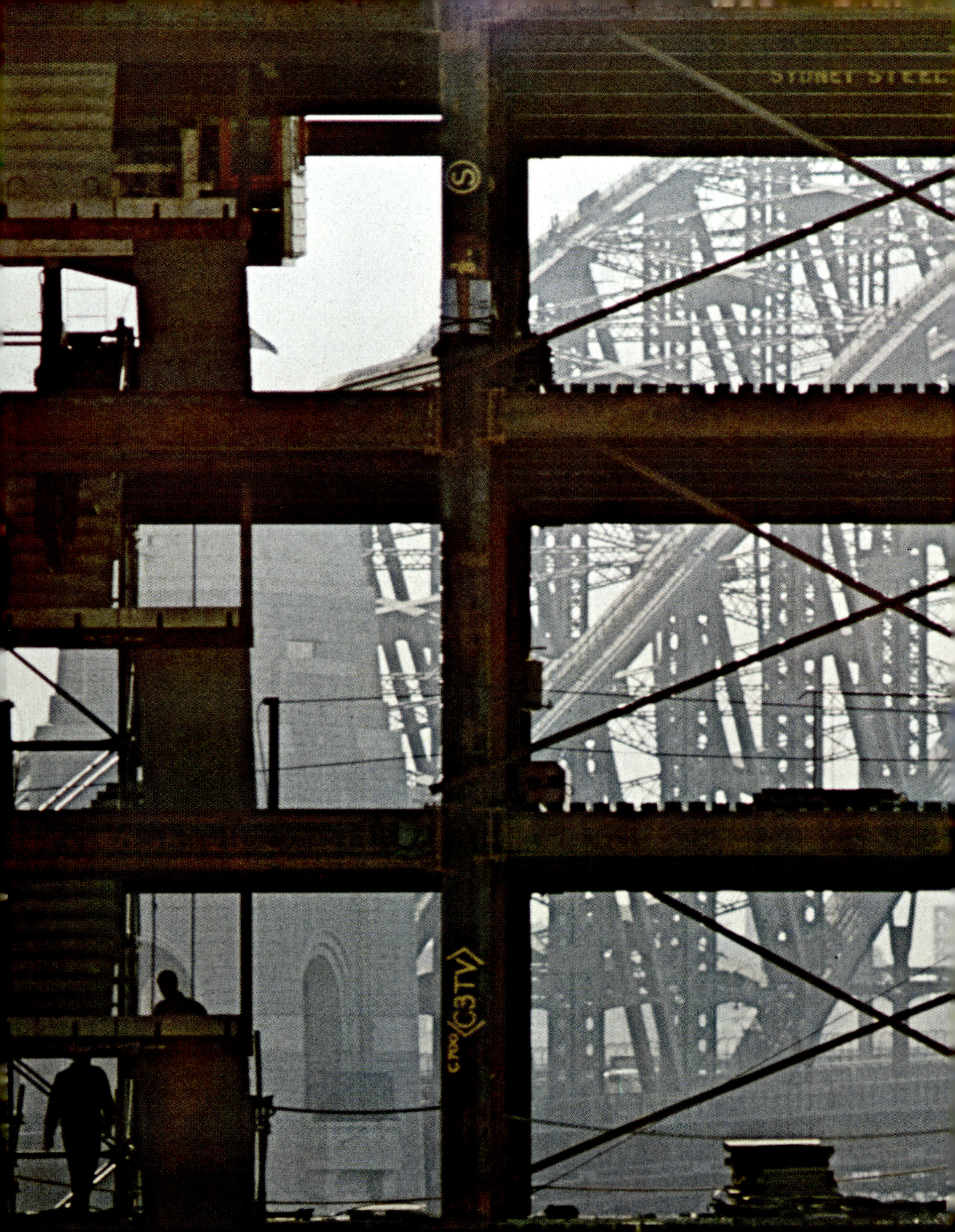
C3TV

Construction, Sydney

cleared, fences put up, ports built, homes erected and industries started. If what was achieved comparatively early was better than any neighbouring Asian country could show, that was only because our colonial overlords weren't quite as bad as theirs. As a new country, too, we could create our own standards and tradition. Australia has suffered only minimally from the stifling, medieval customs and inefficient outlook codes that even today bedevil full economic growth and development in Europe. Australia is not classless, as some claim, but it is more classless than any other community. That, too, goes back to muscle. The landowner had to get his land cleared, his fences built, his sheep shorn, his wheat sown, his cows milked. Most were small landowners and what clearing, fencing, shearing, sowing and milking they couldn't do themselves they hired extra hands to help. Hirer and hired jointly ran the risk of bad seasons, unsympathetic banks, poor returns. Only muscles could work against all these, and landowner and hired hand jointly threw their labour into the task of staving off disaster. There was neither time nor requirement for colourful overlord-peasantry niceties. Any landowner who tried to introduce them would soon find his "peasants" strolling off to supply their muscles to someone else in need of them. One virtue of under-population has been that high employment has always been a feature of the Australian scene. There has always been plenty of yakka to be done, seldom quite enough people to tackle it all adequately.

For generations Australians could do little more than continue to chip away at the task of establishing a nation. Federation in 1901 brought a kind of unity; involvement in the First World War added pride and a certain internationalism. Development speeded up. But there were still drab lessons to be learned; what we are today is linked with earlier eras which have helped shape and mould us.

To swing into first person. . . . I was born in 1928 and so am old enough to know well from personal experience the previous two important eras that have prefaced our present one. They were The Depression and The War. I used to say—and believe—that The Depression hasn't affected me or my family. Certainly it brought no immediate hardship. In the street in which I lived, only one family seemed to have been vitally affected. The father there, a semi-skilled worker, was out of work for several years. His children had to go barefoot to school, but we others envied them that particular freedom. We heard, too, that they could afford to eat only bread and dripping and we didn't envy them that. We could sympathise, too, with their embarrassment at the sight of their father in the dole queue outside the police station, lining up with the other unemployeds for handouts of money and groceries. But our family and the rest of the street maintained what was then considered the lucky and normal way of life. They were civil servants, small shop keepers, accountants, some old people retired on reasonable savings and pensions. In our typical lower middle class way, we reasoned it was only the "others" who were hit by The Depression: the semi-skilled and unskilled thrown out of work, the doctors we heard about who could get only pick and shovel labour. Not that we knew of any doctor who had to do that, but we heard of lots.

Few of us seemed to realise then, or even later, how much the exigencies of that era pervaded our thinking and produced what are now surely curious effects. It was a time of scare and caution. You had to be careful: just mend the old fence posts, don't start thinking of building new ones. I recall a grade five exercise in which we had to write one of those essays on What I Want To Be When I Leave School. Most of my fellow students wrote that their ambitions were up by the public service, banking, accountancy, the ministry, teaching the police force. There was scarcely any entrepreneurism breeding in our mildly fearful grade five minds. Sadly, what back-checking I've been able to do indicates that the sad dies cast by The Depression still mark most of my class mates today. Most have been swallowed up by the public service, banking, accountancy, the ministry, teaching and the police force. If there had been any vague seeds of self-enterprise, science or culture scattered there, the times then and immediately since were too infertile to allow them to flourish. Maybe they were in my two former school fellows who have now achieved criminal records, the one who disappeared out West hoboing, the one who turned drunkard or maybe the one who has taken to drugs. I can't classify the one who went into politics and has won his kind of security there.

The Depression was an era of, at best, pause; at worst, stagnation. The period saw little change on the Australian landscape; such as did occur were the products of an unimaginative necessity to create work for the unemployed, under a general financial advisory policy dictated even then by the Bank of England "experts." The Great Ocean Road was built in Victoria, the City Hall in Brisbane. It was a time of having and holding. Even the old chipping away process that had begun in 1788 stalled. Looking back, perhaps the best lesson that era taught was a kind of discipline. Maybe because of The Depression we are today such avid home-owners and are prepared to make great efforts to keep employment figures high. It was a lesson to those of us who knew it to save some money, work hard and not take good times and opportunities for granted. Be glad when they come, because we know they weren't always here.

The War era, of course, brought its own changes. There was a demand for brains as well as muscles—war was a scientific business. The War produced the first significant Australian-American alliance, which was something we thought we could benefit from. Inversely, it just about severed for all time the mother-son link with Britain. Singapore, the Churchill-Curtin rows, Britain's post-war decline in power and influence, then her apparently clear wish after a few years to be shed of the dreams as well as the realities of empire washed up any semblances of colonialism that were still lingering. We still weren't prepared to ditch the old Greensleeves tune for the American hit parade, but we were more prepared to listen to it and see what we could learn and adapt from it.

184, 185) Khancoban switching station, N.S.W.

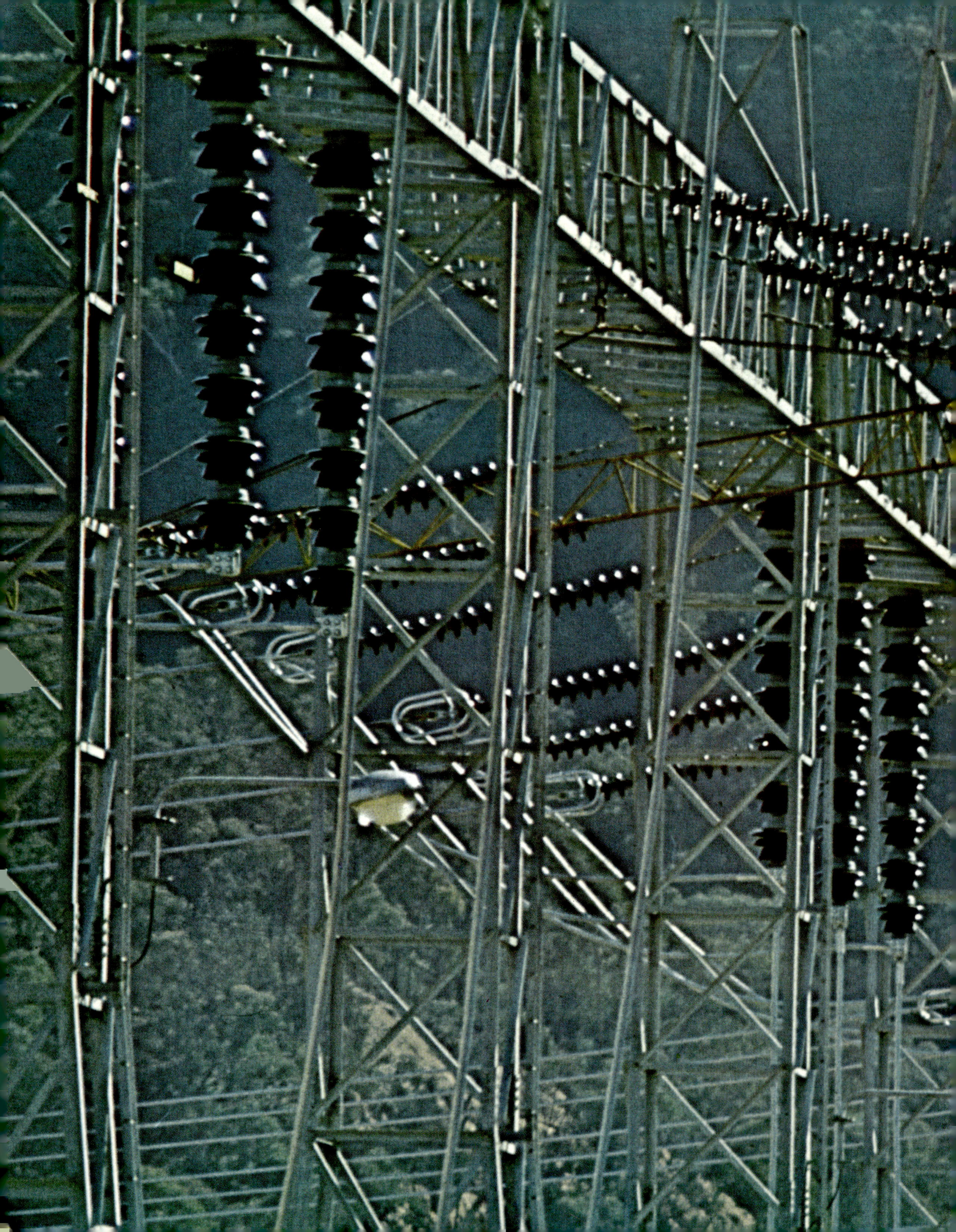

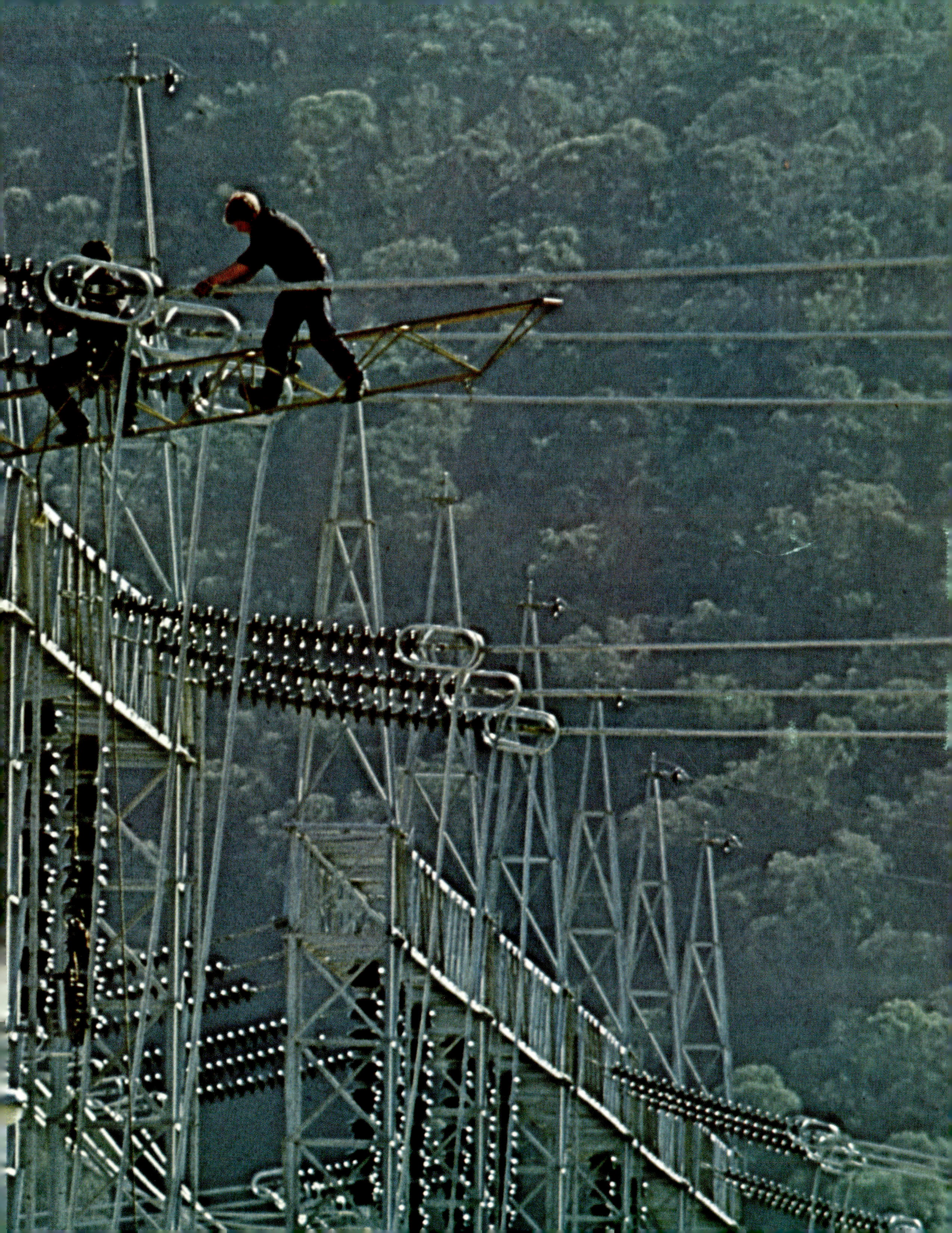

The War era brought for Australia a major switch from ruralism to industrialism in thinking and planning. It stopped us marking time, as we had been doing in The Depression. It forced us into a new national maturity. Darwin was bombed, Sydney Harbour raided by Japanese submarines, cities all around the coast had air raid alerts. We suddenly saw that after 150 years of chipping away at our continent we were still terribly vulnerable. That would have to be changed.

Curiously, it was wool from our rural background that provided the first major financial fillip. In the Depression '30s, it sold for sixpence a pound. By the '50s it was bringing 20 times that. The period produced a ferment that made money that brewed jobs that made more money that generated more ferment . . . and so the process took hold. There were new opportunities, new jobs. Old Depression-style fears and inertia faded. But for those of us who remembered the Depression, it wasn't always a clear-minded progression. I can recall the 1957 dinner party—it was a Saturday evening—when a group of us, all of similar ages, heard the news of the launching of the first sputnik. There were some in that gathering who queried: "But is that sort of thing really so important?" The Depression that raged 20 years earlier had left its crippling scar. It is only now that the grade fives, asked what They Want To Be When They Leave School, plump for the sciences, law, medicine, the arts as their vocational aims. Nowadays the public service, banking, accountancy, the ministry, teaching and the police force all have to mount advertising campaigns to attract Australian minds and bodies. It's no longer a bar to some banks if applicants are of certain religions. Nor to the ministry if they come from lowlier districts or homes. Today's full employment seems to have knocked away, finally I imagine, old bogeys like those.

As a young developing country, we still need all the brains and muscles we can get. We cannot afford the talent wastage many European countries and, to a lesser extent, North America still indulge in. The years 1959 to 1961 that I spent in Europe produced regular bouts of disgust and disdain for a system that denies opportunity to someone simply because he has the "wrong" accent or the "wrong" religion or comes from the "wrong" area. Ask any East or South Londoner his job chances, then check the result with any Australian from a lower class area; the Australian is incomparably better off. The East and South Londoner knows from the start that his field of operations is going to be limited, unless he's a very rare character or turns spiv. His Australian counterpart knows few such limitations. The Jack's-as-good-as-his-master attitude in Australia can sometimes be galling when it comes from bad-tempered taxi-drivers but it's the Australian system of unlimited job opportunities which provides the best national results.

Some of the thrust that was put into the Australian expansiveness of the Sixties came from the over two million migrants, most of them European, who have landed since 1947. There has been little integration at depth, even by the Britons, but they have been an important part of the muscle and brain recruitment Australia has found essential for development. They have also been a vital source of ideas power. I know a broking clerk who couldn't get ahead in the London office where he worked because he hadn't gone to a "right" school. Within five years with an Australian broking firm he had reached an executive position. Both countries need talent such as his. Only Australia was willing to use it properly.

Migrants, skilled and unskilled, today comprise a vital part of the 4¾ million strong Australian workforce. Of these, one-quarter are employers or self-employed. So keen is the demand for manpower that among employees there is one female for every three males. There are now 600,000 married women working in Australia—more than double the number in the mid-'50s. Changes in demand and opportunity are reflected by switches in the various workforce patterns. Between the mid-'50s and the mid-'60s the numbers employed in primary production fell from 500,000 to 440,000. By the mid-'60s, Australian factory production had raced ahead until it was almost double the value of primary production: the gross value of factory output reached $6,000 million, while primary production was just above $3,000 million. Improved production techniques have enabled factory outputs to increase in a period when the trend is away from blue collar to white collar work. Mining and quarrying production, for instance, increased between the mid-'50s and the mid-'60s, yet employment in these fields fell from 57,000 workers to 50,000. In the same period there were dramatic increases in numbers employed in white collar occupations: finance and property employment rose from 90,000 to 162,000, retailing from 287,000 to 406,000, education from 88,000 to 162,000.

This revolution has been wrought with a minimum of industrial friction. As a new country, Australia could afford to experiment with social and industrial legislation. In 1896 Australian women voted for the first time at a South Australian State election; other States soon adopted the practice. As long ago as 1907 a Government-appointed court laid down a legally stipulated basic wage for the Australian worker that was to be regarded as the minimum to provide "the normal needs of an average employee regarded as a human being in a civilised community." This average employee was taken to be a married man with two children and in 1907 his minimum wage was fixed at $4.20. By 1967 that legally prescribed minimum had increased to more than $36. But such are the demands for labour in the seventies that it would be impossible to find any employee drawing only the bare minimum. The average income earned by the Australian worker in 1971 is $80 a week.

Today Australia is consolidating those early fence-building jobs, but in broader and more sophisticated directions. The vast Snowy Mountains Scheme will eventually yield an output of 4 million kilowatts of hydro-electric power. The railways are being standardised. Existing road networks are being improved and new freeways are

Welder, Snowy Mountains, N.S.W.

Adelaide hills

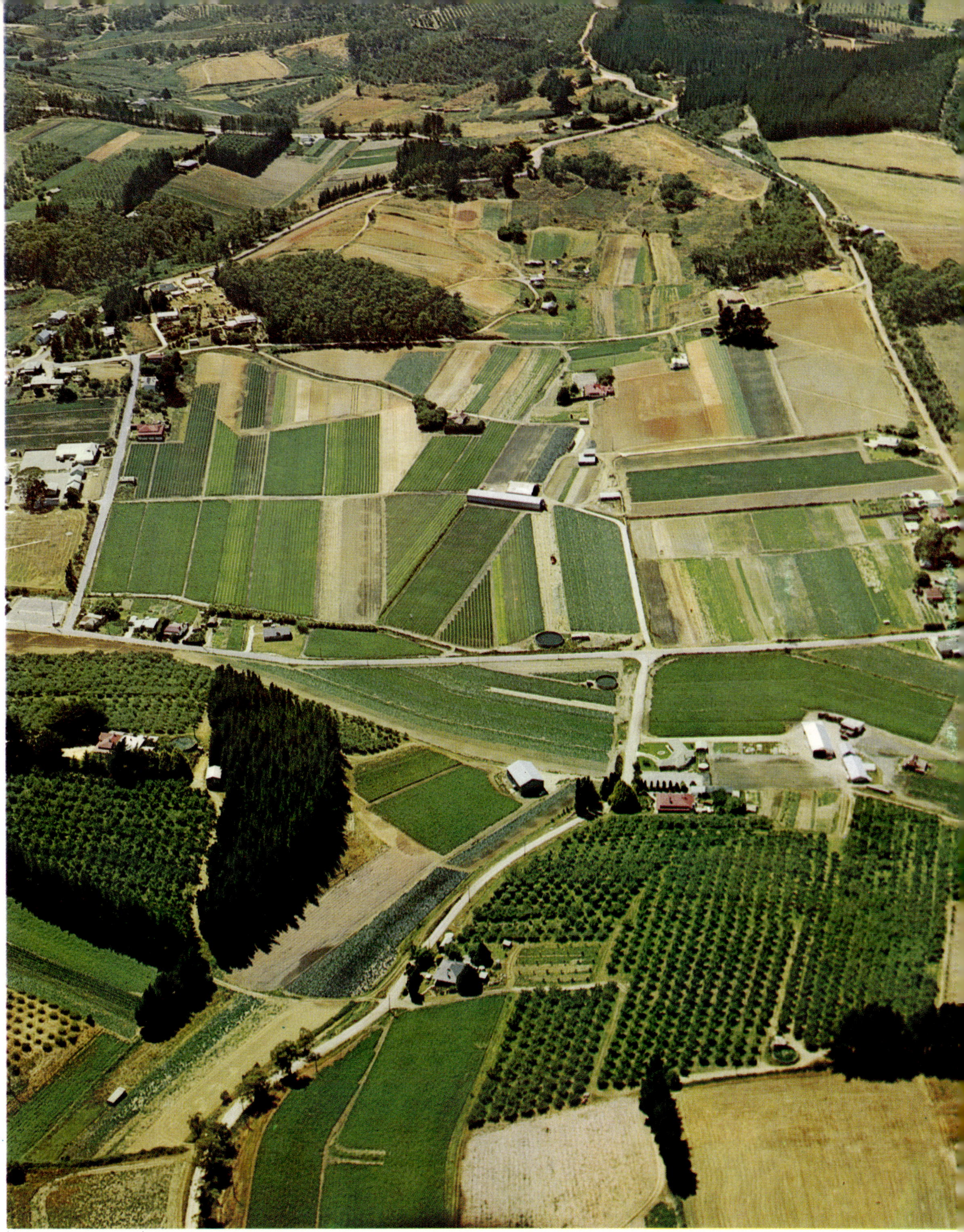

being built to handle the 4 million motor vehicles — double the number in the mid-'50s — now on Australian roads. While all this hard-core nation building goes on there have been new scientific breakthroughs. World astronomy and radio communications are aided by modern installations at Parkes and in the north-west of N.S.W. Woomera in South Australia is the site of rocket and satellite launches. In medicine, just as the Australians Florey and Bazeley played important roles in the development of penicillin and Salk anti-polio vaccine, local teams are pushing ahead with research into cancer, heart disease and human organ transplantings. There is now time and scope to develop these upper layers of modern progress. Profits from the ore-rich Hamersley Range in Western Australia contribute to the development of freeways, concert halls, medical research.

The Australian in The Seventies finds himself with broad job opportunities. He can cut cane in North Queensland or pick hops in Tasmania. One week's work will provide the train fare from coast to coast. Unemployment rarely rises above a low 1 per cent of the workforce, and since the 1940s a week's work means no more than 40 hours. This is just one of the many important benefits the Australian workforce has enjoyed for many years—along with an arbitration process to settle industrial disputes and adequate (if not grand) sickness, unemployment and holiday arrangements.

With all this outburst of energy there are naturally distortions. Vital services such as roadways, sewerage and public transport have been unable to keep pace with city growth. The cities are choked by traffic jams. With the decline in business in the city centre, public transport faces a serious problem. The increasing number of Australians who own their own cars doesn't help. Traffic experts estimate that the average worker saves 20 minutes a day each way on his trip to and from work by driving his own car. It also costs him $1 a day more in running costs, but he apparently values his leisure time at the rate of 2.5 cents a minute or $60 for a 40-hour week. This is, to him, one of the freedoms of the affluent society he has helped create and now wishes to enjoy. As an indication of how confident he has become that most of his industrial battles are behind him, union membership between the mid-'50s and the mid-'60s fell from 60 per cent of the workforce to slightly above 50 per cent.

The standards of living of different countries are almost impossible to compare. Americans, Canadians and New Zealanders have more motor-cars per head of population than Australians. Americans also spend longer at school, and have more refrigerators, television sets and radios. But on his visit to Australia late in 1966 President Johnson was impressed by the low unemployment figures and the high home ownership figures (the highest in the world) Australians have achieved for themselves. Perhaps, he admitted, it was on such things that a true overall standard of living could be best judged. Certainly Australians have always thought it more important to have a job and a home than to surround themselves with a repertoire of refrigerators and television sets. It seems the right emphasis. Australians can be as proud of that as they can be of what they have achieved since that day, 180 years ago, they began chipping away at creating a new nation.

Night harvesting

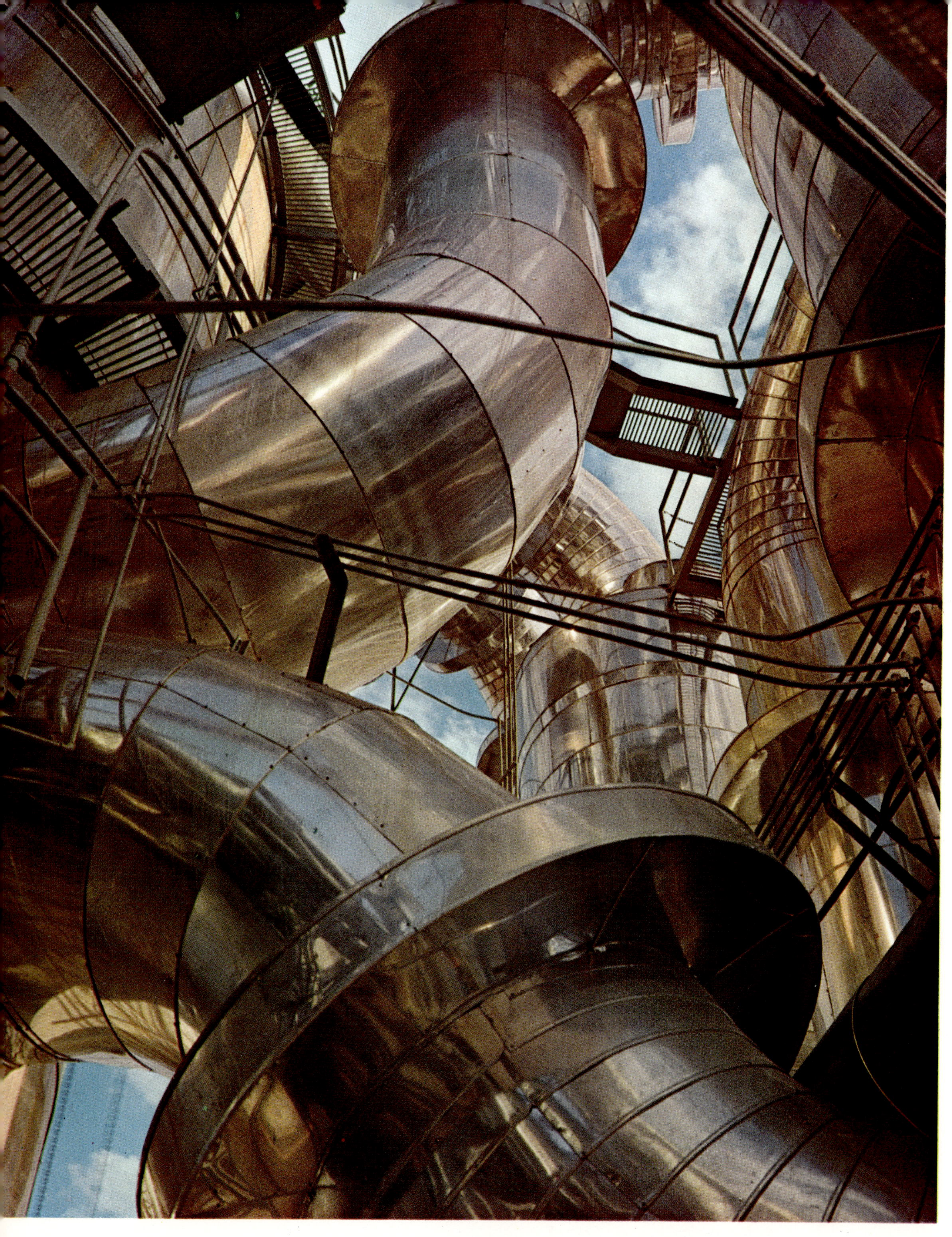

Iron ore workers, Hamersley, Western Australia

Refinery complex, Victoria

YOUNG AUSTRALIA

PACEMAKERS FROM THE CULTS

Richard Walsh

At first impression Australia is a young person's paradise. That has always been its proud claim and international attraction. It is the image the PR men who service the immigration centres abroad have attempted to convey. Forty per cent of Australians are under 20 and for the purposes of national propaganda they have usually been pictured as sharing their time between the surf and the tennis court, so that Europeans must sometimes wonder, as with the flies, where they all go in winter.

Yet until very recently this popular image of a young virile country moving, almost hormonally, towards self-realisation was so grossly at odds with the truth that it began to constitute a case of deceptive international packaging by a country obviously over-eager to attract new citizens. Four years ago the Adelaide poet and publisher Geoffrey Dutton wrote: "Alas, how embarrassing the truth would be if one were tactless enough to tell it, namely that youth in Australia controls nothing except, maybe, the teenage gramophone record business. This may be symbolic; youth is governed by its elders to a maximum of 45 rpm. Australia as a nation is run by old men and is subservient to senile institutions."

Today that judgment is almost valid but its truth is beginning to falter. In the last few years political power has swung away from the very old to the mediumly so; great social changes have occurred and some can be traced back to the young; a new awareness of young achievement has grown up and the voting age has dropped, at least for those young men prepared to risk their lives for the current national cause. Youth in Australia is beginning to make its presence felt, and its leaders are often the same age as those being led. The turntable is speeding up.

Youth begins at school, which is a muck-up from 9 to 3 and sport thereafter. Football, in one of its many guises, and cricket are played in school teams. Most schools have swimming and athletic carnivals as well but, oddly enough, there is little formal place for tennis (except in the girls' schools; despite international prowess, tennis is regarded in many young quarters as rather "sissy"). Golf is learnt on almost an apprenticeship system, with kids making extra money as caddies or selling repainted golf balls and then busting the proceeds on an eighteen. It is a "grown up" sport where you practise bad language on the duffs and learn such miscellaneous arts as throwing down your fag to make a shot. You learn to smoke at about 8 because, like sex, there is a great reluctance to tell young people the facts about lung cancer (or contraception) until it is too late. Sailing is for the toffs and ice-skating for the proles.

At 15 youth divides into that great watershed of modern man: the skilled and unskilled. In working class suburbs it is not unusual for kids to leave school right on their birthday. School is not too bad (though few would admit it), but earning money is better. The good money Australians offer early school-leavers is perhaps one of the most disastrous features of its economic system. The low participation of working class children in post-school and higher school education is often cited as evidence of the lack of real opportunity in Australia. This is seen at its worst at university, to which the sons of unskilled and semi-skilled workers, comprising one-third of the general population, contribute a mere 8 per cent of the undergraduate population. These children, however, are from homes where education is almost despised and cash-in-hand is the only measure of success. It is not that their parents cannot afford to educate them further (though, of course, there is always some element of this), but rather that neither adults nor children can see any point in continuing study.

It's a shock to leave school at 15. Work means an eight-hour grind without the mental stimulation to which even the loafer is intermittently exposed at school. Evening telly-watching, once associated with the background guilt of undone homework, now becomes grist to fill the vacuum between 5 and bed-time. Suffering the witticisms of their older workmates, exposed to sex-talk almost too sophisticated for their comprehension, there is initially a fantastic demand on their powers of assimilation. Yet it is estimated that within a month of beginning work of this kind these youths are able to adopt the familiar mentality of careless nonchalance that characterises the Australian worker. Many of them become drifters, chucking their jobs in when a few dollars mount in the bank account, and they are often the unstable element that creates industrial unrest, even though they show no real interest in the union movement or any of the old workers' causes. Their work creates a vacuum which their limited attempts at leisure cannot fill.

Entertainment, apart from the television set, is usually restricted to weekends. Sport after leaving school is more usual among the well-to-do than the unskilled, apart from professional sport and the two Great Australian Sports, surfing and spectatorship. Saturday, where possible, means swimming in summer and in winter going to the football match. Girls also go to the football, dividing their attention between the play and their favourite spectators. Or they may spend the whole of Saturday in elaborate preparation for the evening, which is spent at the cinema, the drive-in, public dances or private parties. The girls indulge in a little unionism of their own, exerting subtle pressures upon wayward men to "do the right thing." In this world, there is little disguising who does the chasing: marriage at an early age, often "shot-gun," is very common as a respite from the boredom and one of the ways of leaving home. Where once a girl wanted a husband and kids, she now wants a husband and kid (it is the bourgeoisie that desires two, the standard Australian family). It is not infrequent for a girl, by the time she is twenty, to have achieved all the life-goals she ever set herself.

This drab, relentlessly unstimulating picture is, of course, a far cry from the life cycle of Glamour Youth, the *toujours gaie* young hedonists that slick journalism has recently unearthed and amateur sociologists adore. But, despite their publicity machine, Glamour

Youth is atypical. Glamour Youth, for girls, means at least an extra year at school and then on to typing school. Or it can mean art school, teachers' college—even university. For boys it means, at the worst, clerical work, or anything that keeps them in the city and away from the industrial areas. It is not merely a socio-economic matter since a good apprentice is holding down a much better future than the pasty-faced little mod messenger boys in high collars and winkle-pickers who take their cut sandwiches to the lunch-time discotheques.

Wherever they are, youths have their groups or, as the sociologists like to call them, their *peër groups*. In his study *Growing Up in an Australian City* (Sydney to be exact) Professor W. F. Conell has made an intensive study of these groups, particularly amongst 14-15 year olds, though the results remain applicable to older age groups as well. He found that 70 per cent of boys and 80 per cent of girls belong to such groups, which usually have 7-12 members with the average 9. There is usually only a small age range and they are all of the same sex. While at school these groups begin to take up the adolescent fads in dress, music and dancing. Girls lead the way, dress-conscious and maturing rapidly enough to be susceptible to the rhythm of the pop craze. They shriek their heads off at their pop idols and haunt the discotheques. First they go in their groups, even dancing together when they are young. Gradually, like some primitive ritualistic evolution, the males begin to get the message. One by one they are seduced from their own tight groups to partner potential girlfriends and to respond similarly to the big beat. They are always a bit self-conscious about mod gear—they suffer worse than girls at the hands of their parents, for whom long hair and kinky clothes are a radical departure from adult sartorial preconceptions—and sit rather stolidly through the teenage shriek shows. But they are good dancers and somehow meet all the demands placed on them.

Australian youths learn sex by the trial-and-error method and there is plenty of the latter. Six and a half per cent of all children are illegitimate and of these fatherless babies some 38 per cent are born to girls aged between 15 and 19. A cruel, destructive vocabulary has emerged to characterise the unfeelingness of early sexual contact. Every district has its "bicycle," the neurotic girl who will take all comers in her compulsive craving for attention and/or affection. She is the classic "raving case," but for every one such there are hundreds of "pigs" who fall easy prey. A lot of mass rape makes the papers, but a lot of it is semi-rape with the girl intoxicated or half-willing, the so-called "gang-bang" with the tail-ender "stirring the porridge." As in other cities and towns in the rest of the world, this is the impersonal way in which young people learn about sex at first hand. (It is only Australians who want to deny that this is so.) The pattern extends from the socio-economic lowliest into the very highest echelons, amongst whom it is particularly associated with the surfing cult.

But amongst the uppers there is a competing pattern. The uppers are impeded by their attendance at private colleges, which are never coeducational, are often boarding schools and battle against the undercurrent of overt homosexual experimentation. Such children are supposed to be "late developers" anyhow and, one way or another, seem to be less free and easy with the opposite sex than are their state school counterparts. Their heterosexual contacts begin with flirtations on buses and trains, graduate to milk bar rendezvous after school and football dates, and flower into "pashing parties" held under the influence of alcohol and the aegis of tolerant parents, where the lights are out most of the night and they lie around fondling exploratively. Through all groups there is great emphasis on "steadies" and the pop songs do not plug the theme of fidelity for nothing because that is the dominant ethos. The idea that premarital sex is not entirely wrong within such relationships is rapidly gaining ground even among parents, so that white weddings are becoming as passé as confetti.

Glamour Youth is amoral and hedonistic and, above all, susceptible to the crazes that sweep through its ranks like prairie fire. First there was Rock-'n'-Roll, which always had a strongly American flavour and so fell rapidly from favour when the Beatles and, later, the Carnaby Street kick came along. It is quite clear that working class youth prefers to adopt an American life-style and the big R. & R. has lingered on with the phenomenon of the rockers, who still cling to their leather-jackets, slicked hair and a swagger that is slightly bowlegged from continual drag bike-racing. Little r. & r., of course, is the rescue and resuscitation of the life-saving clubs, a fine old Australian tradition that has been perverted into the surfie cult. The life-saving movement, like the National Fitness movement (in fact like all organised youth activities in recent years) is failing to attract new members, who resent its authoritarian flavour—particularly when the leaders are fairly senile youths—and the high-sounding ideals, which are more notable in the breach than in the observance.

While organised movements decline, fads no less (but more inconspicuously) organised arise like phoenixes from the ashes of their predecessors. There has been a half-hearted attempt to get the kids interested in Op-art with a few uninspired check shifts and umbrellas. There was a mediocre attempt at launching Pop. But over the last decade it was perhaps the 'go-go' groove that attracted all the sharpest kids. The go-go was a free expressionist kind of dance form uninhibited by the old necessities of a regular pattern. It involved every part of the body that could muster a twitch and maintain it vaguely in rhythm with the music. The natural habitat of the go-go was the discotheque. The discos began about five years ago and at their height Sydney was able to support about twenty of them. At their best they are fitted out with opulent mirrors, hatstands, couches and other Edwardian bric-a-brac, and they provide live bands. At their worst they have laminex and recorded music. At one or other end of the scale, depending on your taste, are the "sophisticated" discotheques, licensed and catering for older trendies shamelessly regressing.

At its beginning the go-go seemed to have absorbed the stomp, the surfies' old free-form dance, with which they pile-drove many a good dance hall back into its foundations, and it is still not uncommon to see threshing arms attached to stomping feet. More lately the craze has absorbed some of the hippy back-lash, with attempts to introduce psychedelic lighting and art nouveau decor into the discos. Psychedelicism in Australia, as so often happens with local crazes, has been pallidly imitative.

The groovers not only absorbed the surfies but inherited its old enemies, the rockers, later transmogrified into "sharpies". The sharpies had abandoned the James Dean look somewhere east of Eden and moved over to a modified clean-cut all-American look with short hair, T-shirts and bike-chains as optional extras. Beating up mods has replaced the old surfie massacres. This rivalry still represents a dichotomy of life-style between the American and British mods replaced the old surfie massacres. The rivalry still reprehostilities. It is a rift between the underprivileged and the not-so-underprivileged; only the second group can afford the upkeep of the hellishly expensive mod trappings. The really privileged, let it be added, indulge in such things only as an occasional whim and have a wider range of leisure activities than addiction for discotheques, and more adult pretensions than to allow themselves to become fully committed to a cult.

Yet it is Glamour Youth, the mods, that provides the driving force behind young Australia, and they are creating the changes. They are selfish and unfeeling, but these are the traits with which they feed their ambitions. It they can find a short cut, they want to be rich. If they can avoid marriage they want to travel and, if they succeed, they will go as bludgers of the very first water. They are the prototypes of the driving middle class that will characterise Australia in the '70s, though many of them have their origins at the lower border of this class, in a society which of course still pretends to be classless. For all their faults, they are honest about their aims and frank about their methods. They lack the hypocrisy of their elders and not only practise, for example, premarital sex but believe in it, the more insistently the older they get. Moreover they have evolved their own heroes, who are sometimes worthier than their worshippers and point more definitely to the future.

These are the so-called Pacemakers, the Super Glamour Youth who are making good even by adult standards. They are young men and women in their early twenties who are succeeding as entrepreneurs of one kind or another. Sometimes they are mere traders, sometimes fashion-designers or otherwise engaged in the creative arts; sometimes they are entrepreneurs for themselves. Youth is now being catered for by youths: their fashions, their reading matter, their music are the products of people their own age. The young are beginning to control their own destiny, and it is evident that their destiny is very different from that of their fathers.

Surfgirl

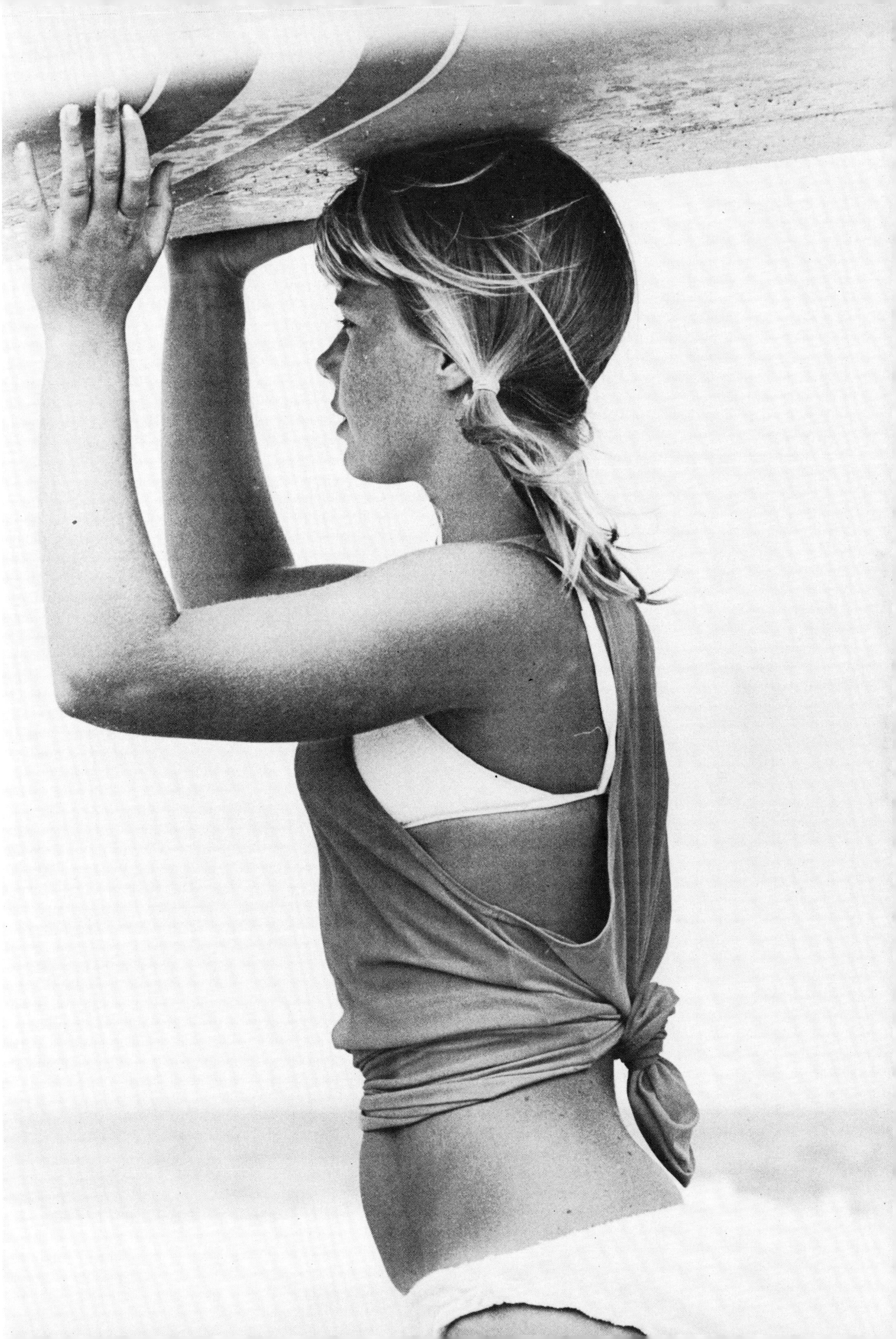

Follow the leader, Sydney

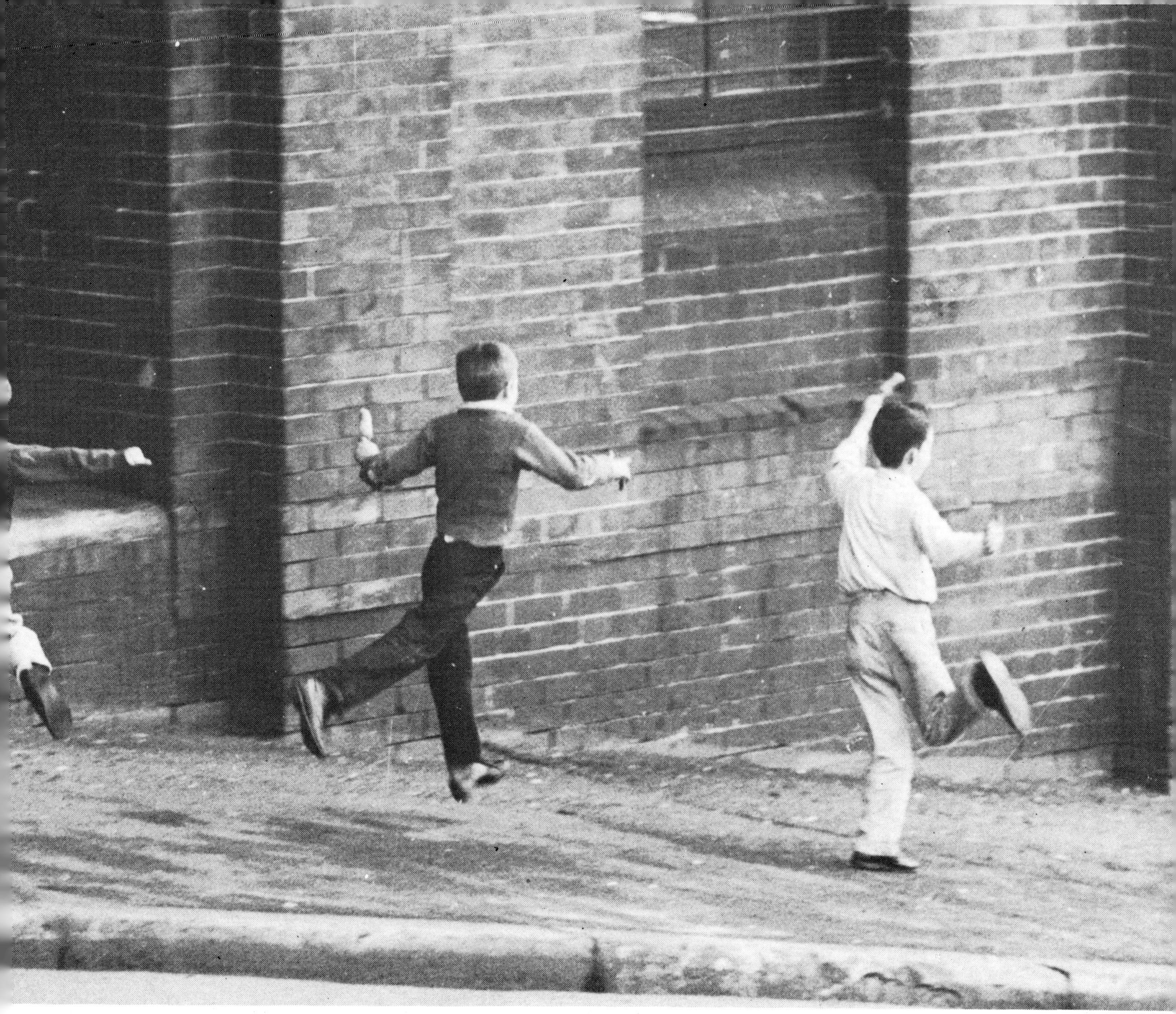

It was inevitable that there would be a gulf between the members of this new generation and their parents. There is always some gulf between generations, but in this case the difference in outlook is obvious and vast. When the fathers of the present generation came back from the Second World War some married quickly and often ill-advisedly. Others returned to old marriages, but they had been profoundly altered by their ordeal. They had known not only the physical hardships of war but the emotional privations of the Depression; some were strangers in a new land, some had known the horrors of racial persecution. These men fathered the post-war baby boom, children who would face opportunities that they had never known.

Yet there is not merely a difference in opportunity and affluence between the generations but a difference in identification probably unlike that in any other country today. The men who marched off to the Second World War were as surely British in their instincts as Winston Churchill, their acknowledged inspiration. They fought hard for Australia, which was a beaut little country but always little in their eyes and never God's own, as the new nationalistic spirit will teach their children. Today Britain is a non-power, and a new jingoism is arising in Australia. It is a slow, subtle process that affects everything from a revival of republicanism to the waning of the expatriate vogue. But, however subtle, it is there and it drives its wedge deep, not only between current youth and its parents, but between youth and the people only five or ten years older

In intellectual circles the gulf becomes a rift. In their 40's are men like Donald Horne, who once told a newspaper columnist: "All the main rebellions of the twentieth century were over by 1910. Our lot—Hope, McAuley and I—knew something of the history of rebellion: that ours was second-hand. The present generation, enacting all this again at fourth-hand, does not realise this. They think it is new." These are the words of an ageing, disenchanted Pacemaker. Horne was one of the 1940s men who passed out of undergraduate life into academic posts and other positions of intellectual influence. In their youth, despite his hindsight wisdom, they also thought they were doing something *genuinely new,* and they are resentful that today's youth may be succeeding where they failed. In their 30's are the intellectuals who have either returned from long periods of expatriation in Europe or, for one reason or another, missed out on the Brain Drain and have resented it ever since. For them, to have their own programme on the B.B.C. or to hit the West End is the life-goal. They are incurably alienated from any Australian aspirations. Their attitude is not so much resentment as indulgent amusement that anyone should care about succeeding in Australia.

These older men are not without their influence in Australia, but their influence is confined to matters of taste. They give direction to our cultural and intellectual life. But they have failed to revolutionise Australian attitudes away from a kind of apprehensive self-consciousness. They have failed to inspire a new spirit and create

Sunday afternoon, The Domain, Sydney

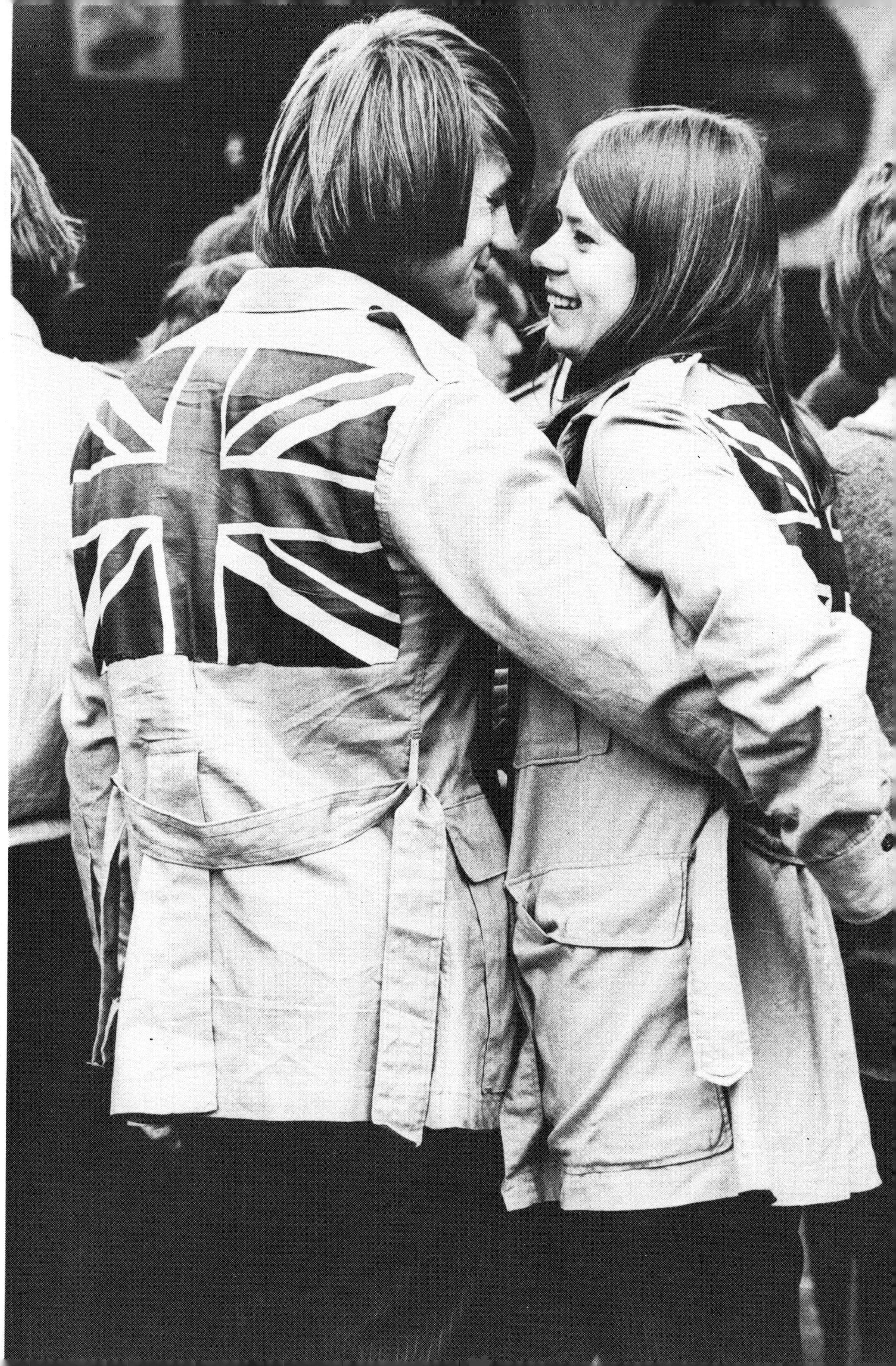

a new society. The younger generation seems more determined to force its demands through—so much so that, in the universities, the older men in power are beginning to be gripped by Berkeley-phobia. Yet the university authorities think more in terms of repression than in attempting to appreciate or comprehend the new spirit that demands freedoms Australians have never previously enjoyed and, by so doing, fan the flames they fear.

As the post-war boom babies gradually become enfranchised their attitudes will begin to have some effect. They are already starting to exert influence; one day they will experience power. As this happens Australia will take on a real, perhaps dangerous, nationalistic character. Yet because Australia has so little tradition, youth has a free hand to mould its society exactly according to contemporary needs. Despite the lures of hedonism and affluence, it is quite clear that its leaders will attempt this. The historical judgment will be made of their efforts, not of the kinky cults from which they emerged.

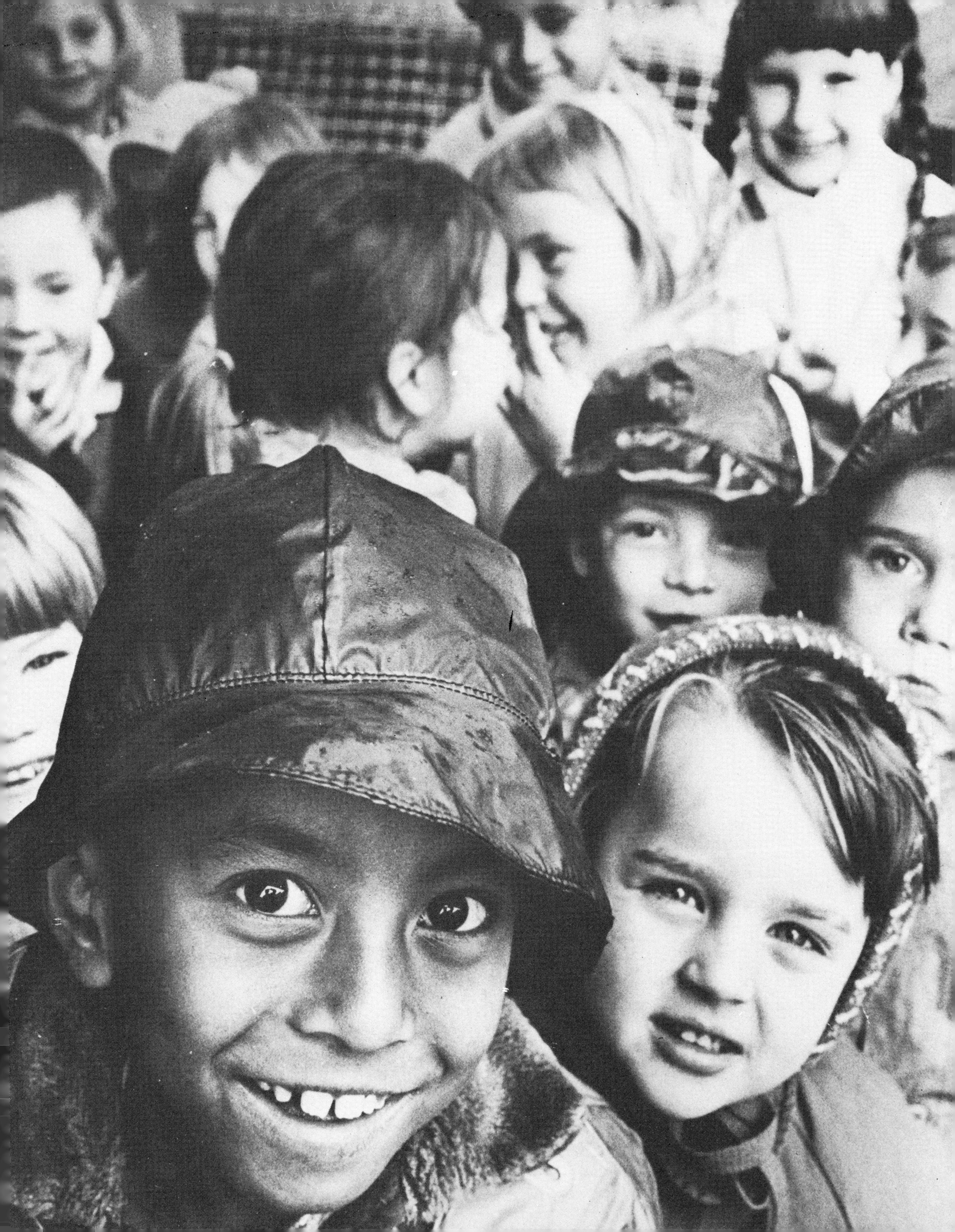

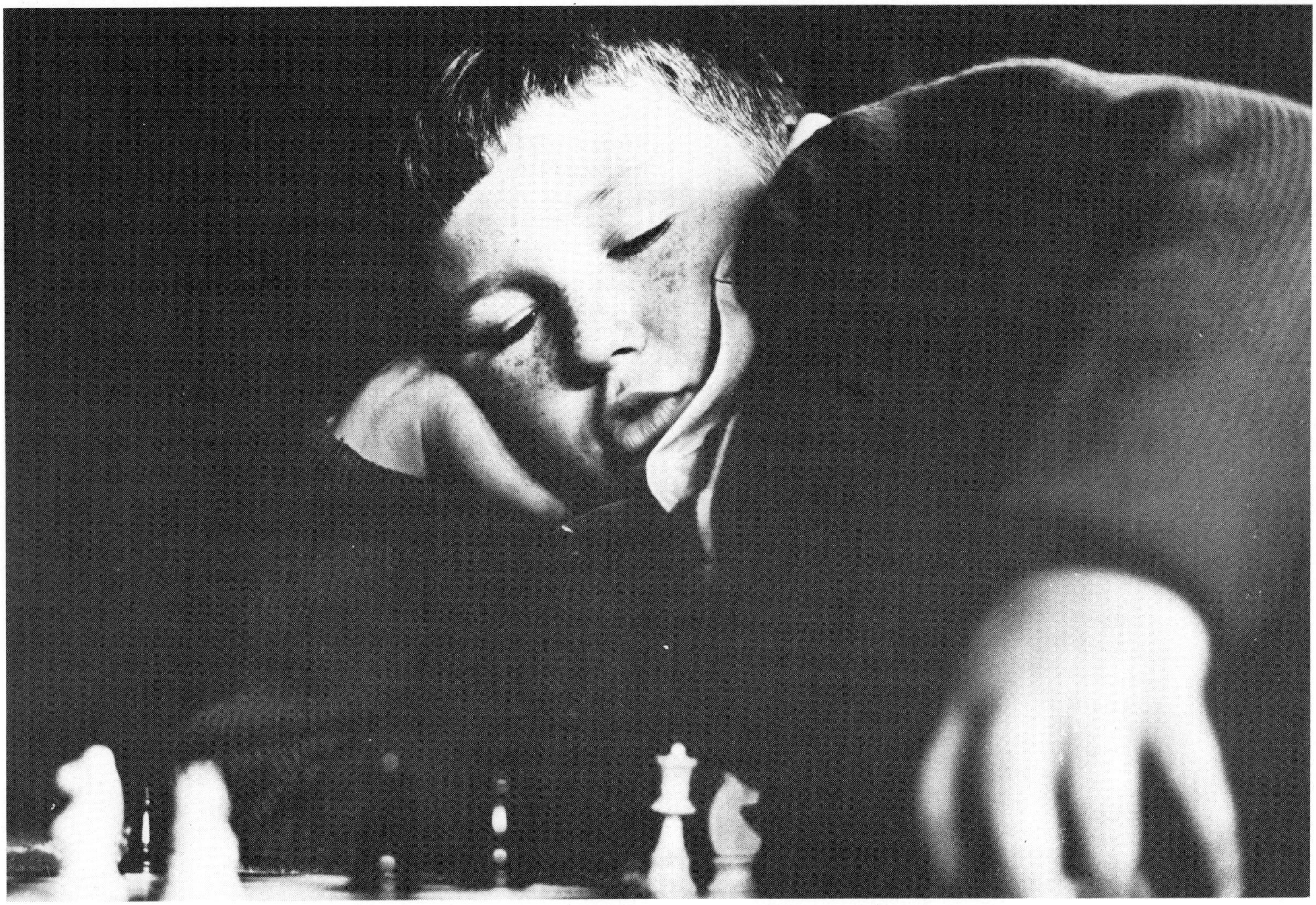

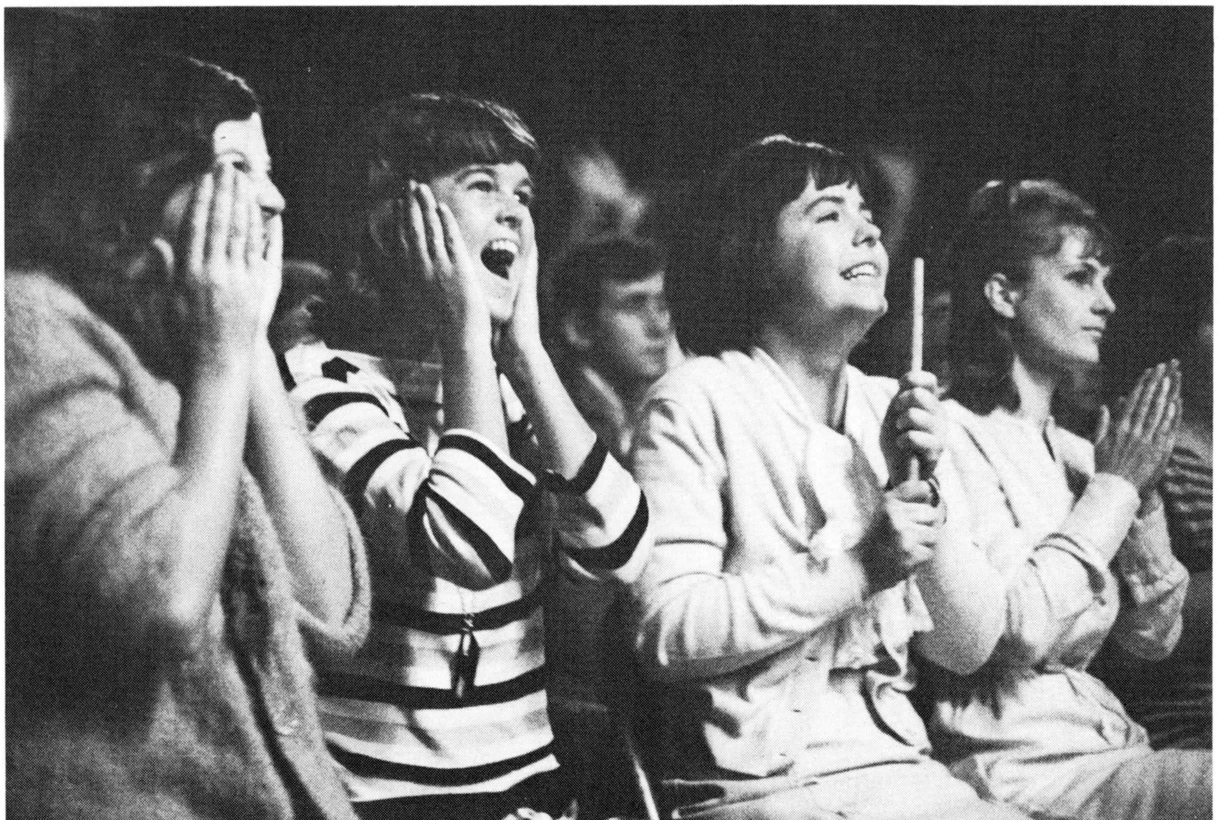

Youthful activities

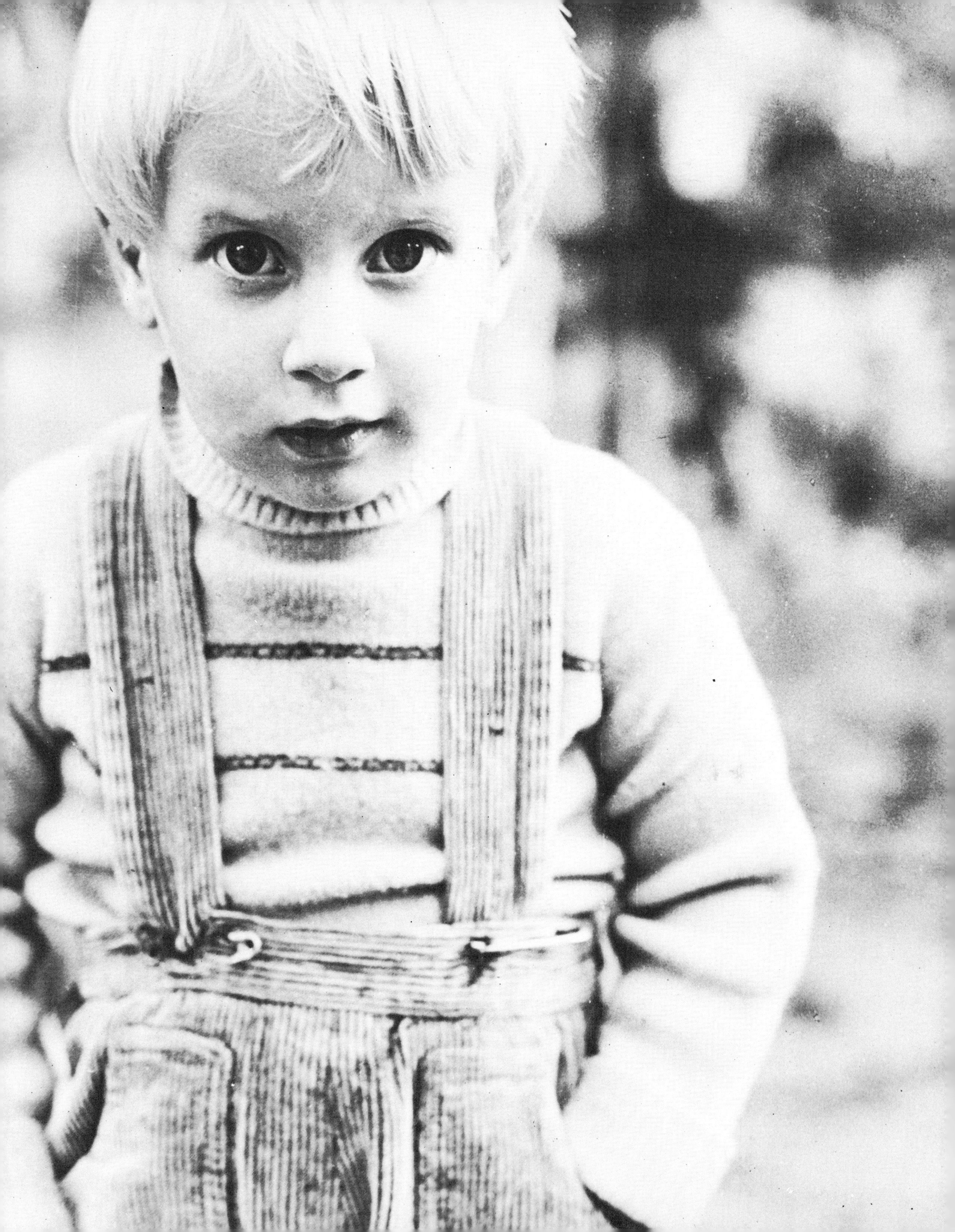

Lunch break, The Domain, Sydney

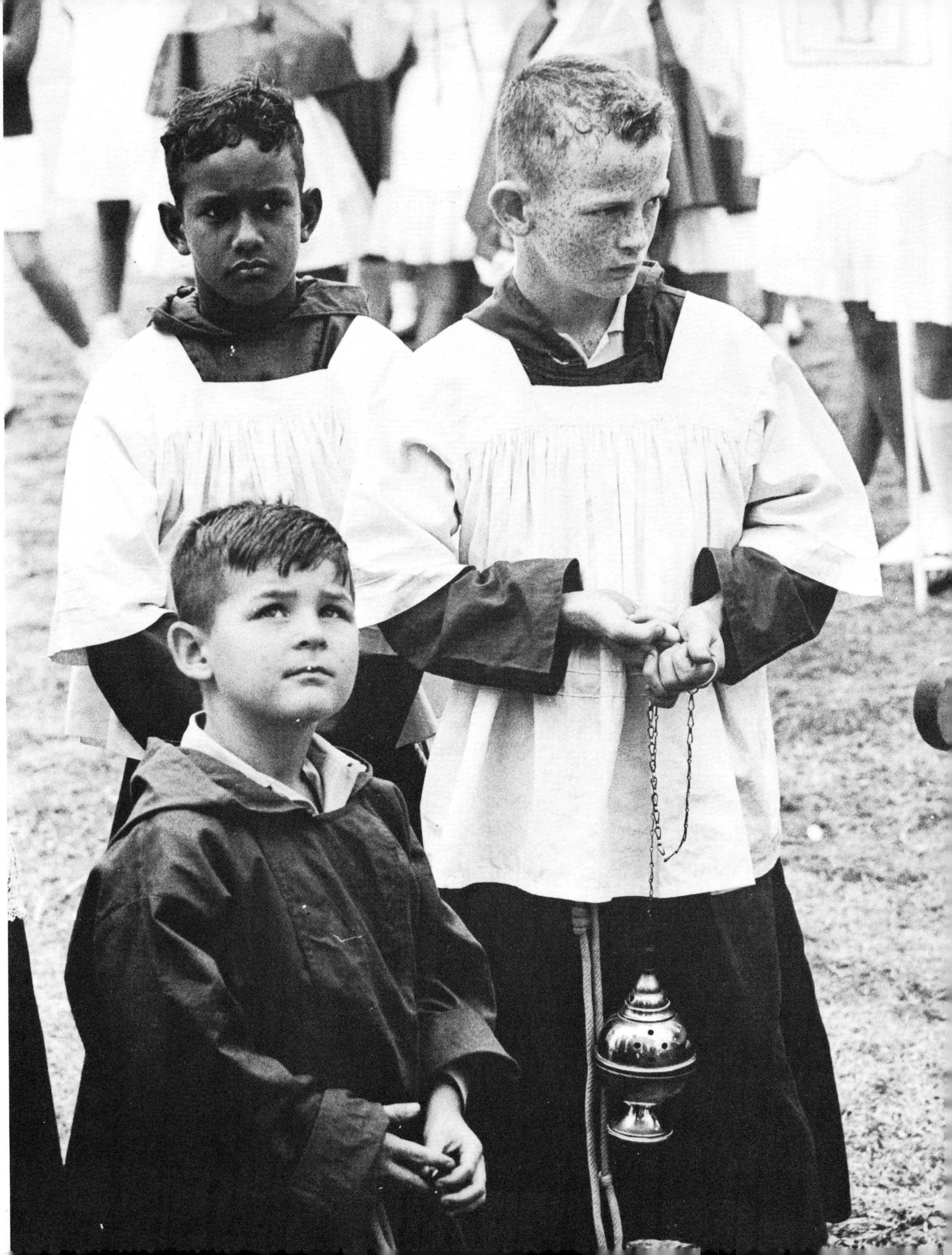

St. Anthony's Feast Day,
Bemerside, Queensland

One a.m., Sydney

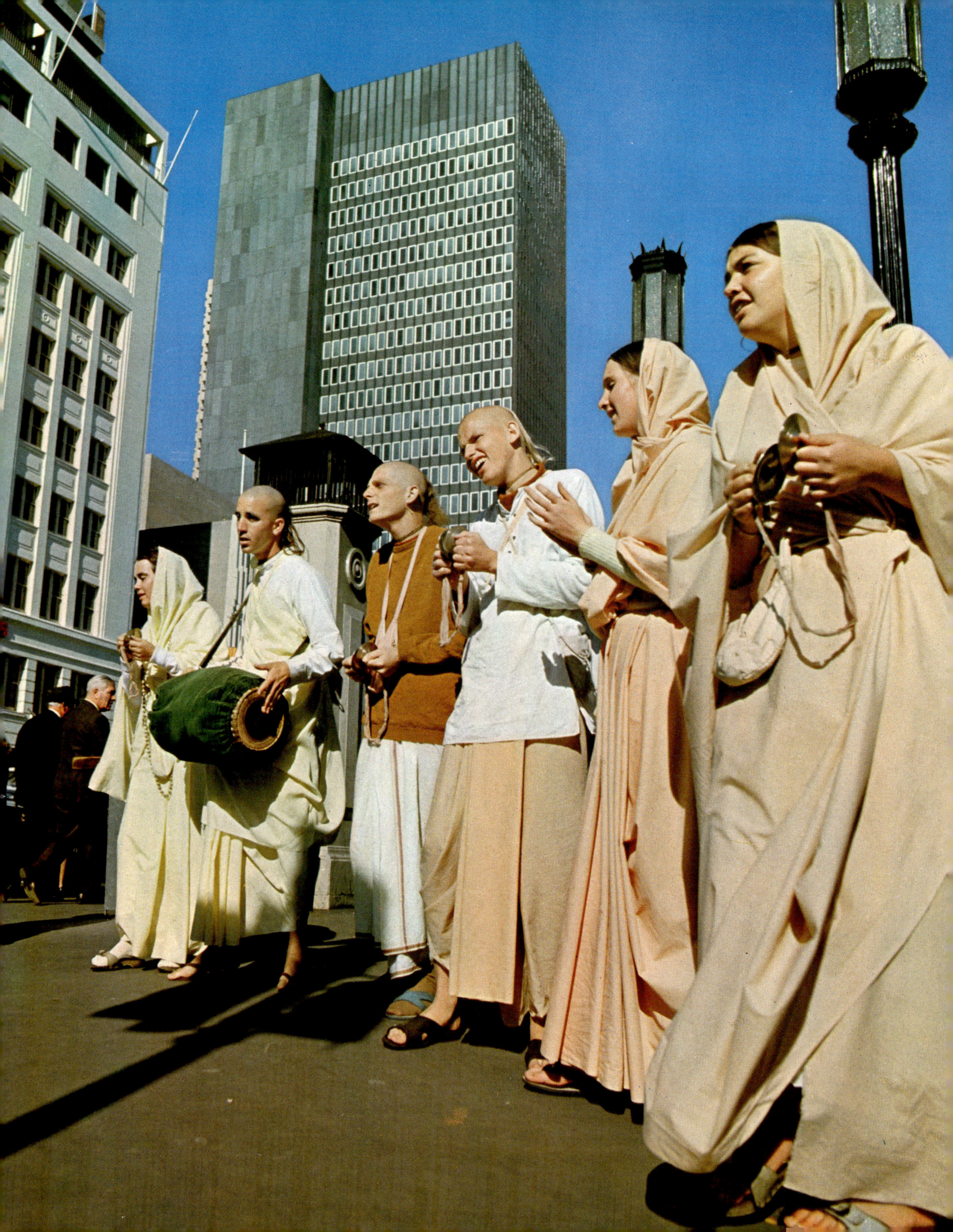

Sailing enthusiasts, Adelaide

Hare Krishna, Martin Place, Sydney

213

Belltrees public school, N.S.W.

Water-ski display, Yarra River, Melbourne

216, 217) Iron and steel plant, Port Kembla, N.S.W.

215

THE FUTURE

John Douglas Pringle

No one can foretell the future of Australia, for a very simple reason: no one can foretell the future of the world. Obviously Australia would be affected by a nuclear war, by the expansion of Chinese power in the South Pacific, by the emergence of a new revolutionary power in Indonesia, or by many other eventualities which we cannot foresee. All one can do is to make guesses. But one thing I do now believe—that Australia has a future as an independent sovereign State in control of its own destinies.

Not everyone would agree. Malcolm Muggeridge has expressed the view that all our brave hopes are vain and that our inevitable fate is to be taken over by some Asian nation. I myself once put forward the possibility that some world government or regional government might weary of our slow development and might hand over the North to Asian migrants for intensive cultivation. Neither of these destinies now seems to be likely. I can see no Asian Power—not even Red China—which either could or would threaten our independence in the foreseeable future, and I no longer think that a world government will be formed in this century. Moreover, Australia's own development seems at last to have got off the ground and to be gathering impressive speed and power. I have therefore written this chapter on the assumption that we shall go on pretty much as we are now, as an independent nation in control of its own affairs, even though inevitably affected by what happens on the mainland of Asia to our North.

This, however, leaves out one important—though by now slightly boring—consideration. Will Australia remain predominantly a white nation peopled by men and women of European stock or will it, of its own volition, take in enough Asian migrants to change significantly the present composition of the population or even to make this a multi-racial society? Here, I think, a new factor is emerging. Hitherto the debate has been between a minority of liberal idealists, who oppose the White Australia policy on the ground that it is morally indefensible, and a majority of hard-headed realists who point, with some reason, to the difficulties of absorbing coloured minorities in other countries. I suspect, however, that this may soon change. Because of the steady fall in the number of European migrants the liberal idealists may soon be joined by a new party of hard-headed realists who will argue that only by taking some Asian migrants will Australia be able to build up its population fast enough. When this happens—and I think it will happen—the whole nature of the debate will change and the White Australia policy will crumble.

This point seems to me to deserve some expansion. During the last 200 years migrants have left their homes in Europe for Australia and North America for one of three reasons—to better themselves economically, to escape from war and political or religious persecution, and, during the last fifty years, to find a better climate. Of these three reasons the last—and most trivial—is the only one that is still valid for most Europeans. Except in Spain, Portugal, South Italy and Greece (where the climate is as good as ours) the standard of living in Europe is now very little lower than that in Australia and the standards of public welfare may actually be higher. War is today rather more likely in Asia than in Europe. Indeed Australia is at this moment committed to a war in Vietnam whereas no European nation is at war anywhere in the globe. I admit that no one can be certain that war or persecution will not again break out in Europe; indeed some persecution exists now in Spain, Portugal, Greece and the Communist countries of Eastern Europe. Yet, since one is peering into the future, one is bound to say that the signs suggest that this may diminish rather than increase.

This leaves the climate, which has become an increasingly powerful factor in our century when, for the first time in history, men have been able to see other lands and so become discontented with their own. This is a world-wide trend. Northern Russians tend to migrate to the sunny Crimea. North Americans go south to Florida or West to California. Europeans go south to the Mediterranean for holidays and to retire, even if they cannot go there to live and work. Only the British, now thoroughly dissatisfied with their damp, grey climate (which they used to think the finest in the world) have no "South" of their own and must look beyond the seas to South Africa—a somewhat hazardous health resort—or Australia.

I don't think we should underrate the force of this attraction. Sun is a powerful drug. Some Britons, having once tasted the joys of blue skies and warm seas on their Mediterranean holidays, will continue to seek these things in Australia. But even so we must consider the possibility that when Britain enters the Common Market, if the Common Market continues to develop and to break down barriers to movements of men and capital, Britons too will go to look for the sun in Spain and Italy and Greece rather than overseas.

This leads naturally to a vital question. Apart from the sunshine, why should anyone now come to Australia? What have we to offer that is richer or more satisfying? A higher standard of living? I have already argued that this is no longer true at least for Britain, France and Germany and may soon not be true for Southern Europe as well. Better welfare? Not now. A richer culture? Certainly not. More opportunities for young people? Yes, perhaps. It is still easier for boys and girls to get a higher education in Australia than in Europe though that education, when you get it, may not be so good. It is certainly easier to get jobs and make money. More space, more room to breathe? Yes; this too is a genuine attraction, especially to the British, whose islands, except for Scotland and Wales, are noticeably overcrowded.

Yet anyone who does this exercise honestly must recognise that there are now no very obvious or overwhelming reasons why Europeans should leave their homes to try their luck in Australia.

Of course this is not true of Asia. There are still millions of Asians to whom life in Australia would be a paradise, and I cannot believe

220, 221) Opera House, Sydney

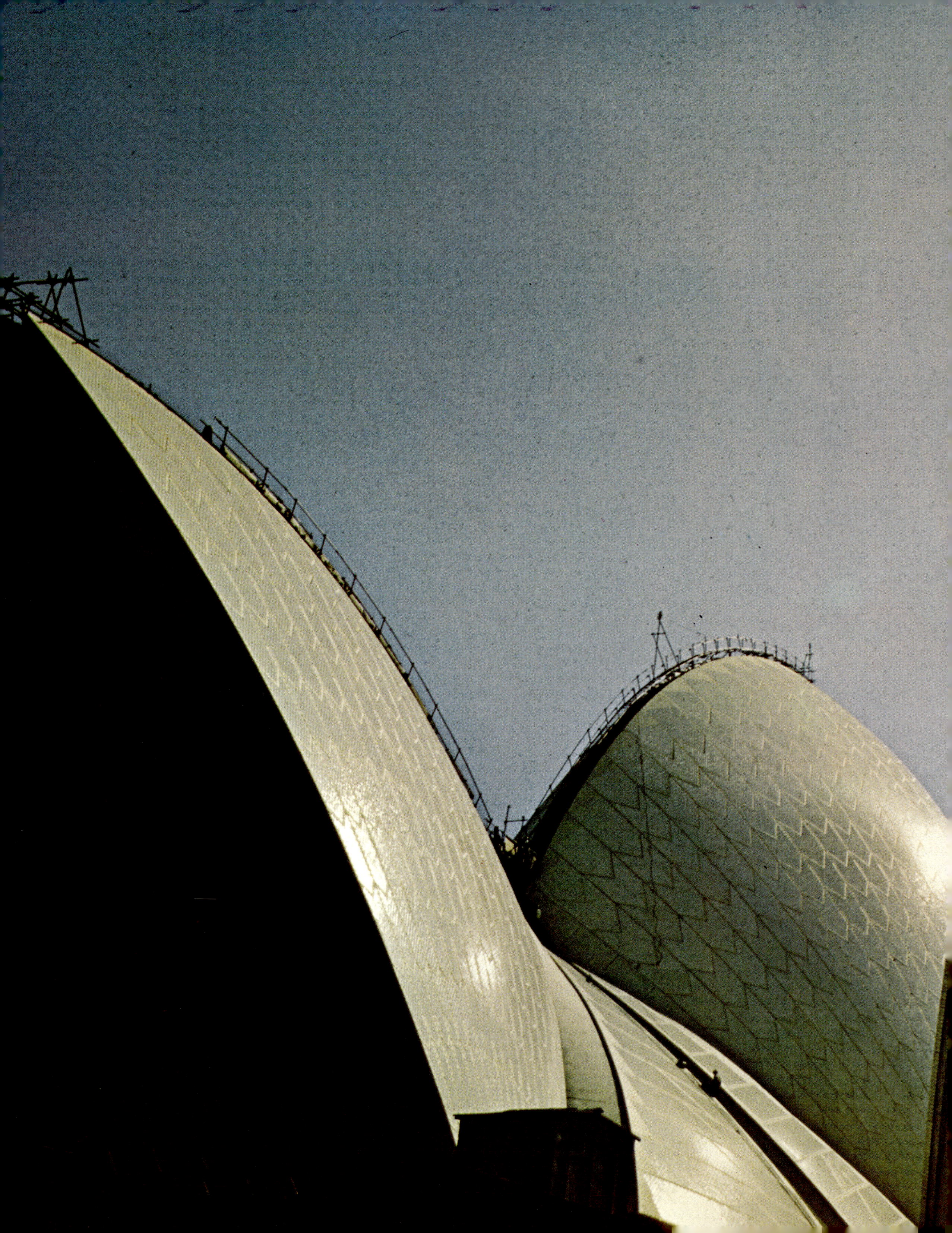

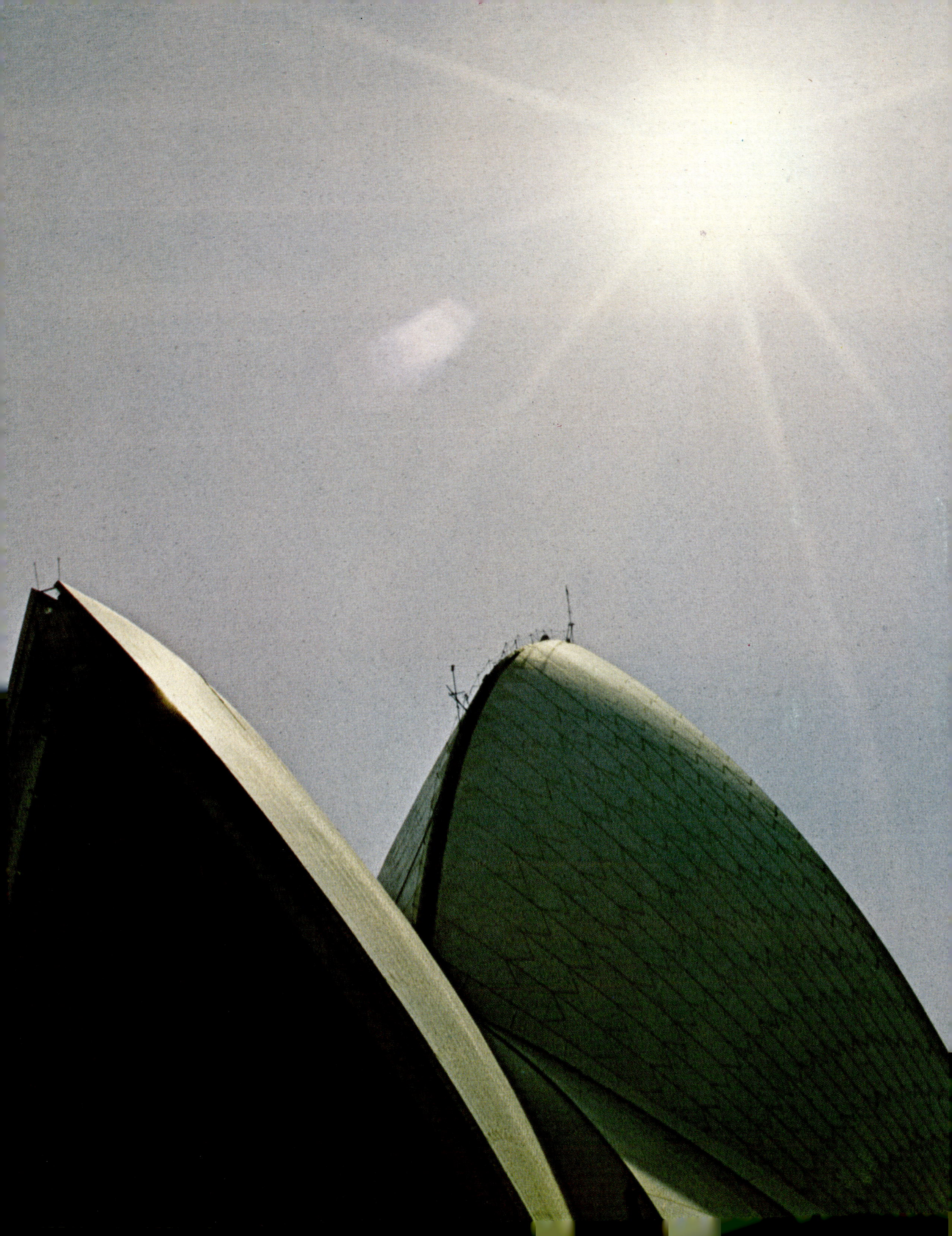

Stock Exchange, Sydney

Dam construction, N.S.W.

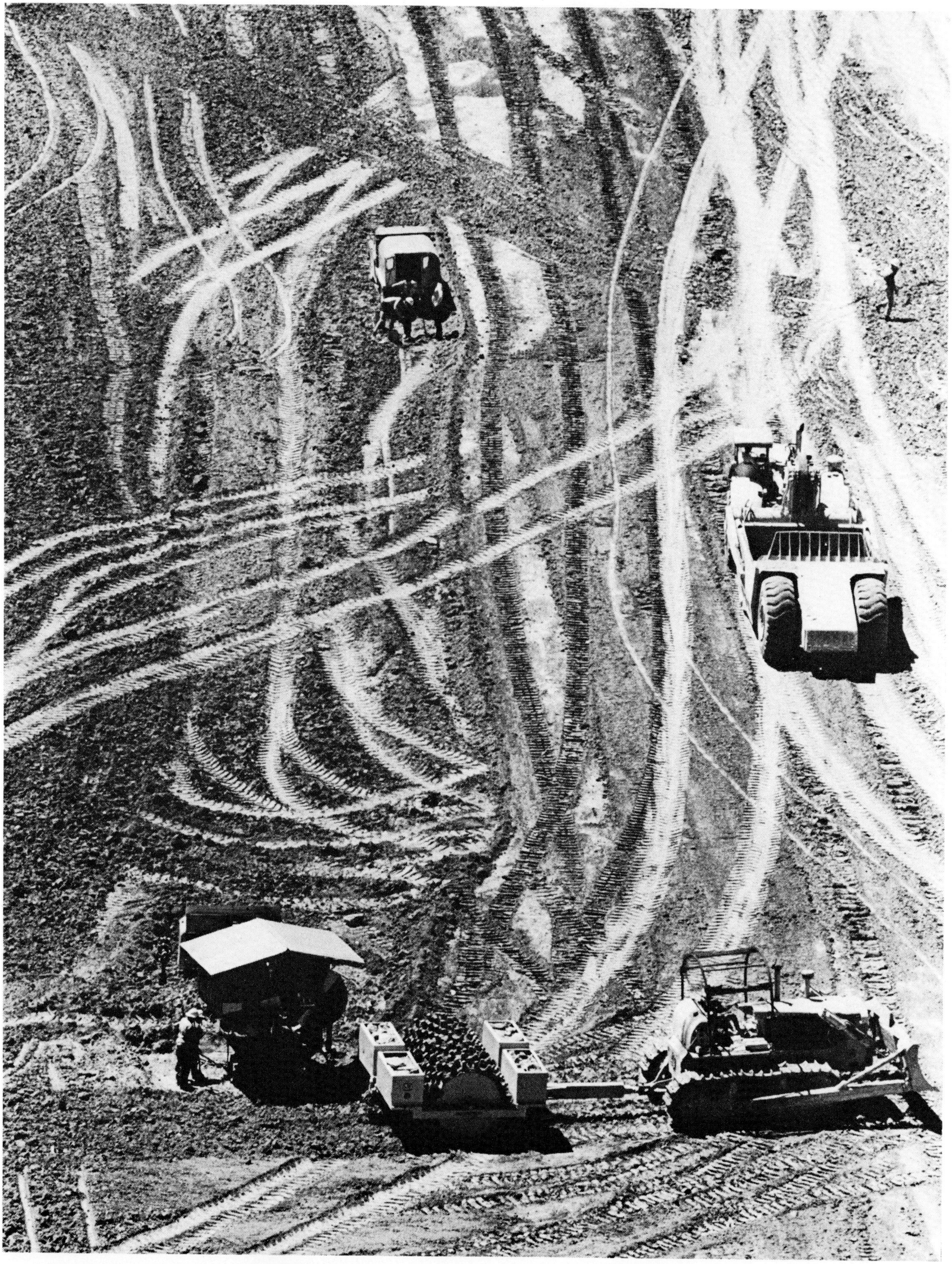

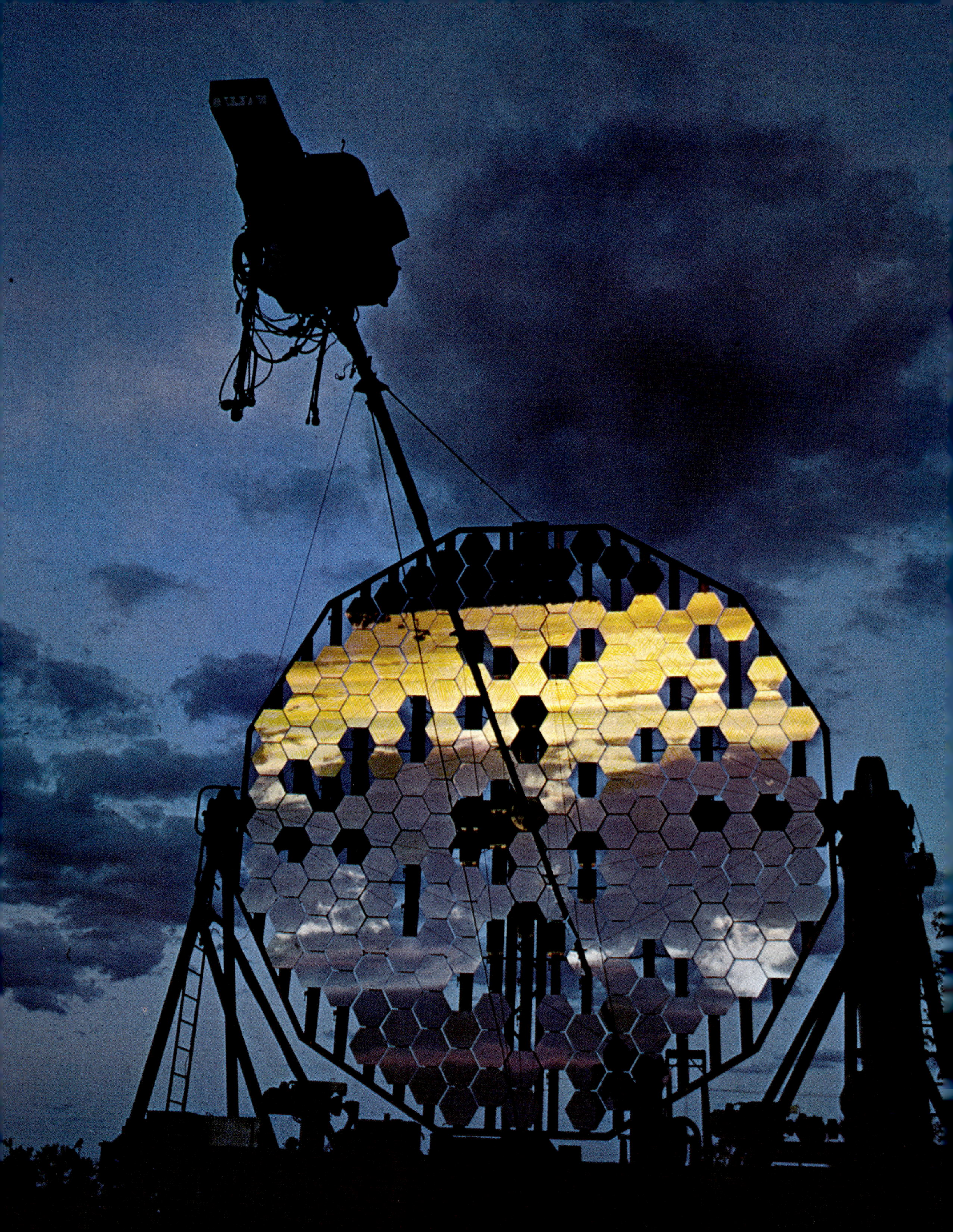

that we would have any difficulty in finding Asian immigrants if we wished to do so. My guess is that we shall soon reach this point and that we shall start by taking in small numbers of Japanese, who are honorary Aryans even in South Africa because of their wealth and industrial importance, and of the extraterritorial Chinese from Hong Kong, Singapore, Malaysia and Indonesia whose future in these countries is increasingly uncertain. After that we might risk a few Papuans, for whom we have a special responsibility, and Fijians who have the supreme qualification of playing Rugby football! But it would take a very considerable influx of Asian migrants to alter the overwhelmingly British composition of our population and therefore of our customs, traditions and habits of thought. I find it difficult to conceive of such large-scale immigration in this century.

Very well, then, we must make the best of what we have got. But do we want to change? I find myself divided on this question. In some ways it seems to me a pity that Australia was not granted another century of isolation so that it could have further developed and hardened the Australian character of its people. For there is much in that character which seems to me admirable. I would not, for instance, want the Australians to lose their natural virtues—their common sense, their dislike of anything pretentious, their healthy suspicion of those in authority, their genuine kindness and humanity, and, above all, their strong egalitarian instincts. On the other hand I would like them to become better informed, less apathetic about ideas and world affairs, more respectful of intelligence and the arts, more tolerant of individual differences. There are those who tell me that the younger generation will combine these virtues and will produce precisely the mixture I desire. I confess that I am sceptical about this. I see all too many signs that the young of all classes are succumbing too easily to the worst influences from the United States. Instead of imitating American idealism, they are adopting American materialism. Instead of copying the American appetite for knowledge and information, they are succumbing to that universal American tendency to think and talk in cliches.

That is why I wish that Australia had been granted another century of isolation. The Australian character and, still more, Australian culture, are not mature enough to stand the impact of a stronger culture. Even Europe, confident in the immense wealth of her own civilisation, has been hard put to it to keep out the American way of life. Is it likely that Australia will do so? Already we watch American programmes on television, read American magazines published in Australia, imitate American fashions in clothes and advertising, train our young men to be second-hand American executives. The man from Snowy River is hard put to survive.

In fairness we should recognise that it is the American century, that the immense power of American technology has swept over the world so that every Western country is to some extent affected by the same revolution. What America did yesterday, we all do today: what America does today, we shall all meekly do tomorrow. What haunts

Stellar Interferometer, Narrabri, N.S.W.

Artist, Mrs Macquarie's Chair, Sydney

Lecture hall, Sydney University

226

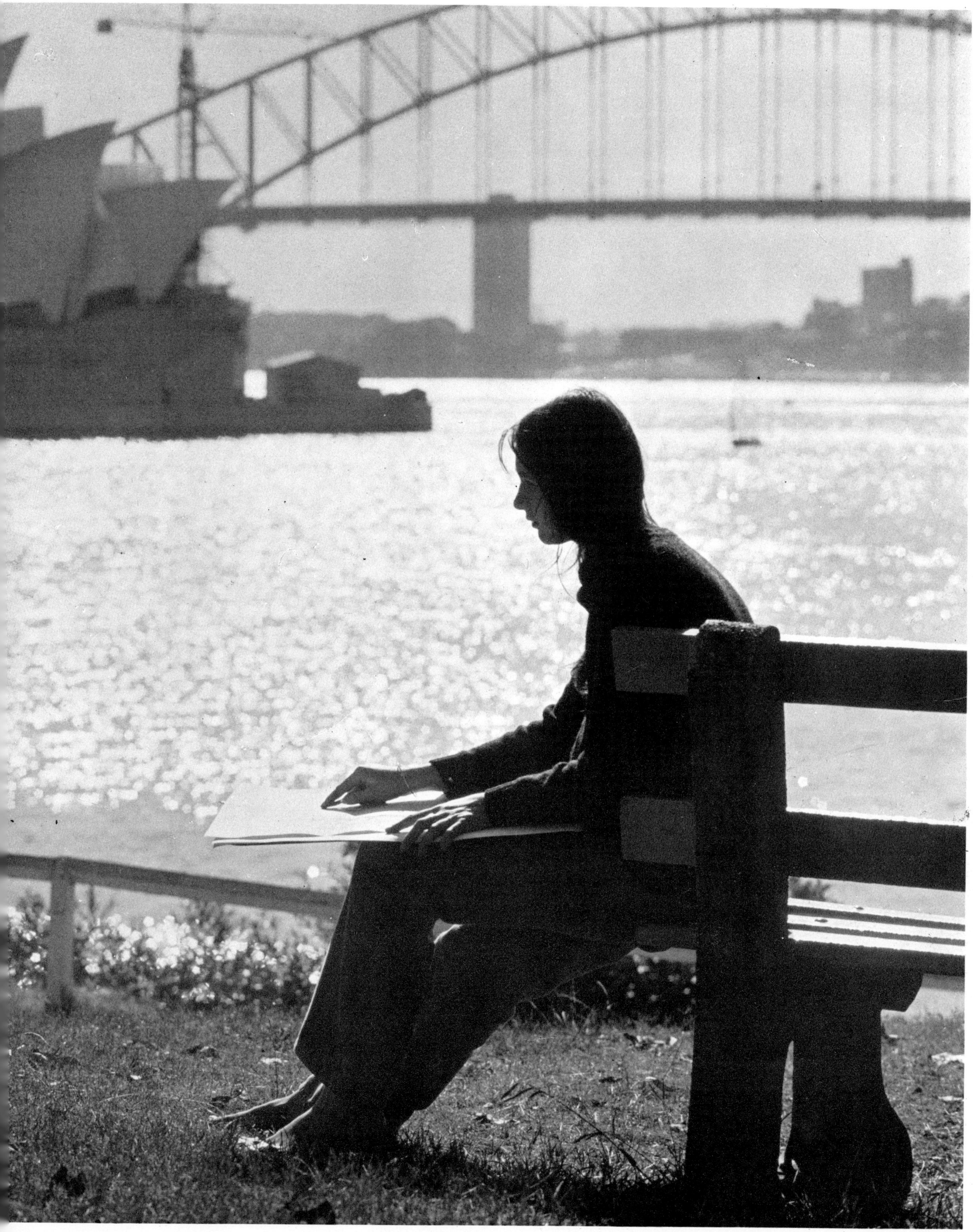

Another generation

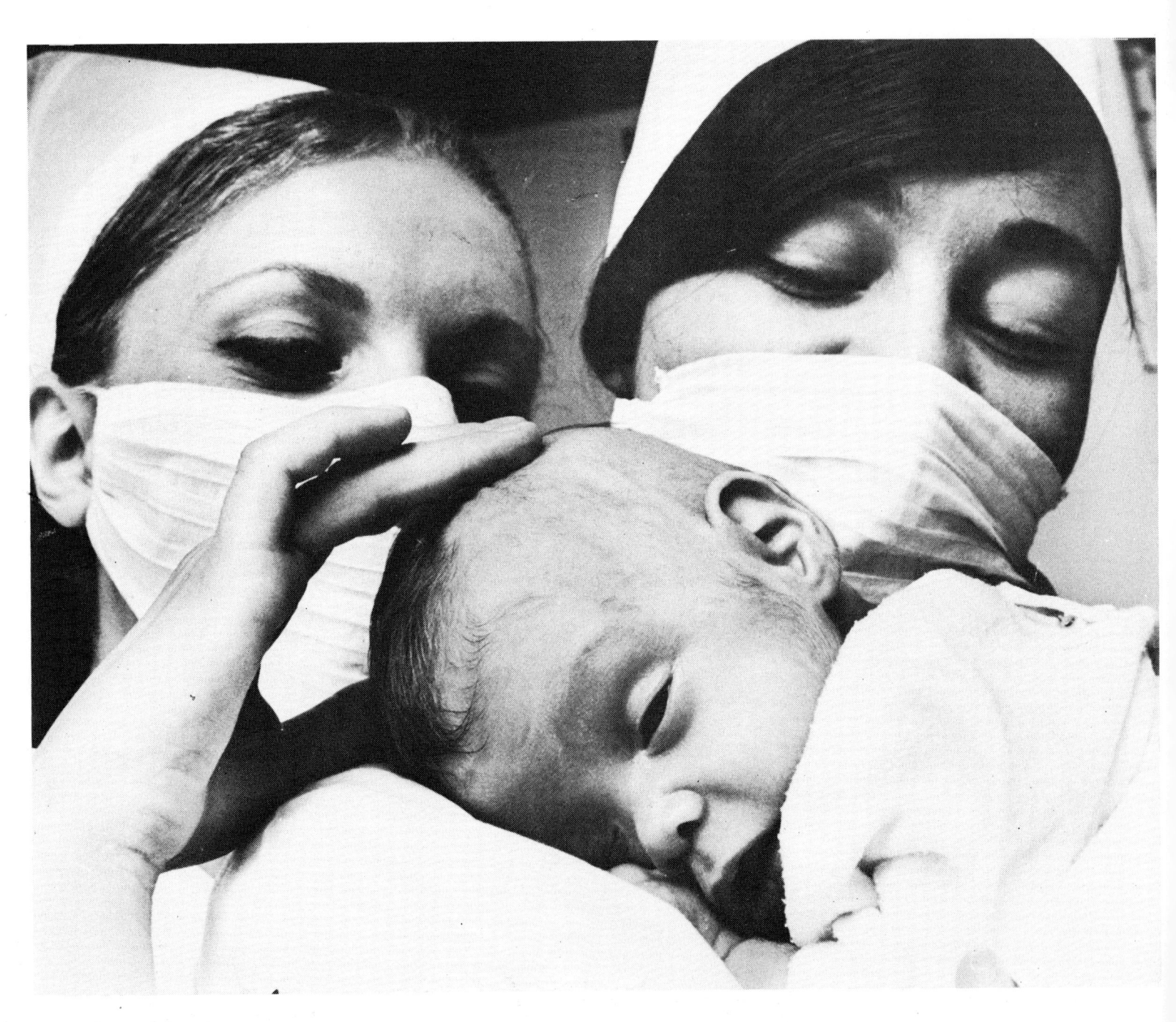

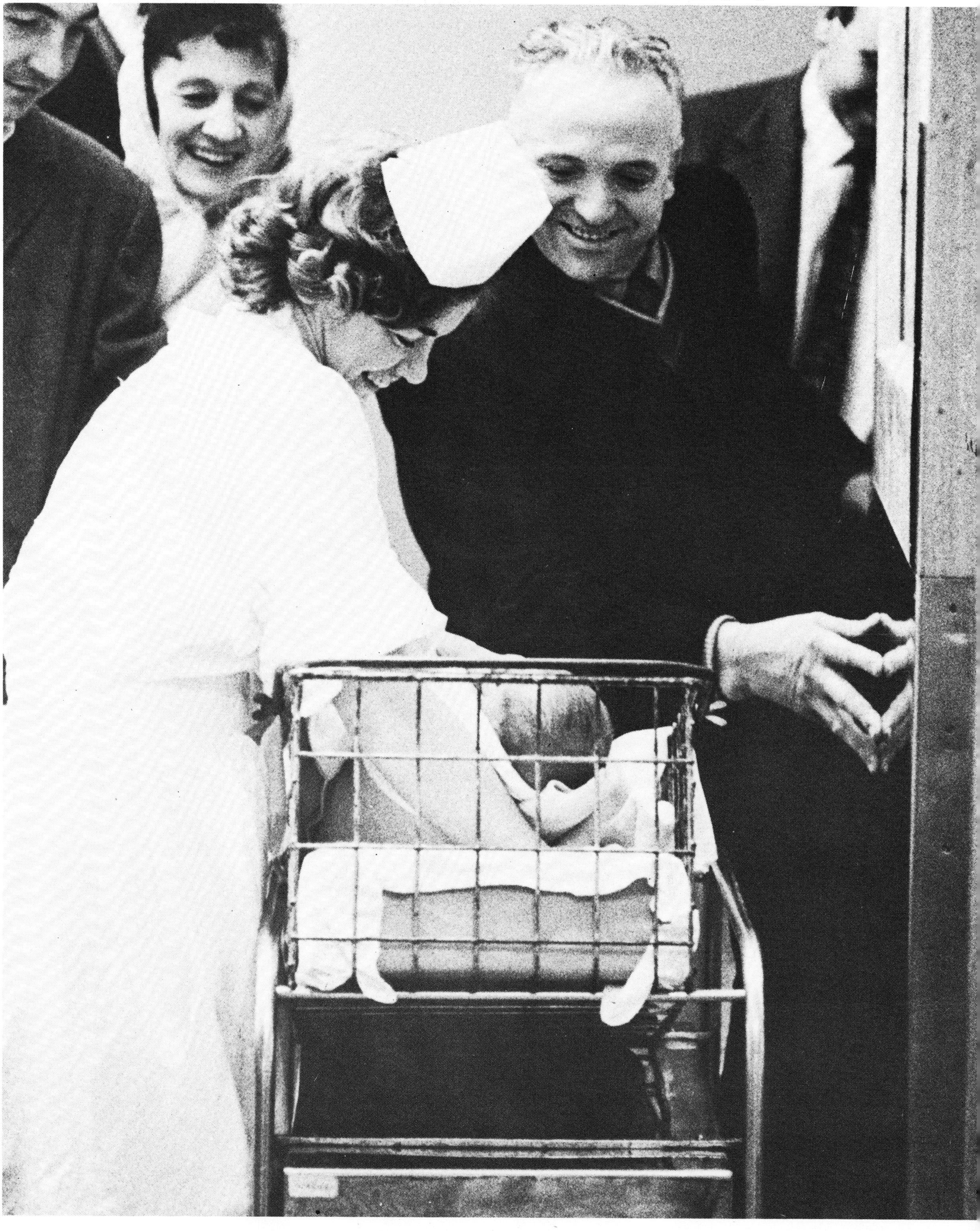

me is the fear that Australia has too little confidence in her own qualities to save anything from the past. The fact that the American way of life has many admirable virtues mitigates but does not remove this fear. I would wish Australia to remain Australian.

The American revolution has its advantages. It is already helping us to develop our resources more rapidly and more efficiently. It should soon help us to re-design our roads and cities and so make Australia a pleasanter place to live in. I believe, indeed, that Australia is exceptionally well-placed to take advantage of the latest knowledge and techniques in town-planning and architecture. Our brilliant light and empty spaces, our unspoilt bush and superb coastline are waiting for the men who can do justice to them. It may be a little late for Sydney and Melbourne, grown old and crusted in their bad habits, but already two new cities, Perth and Canberra, are taking advantage of the new knowledge and it seems certain that still newer cities will be created during the next 100 years. Not, I think, inland—I believe that is a dream that is already out of date—but on the coast of Queensland and Western Australia and, perhaps, northern New South Wales. These cities should be incomparably better planned than anything we know today.

Private housing will improve out of all recognition both in the quality of design and in convenience. Here again no country in the world offers such opportunities to architects. I'm afraid that it is inevitable that the tropical coast of Queensland will be developed, though one hopes that this development will be controlled more highly than it has been near Sydney. Perhaps the rich will prefer to have their week-end and holiday homes in the desert, which might easily become fashionable as it already is, to some extent, in California and Arizona. It is not difficult to imagine wealthy men commuting to the Far West or even to the Centre where—at a cost—water will make their gardens cool and green among the red earth and rocks of the inland.

All this is easy. Australia, already technologically advanced, will share in the new technical revolution that is coming to all the Western World and will add to it her own special qualities to make life pleasant. It is far harder to imagine the quality of life itself. The climate should help to preserve the easy-going, good-natured side of the Australian character against the stresses of the acquisitive society. The last traces of Victorian Puritanism will surely disappear, though I sometimes think that Australia will be the last nation to have a literary censor as well as the last nation to be a colonial power. We shall certainly become more sophisticated in our tastes. I do not believe that organised religion will maintain its present hold on a people that is deeply materialist in outlook, especially when the churches themselves show so many signs of dissolution and decay. For our spiritual values we may depend on the artists—several writers have pointed out that art is becoming a substitute for religion among advanced societies—and there the outlook is not discouraging. For twenty years now the arts in Australia have been simmering quietly. Chance alone makes it probable that we shall produce a major artist or writer or composer in the near future, but I do not think that we need depend on chance. History seems to show that great periods in the art and culture of a nation coincide with periods of political and economic expansion. The energy that flows into the one spills over into the other. Whatever criticisms can be made of Australian society today, I do not think it can be denied that it is marked by great vitality, and all available evidence suggests that we are at the beginning of a period of intense development. I should be surprised if this does not also produce a flowering of the arts before the end of the century. The influence of this on the whole people might be profound.

I would guess that there will also be strong movements of dissent, especially among young people, from the material conformity of organised society. Perhaps we have already seen the first of such movements among the surfies. To live on the beach and follow the waves may be the Australian equivalent of the beats or the hippies in California. I remember a friend once telling me that, when driving in the far North of Queensland, he had given a lift to two young men who were walking along the road. He asked them what they did for a living. "We cut cane for four months and make a bit of money," they replied. "Well, what do you do the rest of the year?" my friend asked. "Oh we live on the beach the life God intended us to live."

It was, in a way, a good answer and one which is not easy to refute. What life *did* God intend us to live? The life of a businessman in Sydney or Melbourne, driving to work each morning through the traffic, buying and selling all day, watching television in the evening, or the life of the young men on the beach? "They toil not, neither do they spin." It seems certain that this question is going to be asked more and more frequently during the next fifty years in all Western societies and that Australia, in a curious way, is well adapted for whichever answer you may choose to give. I can imagine communities of dissenters, living a simple life and sharing their few possessions, living on the Queensland coast a few miles away from some new industrial centre where men toil to refine the rich ores of the earth so that the nation may become still wealthier so that individuals in their turn may have still more possessions. . . .

But is it possible that we may produce our own answer, a sensible, down-to-earth Australian compromise, rejecting the extremes of either way of life? There are, I like to think, faint hints of this already—a sturdy refusal to work too hard just to make more money, a universal appreciation of the value of leisure, a cult-free but genuine passion for sun and sea and bush. Australia is a nation of nature-lovers without all the nonsense that sometimes goes with it, and in spite of our unrivalled destructive capacities we still, thank heavens, have a lot of nature to love.

This, at least, is my own dream for the future of Australia: that we may take what is best in modern technology without becoming slaves to the machine; that we shall have no poor and not too many rich; that we shall gradually come to accept some limitation on our needs so that our children do not become victims of the endless drive for a higher gross national product; that we shall have still more leisure and that we shall continue to use some of it for surfing and sun-baking and picnics in the bush but use rather more of it for the cultivation of the mind; that we shall retain a strong sense of individual humanity and continue to suspect the wisdom of those set in authority over us.

We shall not and should not grab at world power—not for us the imperial destinies of a Rome or a Britain. Instead we should cultivate our own vast spaces and give what surplus we can afford to help our less fortunate neighbours in the North.

I would like to think that Australians will always question the latest fashions, whether in clothes or consumer goods or ideas, instead of swallowing whatever is poured down our throats. We are no longer bushmen, but it would be excellent if we could preserve something of the bushman's scepticism and common sense. But above all I wish that they may rediscover the admirable virtue of simplicity, so well illustrated by our own forefathers who cleared and settled the land with their own hands or by those still earlier Australians who wandered across the continent naked, with a handful of spears, a wooden dish and a fire-stick. It seems to me that a certain hardness and austerity are fitting for a desert people and probably pleasing in the sight of God.

Steelworks, Newcastle, N.S.W.

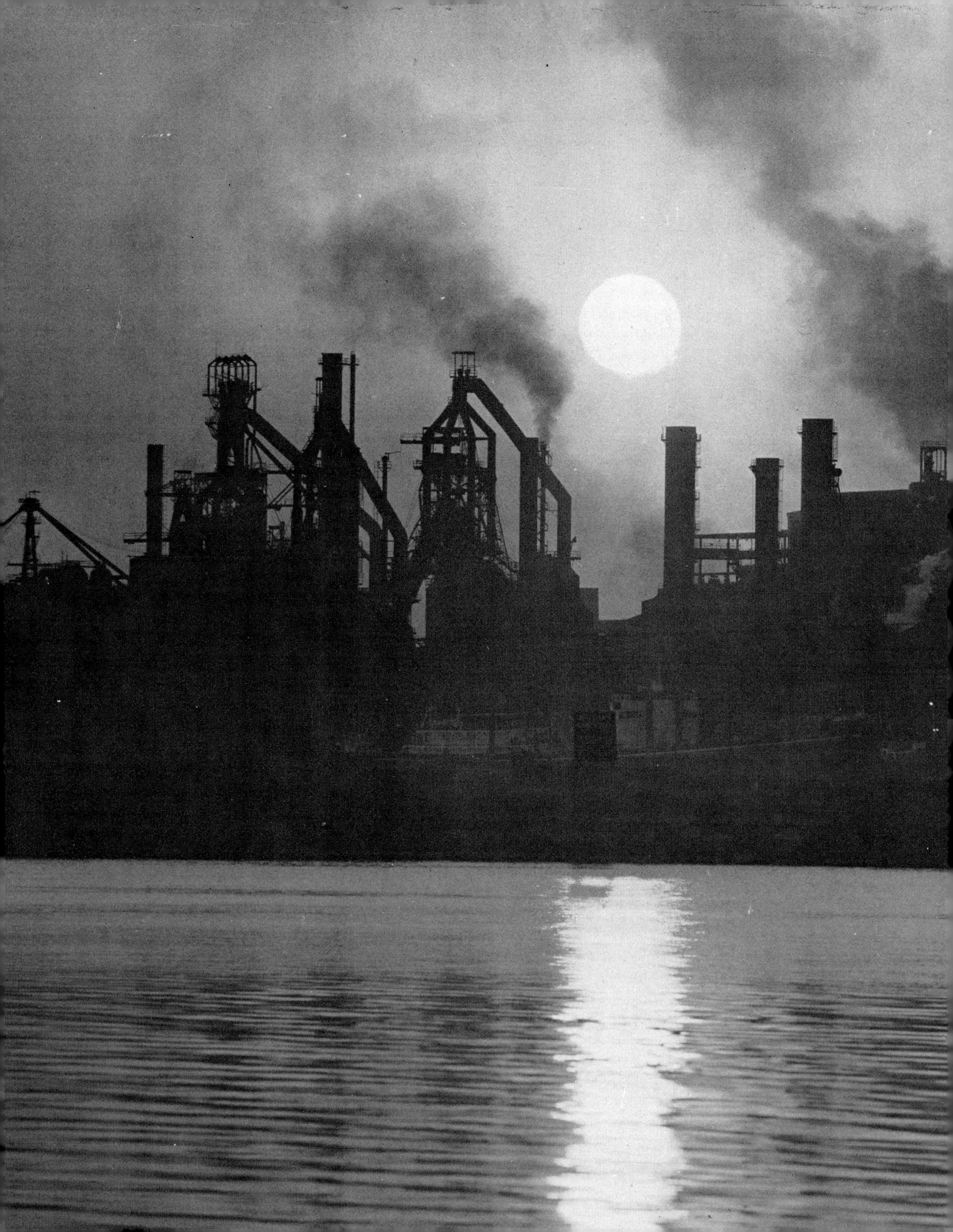

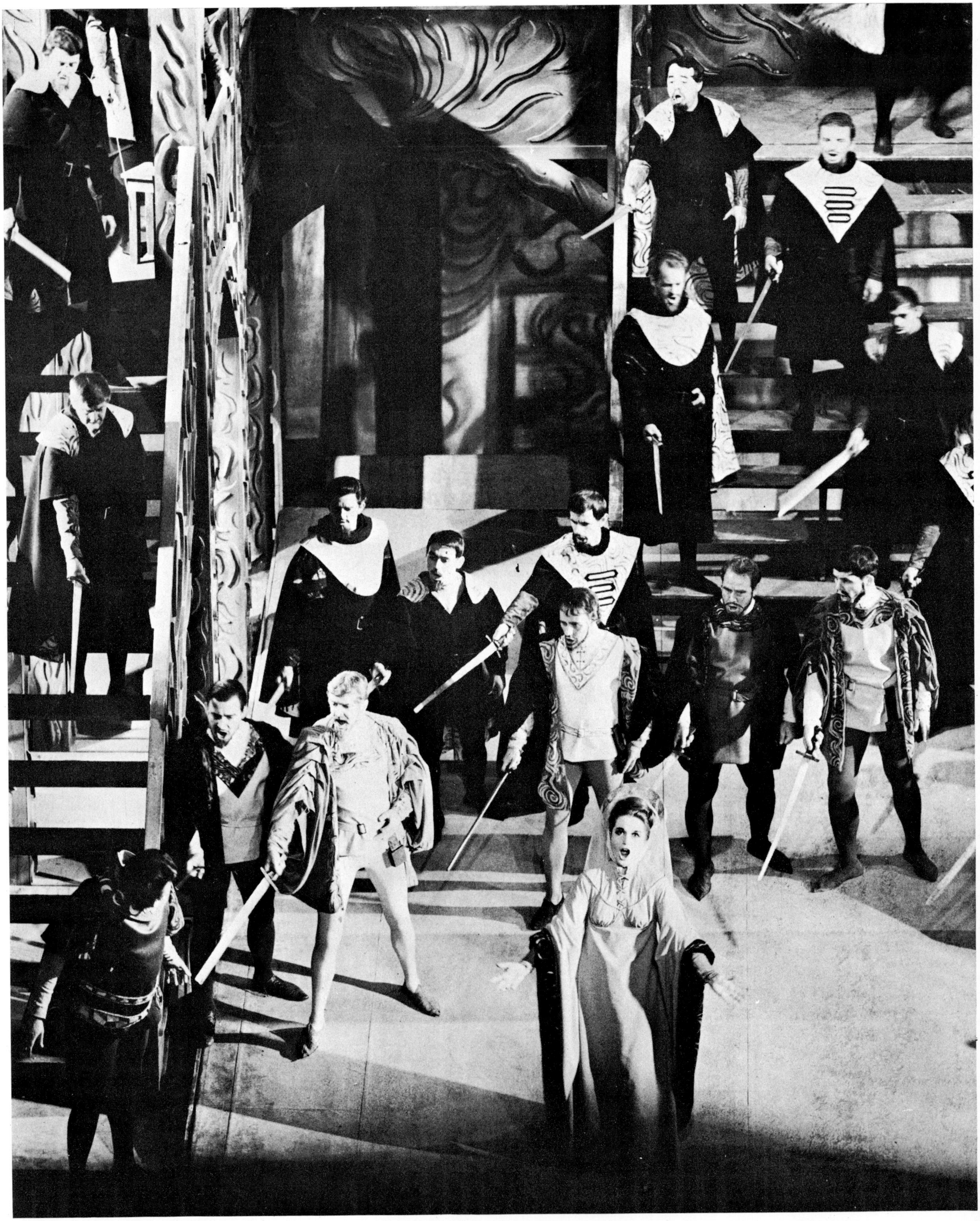

Grape pickers, Barossa, South Australia

Festival of Arts, Adelaide

Photographic Credits

endpapers, *Robin Smith*
title-page, *Helmut Gritscher*
12-13, *Beverly Clifford*
14, *Jozel Vissel*
17, *Robin Smith*
18-19, *David Moore* for Sports Illustrated, Time Inc.
20-21, *David Moore*
22, 23, *Robin Smith*
24, *Robin Smith*
25, *David Moore*
26-27, *David Moore*
28, *David Beal*
30-31, *Peter Rae*
33, *Kerry Dundas*
34-35, *Helmut Gritscher*
38-39, *David Moore*
42-43, *Robin Smith*
45, *Robin Smith*
46-47, *Robin Smith*
48-49, *George Lipman*
50-51, *Robin Smith*
52, *George Lipman*
53, *John Carnemolla*
54, *David Moore*
55, *David Moore*
56-57, *Robin Smith*
58, *Robin Smith*
60-61, *Robin Smith*
64-65, *David Beal*
68, *Robin Smith*
69, *Robin Smith*
71, *Nick Bauman*
72-73, *Robin Smith*
74, *David Potts*
75, *David Moore*
76, *David Beal*, c. ANTA
77, *Robin Smith*
78, *Helmut Gritscher*; bottom, *Robin Smith*
79, *David Moore*
83, *David Moore*
85, *David Beal*
88, *Lance Nelson*
89, *Jane Marston*
91, *David Moore*
92, *David Beal*
93, top, *David Beal*; bottom, *Jane Marston*
94, *David Moore*
95, *George Lipman*, c. SMH
96, *David Beal*
97, *David Beal*
98, left, *David Beal*; right, *John Witzig*
99, *Helmut Gritscher*
100, *Jane Marston*
101, *David Beal*
102, *Robin Smith*
103, *Jozel Vissel*
104, *Robin Smith*
105, *David Beal*, c. ANTA
106, top, *Helmut Gritscher*; bottom, *David Moore*
107, *Helmut Gritscher*
108, *Lance Nelson*
109, *Robin Smith*
112, two photographs, *David Beal*
113, *Robin Smith*
116, *David Beal*, c. ANTA
117, *David Beal*
118-119, *David Moore*
121, *Robin Smith*
122-123, *Robin Smith*
124, *David Moore*
125, *Robert McFarlane*
127-127, *Helmut Gritscher*
128, two photographs, *David Beal*
129, *Robin Smith*
130, *Robin Smith*
131, *Helmut Gritscher*
132, *David Moore*
133, *Helmut Gritscher*
134-135, *John Carnemolla*
136, *David Moore*; bottom, *Helmut Gritscher*
137, *Jozel Vissel*
145, *Rennie Ellis*
147, *David Moore*
148-149, *Helmut Gritscher*
150, *Helmut Gritscher*
151, *Helmut Gritscher*
152-153, *David Moore*
154-155, *David Moore*
156, *Brian McArdle*
157, *David Moore*
158, *David Moore* for Sports Illustrated, Time Inc.
159, *Brian McArdle*
160, *Helmut Gritscher*
161, *John O'Grady*, c. SMH
165, *David Moore*
170, *David Moore*
172-173, *Gregory Weight*
174-175, *David Moore*
177, *Leo Duyckers*
178, *Lance Nelson*
180, *Lance Nelson*
181, *Ern McQuillan*
184-185, *David Moore*
188, *David Moore*
189, *Wolfgang Sievers*
191, *Ern McQuillan*
192, *Pat Crowe*
193, *Richard Woldendorp*
199, *Helmut Gritscher*
200-201, *Lance Nelson*
203, *John Wong*
205, *George Lipman*, c. SMH
206, top, *Mark Strizic*; bottom, *David Moore*
207, *Helmut Gritscher*
208, *Richard Woldendorp*
209, *Helmut Gritscher*
210, *Beverly Clifford*
211, *Robert McFarlane*
212, *Jozel Vissel*
213, *David Beal*
214, *David Beal*
215, *Robin Smith*
216-217, *David Moore*
220-221, *David Moore*
222, *David Moore*
223, *Helmut Gritscher*
224, *David Beal*
226, *David Moore*
227, *Robin Smith*
228, *George Lipman*, c. SMH
229, *Mark Strizic*
233, *Robin Smith*
234, *Robin Smith*
235, *Robin Smith*

The Editors

Craig McGregor

is the Sydney writer and critic whose *Profile of Australia* has become a standard work. He is the author of *People, Politics and Pop*, co-author with Midget Farrelly of *This Surfing Life,* and wrote the text for Helmut Gritscher's pictorial book, *The High Country*. He has recently published a novel, *Don't Talk To Me About Love*. He was co-author, with David Beal, of the book *In the Making*. An absorbing interest in contemporary life and the visual arts has made him the natural choice to co-edit LIFE IN AUSTRALIA. He also wrote the introduction and the chapter on Pleasure.

David Beal,

who is also responsible for a number of the photographs in this book, is one of Australia's foremost photo-journalists. He was co-author with Donald Horne of the best-seller *Southern Exposure,* and with Craig McGregor of *In the Making*. His photographs appear in *Decor Australia* and with his wife, Dawn, he has produced some six children's books. His work appears in *Life, Time* and *National Geographic*; English journals such as the *Sunday Times* and *Observer* colour magazines; and many European publications. After early training on Australian newspapers and magazines, he moved into the competitive world of freelance photography.

The Writers

Geoffrey Dutton,

poet, novelist and biographer, is the author of more than a dozen books. He is the editor of *The Literature of Australia,* publisher of Sun Books, and was for several years Senior Lecturer in English Literature at Adelaide University.

Harry Gordon

has written widely on sport in Australia and is the author of *Gold Medal Girl,* a book on the life of Dawn Fraser. He is now the editor of the Melbourne *Sun*.

Douglas Lockwood

has written several books about life in the outback, including the prizewinning *I, The Aboriginal*. He lived for many years in Darwin, from where he made numerous trips into the Australian inland. He now lives in Port Moresby, where he is editor of the *South Pacific Post.*

Ian Moffitt

has been a journalist for 23 years in Australia, Asia, Europe and the United States. He was headquartered in Canton while reporting the Chinese civil war of 1949-50 and was for three years chief of the Daily Mirror's New York News Bureau. He is now a special feature writer for *The Australian.*

John Douglas Pringle

is one of Australia's most distinguished commentators. He is the author of *Australian Accent* and *Australian Painting Today* and is former editor of the *Sydney Morning Herald.*

Gavin Souter

is the author of two books, *New Guinea: The Last Unknown* and *Sydney,* and has recently written another on the Australian colonies in Paraguay. He is a feature writer on the *Sydney Morning Herald* and won the 1960 Walkley Award for Australian Journalism.

Patrick Tennison

is one of Australia's leading freelance journalists and is well-known as a TV personality. He has worked in Fleet Street and on the Melbourne *Sun-Pictorial*, and is a regular contributor to a number of Australian newspapers and journals.

Richard Walsh

was for some years co-editor of *Oz* magazine. He contributed a chapter to *Australia and the Monarchy: A Symposium* and has edited an anthology of cartoons. He is now editor of the *Review.*